AF395201

CRUNCH
TIME

CRUNCH TIME

NARENDRA MODI'S
NATIONAL SECURITY CRISES

SREERAM CHAULIA

RUPA

First published by
Rupa Publications India Pvt. Ltd 2022
7/16, Ansari Road, Daryaganj
New Delhi 110002

Sales Centres:
Allahabad Bengaluru Chennai
Hyderabad Jaipur Kathmandu
Kolkata Mumbai

ISBN: 978-93-5520-256-7

First impression 2022

10 9 8 7 6 5 4 3 2 1

Printed by Parksons Graphics Pvt. Ltd, Mumbai

*To India, which is returning to
its original self, Bharat.*

Contents

Foreword

Securing the territorial integrity and physical safety of citizens from hostile external adversaries is the core dharma of a state. This has been true since time immemorial, since the age of ancient civilizations and empires to the modern period of nation states. The guru of Indian statecraft, Kautilya (375–283 BCE), identified three core duties of a ruler as follows:

> ...*rakhshan* or protection of the state from external aggression; *palana* or maintenance of order within the state; and *yogakshema* of the state or safeguarding people's welfare, prosperity, protection and peace [italics in original].[1]

Without rakhshan, there can be no prosperity and welfare of the state's residents. Defence against foreign threats is the prerequisite for all other functions of governance and rule to be fulfilled. Therefore, strategic thought has focused on the key dimension of external threats and how they can be deterred, depending on the intent and conduct of the foreign foes, their capabilities and alliances.

Undoubtedly, there are also threats to a state within its own frontiers. These internal challenges could, in some circumstances, be linked to the machinations of external opponents. To that extent, a clear-cut distinction between internal and external threats cannot always be made when it comes to national security. Yet, internal threats often pose a fundamental challenge to a sovereign state or regime only when they receive sustained external encouragement. As long as external enemies are deterred and kept under check, a state has bare minimum security to carry on with the rest of its functions.

In the case of India, the historical and geographical conditions it inherited around the time of independence from British colonial rule in 1947 were such that it was saddled with two seemingly perpetual external threats on its northern and western borders—China and Pakistan. Both these expansionist and revisionist countries, which boast of an 'all-weather alliance', have refused to accept India's territorial integrity, laid claims on Indian land, and harmed the physical safety of Indian citizens through conventional wars, low-intensity proxy wars and terrorism.

It is not coincidental that Kautilya, Sun Tzu (544–496 BCE), Machiavelli (AD 1469–1527), Clausewitz (AD 1780–1831) and many other strategists have focussed much on neighbours and their bearings on the core national security of a state. There can, of course, be benign neighbours who do not pose threats and may even augment a state's national security through coalitions or regional integration mechanisms. But as long as there is a central hostile dynamic in a state's neighbourhood, all of its surrounding countries are impacted by the ensuing insecurity either directly or indirectly.

For India, its relations with the rest of its South Asian and Southeast Asian neighbours as well as extra-regional great powers are thus interwoven with its fundamentally antagonistic ties with China and Pakistan. Managing all these relationships in a way that strengthens India's hand and thwarts Chinese and Pakistani nefarious designs is a core aspect of Indian national security.

This path-breaking book by the leading Indian scholar of international relations, Sreeram Chaulia, deftly weaves a narrative that combines tactical and strategic responses of the Indian state in two interrelated fields—military/defence and diplomacy—to show how India has dealt with its perennial foreign antagonists in the era of Prime Minister Narendra Modi. Since taking office in 2014, Modi has brought to the table a 'New India' that is undergoing a profound transformation into an assertive and gutsy state that has broken many taboos and ventured into bolder realms and methods of defending national security. I do consider this new-found strategic confidence of India as something our adversaries did not factor into their progressive strategies and has, in fact, unnerved them into taking irrational decisions.

Chaulia's contention in this book, which is worthy of wide attention and debate, is that India is no longer a 'soft state' defined by a defensive and ineffective approach to raising the costs of aggression and terrorism by China and Pakistan. The author has outlined in great detail how India has become Bharat during Modi's tenure, how this metamorphosis has triggered deep reforms in India's defence sector, and also the way it has altered the calculus vis-à-vis China and Pakistan through a far more robust attitude towards national security.

The creative and bold use of international alignments to shore up India's position vis-à-vis China and Pakistan has also been highlighted in this book to illustrate the comprehensive nature of national security, which requires an amalgamation of all levers in the hands of a state—military, diplomatic and economic.

Another unique contribution of this book would perhaps be the focus on how Modi has moulded and channelled India's public opinion in order to steer its strategic culture away from the curse of a perceived 'soft state'. As a gifted politician with a mass touch, Modi has made national security a central plank of his appeal. Chaulia shows in this book that Modi has shifted the discourse and the public mood in such a way that giving a befitting reply when India's sovereignty and security are endangered by foreign foes is now an important yardstick for political success in the electoral arena. In fact, for the first time, the term 'comprehensive security' is being given a more focused meaning in India

I must commend Chaulia for his intense focus on major episodes of crises triggered by the malevolent behaviour of China and Pakistan in the Modi years. There is no better point of observation than a national security crisis to discern how the Indian state and its strategic culture have shifted from earlier times. The four crises Chaulia has picked as case studies—the Pathankot and Uri attacks of 2016, the Doklam stand-off of 2017, the Pulwama attack of 2019 and the face-off in eastern Ladakh in 2020—are highly educative about how India as a state and a nation has behaved and risen to the occasion during moments of intense pressure from China and Pakistan. This also alludes to my perception that India's strategic confidence has enhanced with each crisis in the last few years which has actually saddled the adversaries with a dilemma of how far they can actually go with their threats towards India.

Chaulia's deft account of these nerve-wracking crises has the added value of including first-hand opinions and views of Indians who have held respectable positions in the country's national security apparatus. The perspectives of these practitioners make the book a perfect blend of scholarly insight and policy wisdom. I wish that this book is read widely among strategic elites in India and around the world, and also by students and intelligent laypersons who have a strong interest in matters of defence, security and foreign policy. India's outlook and approach to foreign threats has changed considerably since Modi's ascent and I cannot think of a better work that encapsulates this epic shift from a 'soft state approach' to what Chaulia aptly portrays as a state comfortable with its civilizational legacy of using calibrated hard power as a tool of statecraft.

Lieutenant General (retd) Syed Ata Hasnain
Former General Officer Commanding 15 Corps (Srinagar)
Chancellor, Central University of Kashmir
16 September 2021, New Delhi

Introduction

Those who challenged India's sovereignty, be it LoC [Line of Control with Pakistan] or LAC [Line of Actual Control with China], India's brave soldiers gave them a befitting reply in their own language. Whether it is terrorism or expansionism, India is fighting both.[1]

—Prime Minister Narendra Modi, 15 August 2020

A Hellish National Security Crisis

On the night of 26 November 2008, a coordinated assault that began on India's financial capital, Mumbai, shook the nation to its core and left it traumatized. It was the most audacious and sophisticated terrorist attack perpetrated in the heart of India, targeting iconic locations across its commercial metropolis and slaughtering a range of victims, including Indians and foreigners of select nationalities. Over the next 72 hours, 10 heavily armed Pakistani gunmen, who had slipped into Mumbai undetected via the Arabian Sea maritime route from Karachi, went on a rampage—gunning down innocent civilians, taking hostages and planting explosives–effectively holding India under siege.

For decades, India had been at the receiving end of terrorist rage; one bears witness to this rage in the form of repeated firefights, bomb blasts and other violent incidents in the hotly contested Kashmir region, as well as in urban centres such as Kolkata (1993), Hyderabad (2007), Lucknow (2007), Jaipur (2008) and Mumbai (2003 and 2006). However, the deadly attacks of 2008 (popularly remembered as '26/11' to echo with the '9/11' attacks by the Al Qaeda in the United States in 2001), marked a particularly gruesome milestone. Coming on the heels of the devastating bombing of the Indian embassy in Kabul in July 2008—the handiwork of Pakistan's intelligence agency and its dreaded jihadist proxy in Afghanistan, the Haqqani network—26/11 was a shock to the human conscience and to India as a nation.

Strategic analysts noted the 'sheer scale and planning involved' that made the 26/11 attacks a 'watershed' moment involving 'multiple strikes across multiple areas' by sub-teams of terrorists who garnered massive global publicity by going after not only Indian citizens but also Americans, Israelis, Germans, Australians, Canadians, French, British and others.[2] The ruthless jihadists had come logistically prepared for a long struggle until death in the fashion of fedayeen fighters (guerrillas willing to sacrifice their lives) from the Middle East and made more than a statement by killing 166 people and injuring over 300. Pakistan's holy warriors had penetrated deep into India, sown real fear and panic in a live televised spectacle that horrified the world, and exposed India's vulnerabilities like never before.

The transcripts of satellite phone conversations between the attackers and their Pakistani handlers—commanders of the dreaded state-sponsored terrorist organization, Lashkar-e-Taiba (LeT)—which were released by the Indian government shortly after the episode, left no doubt that it was meant to be a fight to the finish. The sole mission was to hurt and damage India and its international prestige, and to ignite a broader clash of civilizations between radical Islam and its foes. They conveyed the stark nature of the threat that India was facing.[3]

India's credibility as a secure and capable nation that was one among a few rising powers in the emerging world order was jolted by this jihadist carnage. Moreover, India's sense of national pride was dented as the saga revealed multiple lapses in coastal and internal security arrangements, which enabled the terrorists to easily infiltrate and inflict maximum damage on India's 'Maximum City'. American investigative journalists revealed damning evidence that the intelligence agencies of India, the United States of America (USA) and Britain had been monitoring online activities of the mission planners of LeT but had failed to connect the dots and coordinate sufficiently to avert the attacks. Calling it 'among the most devastating near-misses in the history of spycraft', the report concluded that had the concerned eavesdroppers pulled together 'all the strands gathered by their high-tech surveillance and other tools', it 'might have allowed them to disrupt a terror strike so scarring that it is often called India's 9/11'.[4] India's then national security advisor (NSA) and former head of the premier counter-intelligence agency, the Intelligence Bureau (IB), admitted later that the national security system had been taken by surprise like deer caught in headlights.[5]

Given the heart-rending drama of a complex attack televised round-the-clock by a feverishly excited news media, much attention has been devoted to what actually happened on the ground in those four dreadful nights in Mumbai and how one terrorist was captured alive and the last team of terrorist holdouts were finally neutralized on the morning of 29 November. Notwithstanding the crucial, early blunders by the state and central governments in identifying the threat and deploying the appropriate means to blunt it, the story of how India's national security units coalesced and finally ended the siege through Operation Black Tornado,[6] and how the National Security Guard saved the day through heroic sacrifices and bravery,[7] has been told. While these factual accounts are useful to piece together the nitty-gritty of the immediate aspects of the worst single terrorist attack India faced, the real issue that hovers over the dense retelling is that 26/11 was a *national security crisis featuring an external adversary* of India.

The attackers and masterminds behind these attacks were not Indian citizens in the vein of Maoist guerrillas or ethnic insurgents, who have posed a plethora of internal security challenges to the Indian state from time to time. The source of the threat in 26/11 lay across the border in Pakistan, and it was a systemic problem rather than a one-off venting of fury.

Enemies Without and Within

The American scholar Stephen Tankel conducted extensive research on LeT, its fanatic jihadist ideology and its fusion with the Pakistani military-intelligence establishment and found that 26/11 was one result of the complicated and overcrowded 'jihadi milieu' that had been building up over decades. With some terrorist creations of Pakistan's Inter-Services Intelligence (ISI) turning into Frankenstein's monsters and attacking Pakistan's own soldiers and officers during the dictatorship of General Pervez Musharraf (1999–2008),[8] there were 'fierce ideological debates among militant groups regarding where to focus their violence'. The plot for a 'spectacular strike against Mumbai' was hatched by the LeT with the encouragement of the ISI to prevent attrition in the former and halt the process of it 'being overshadowed by other jihadi groups in Pakistan'. The

Pakistani deep state endorsed the daring operation because its most reliable proxy, LeT, 'needed to show results in order for the leadership to retain control over elements within the organization.'[9] The dangerous concoction of 'Allah' and 'army'—which has been the bane of Pakistan since its creation as a nation state in 1947—and its externalities were at the root of the Mumbai attacks.

So, the main criterion to judge how India handled or failed to handle 26/11 is by examining how it responded to the foreign attackers—the state of Pakistan and its proxy jihadists. Prevention of such attacks is not primarily a function of beefing up internal security or interdicting terrorists after they have landed on Indian soil or shores and begun their destructive mayhem. In light of the massive infrastructure of terrorism that has sprouted in Pakistan with the official blessings of its military-intelligence industrial complex, it presents an ever-ticking time bomb that explodes every now and then in India, Afghanistan, the West and Pakistan's own internal security. The path to redemption from the wounds inflicted in 26/11 was for India to diagnose the national security crisis without blinkers, take the battle into Pakistan and raise the costs of its cross-border attacks, if not establish deterrence for good.

By their very definition, national security crises mainly arise from foreign threats and derive from the behaviour of international rivals. To the American scholar Robert Pfaltzgraff, a national security crisis 'is a situation that constitutes a threat to the core values or interests of the actors involved, represents a high possibility of military hostilities, has a finite response time, and/or has elements of strategic or tactical surprise.'[10] The British academician Jonathan Roberts concurs with the consensus that national security crises are characterized by high threats, short time for decision-making and surprise. Additionally, he emphasizes a fourth dimension, wherein there is a 'perception of a high probability of involvement in military hostilities' with foreign opponents, thus making 'the study of crisis a microcosm of the study of international relations' and rendering crises into 'conflict episodes par excellence' where there is always a lurking 'fear of war'.[11]

The *international* nature of national security crises is also borne out by the commonly accepted definition of the phrase 'national security' as a dynamic concept that acquires meaning only in reference to external actors. The American scholar Sam Sarkesian's classic definition deserves reproduction here:

> National security is the confidence held by the great majority of the nation's people that the nation has the military capability and effective policy to prevent its adversaries from effectively using force in preventing the nation's pursuit of its national interests.[12]

While the brutal onslaught of 26/11 was underway, ordinary Indians gathered spontaneously across the nation's length and breadth, expressing shock, outrage and frustration at the ongoing catastrophe. Their confidence in the ability of the government to protect them had taken a huge hit, and chants calling for 'the heads of bungling politicians' and 'real action' such as bombing Pakistan and launching a war were aired loud and clear in full media glare for days following the attacks in Mumbai.[13] The then home minister of India resigned on 30 November 2008 in what was interpreted as a 'damage control exercise by the Congress-led United Progressive Alliance (UPA) government'.[14] Yet, questions regarding accountability and competence of the Indian state in managing a dire national security crisis and defending the country's sovereignty and territorial integrity soared and lingered.

Days turned into weeks, months and years with no 'real action' against Pakistan forthcoming and the Indian government settled down into issuing futile diplomatic demarches to Pakistan, demanding that it hand over the plotters and legally prosecute them. The attacks of 26/11 entered the memory bank of Indians and the world as a crisis that proved to be an enduring national embarrassment and a reconfirmation of the much-hated and debated notion that India was a 'soft state' that lacked the will and capability to robustly and fearlessly tackle national security threats. In testimony to the US Congress two months after 26/11, the Indian American defence expert Ashley Tellis rued,

> India has turned out to be a terribly soft state neither able to prevent many of the terrorist acts that have confronted it over the years nor capable of retaliating effectively against either their terrorist adversaries or their state sponsors in Pakistan.[15]

A similarly sobering evaluation about India's seeming impotence in the face of routinized terrorism from Pakistan was made in 2010 by American diplomats in India in a cable classified by the then ambassador but released into the public domain from the trove of the Wikileaks disclosures. This clear-eyed document elaborated on the Indian military's 'Cold Start' doctrine, which had been designed following the 2001 terrorist attack on the Indian parliament in New Delhi carried out by the same LeT and another ISI-favoured jihadist outfit Jaish-e-Mohammed (JeM), and explained why this instrument of hard power was not utilized by the Indian state even though it had been tailor-made for a situation similar to the post-26/11 crisis.[16] The Americans noted that Cold Start was an operational attack plan by the Indian military 'to be taken off the shelf and implemented within a 72-hour period during a crisis'.[17] It was 'not a plan for a comprehensive invasion and occupation of Pakistan' but for 'a rapid, time- and distance-limited penetration into

Pakistani territory with the goal of quickly punishing Pakistan, possibly in response to a Pakistan-linked terrorist attack in India, without threatening the survival of the Pakistani state or provoking a nuclear response.'[18] As to the reasons for India not operationalizing this doctrine after 26/11, the Americans pondered about 'the possible ad hoc nature of decision-making in the upper levels of the Indian government and the role of congress party figures like Sonia Gandhi', and pinpointed that 'while the army may remain committed to the goals of the doctrine, political support is less clear'.[19]

One popular assumption has been that India's 'remarkable restraint' after the Mumbai attacks was attributable to its lack of 'good military options for retaliation [sic] against Pakistani targets'.[20] However, the evidence that has trickled out over the years implicates not an absence of Indian military capabilities to conduct commensurate countervailing operations inside Pakistan after 26/11, but the dearth of *political will* on the part of the Indian government to activate them. In 2020, on the 12th anniversary of 26/11, the Indian security analyst Maroof Raza reflected that 'its wounds will perhaps never heal' and speculated about the road not taken by the incumbent Indian government of that era, a decision that led them to a political failure of epic proportions:

> But the Indian government led by the mild-mannered Dr Manmohan Singh preferred only a measured response, even though he did say that: 'There is enough evidence to show that, given the sophistication and military precision of the attack, it must have had the support of some official agencies in Pakistan.' Had he chosen a tougher response... and the world would have applauded India's willingness to confront terror.[21]

This harsh appraisal is not a benefit of hindsight but a

matter-of-fact assessment of the kinetic options available to the crisis managers at the highest echelons of the Indian government as they were considering the nature of their response during and after 26/11. The former head of the Indian Air Force (IAF), Air Chief Marshal B.S. Dhanoa divulged in 2019 that the Manmohan Singh regime had rejected the IAF's proposal to aerially attack Pakistani terrorist camps immediately following the Mumbai attacks. Dhanoa hit the nail on the head, saying: 'We knew where the terror camps were located in Pakistan and were ready. But it is a political decision whether to carry out a strike or not.'[22] His comments serve as a reminder that national security crises are essentially *political phenomena* with critical choices hinging on the decisiveness and will of civilian political leaders in charge of a country. In functional democracies, the military executes national security tactics and strategies under the express guidance and command of their civilian supervisors, who are politicians of varying degrees and predilections. Whether the politicians seize the moment during a crisis and turn the situation around with grit depends on certain individual and structural factors that bear elaboration. It is fundamentally a question of leadership or its paucity.

Crisis Leaders and Laggards

Roberts identified a detailed set of personality traits of political leaders that matter significantly during foreign policy crises. The key qualities include, among other things, risk-taking orientation, self-esteem, tolerance of ambiguity, intelligence, dominance or submissiveness, need for power, confidence, creativity, initiative, beliefs, motives, emotion, and social, educational, as well as experiential background of the decision-maker.[23] Since no two leaders can be identical in their psychological make-up, the outcome of a crisis will vary depending on which particular prime minister or president is in the saddle at the time of a national security crisis.

In light of the political nature of state power and statecraft, and the oft-cited omnipresence of structural constraints which limit how far a politician can go in responding to crises, the American political scientist Jonathan Keller has developed a binary typology of leaders as 'constraint respecters' or 'constraint challengers'.[24] The former defer to and internalize constraints common in democracies. These include, 'power-sharing arrangements requiring the leader to get other domestic actors' consent', before deciding by what means to respond in a crisis; 'executive accountability to the public', which may or may not want a hard response to the external aggressor; opposition or lack of unanimity about making muscular or risky moves within various bureaucratic arms of the government; and the timing of the crisis vis-à-vis the 'election cycle', wherein a risky foreign policy endeavour may or may not pay off in terms of sustaining the popularity of the incumbent in the eyes of the voters.[25]

On the other hand, leaders who fall within the 'constraint challenger' category do not get bogged down by these daunting problems but have the guts and conviction to overcome them, considering a broader national interest that has to be defended come what may. Where do such politicians get the courage and the tenacity to be different? Keller argues that they are 'guided by a set of inner beliefs or goals' and have a 'more directive management style' that aims to fulfil their vision rather than secure consensus among their subordinates and team members in government. These 'challengers' are driven by distrust and suspicion about the motives and intentions of the foreign adversary country and subscribe to an emotional view of the world where 'one's own nation or group is virtuous, exceptional, and superior in key respects to other nations and groups, which are generally seen as hostile, meddlesome or weak'. The stress these 'crusader' leaders place on 'national honour and identity' is one key reason behind their increased tendency to use force and decrease sensitivity to constraints during national security crises.[26]

Keller's theory is buttressed by Margaret Hermann's pioneering research on how psychological and behavioural factors determine leadership variations in foreign policy more generally, be it in crisis or normal times. She divides political leaders into the categories of 'aggressive' and 'conciliatory'. The former exhibits a manipulative and a controlling attitude with little consideration of the full range of alternative options a state could theoretically exercise when confronting a foreign opponent; has a high sense of nationalism and passion for protecting national sovereignty; is suspicious of the motives of the external adversary and shows a distinct willingness to initiate action without vacillating. In contrast, a conciliatory leader feels the need to establish and sustain good relations with other nations, nurses little suspicion of the motives of foreign countries, carefully weighs a wide range of alternative policy options and has little interest in initiating action or mounting pre-emptive pressure on the external opponent. Hermann says conciliatory leaders, whose description comes close to the stereotype of liberals, 'will attempt to facilitate their nations' participation in the international system'. Conversely, when aggressive leaders who resemble practitioners of *Realpolitik* or *Machtpolitik* feel that foreign 'interaction is necessary, they expect it to be on their nations' terms'.[27]

Political psychology-based analyses of crisis decision-making tend to highlight the worldviews, ideologies and quirks of individual leaders, which are often neglected by more mainstream 'rational choice'-based explanations. But since national security crises are foreign policy crises, *geostrategic* or *international structural constraints* are exigent determinants of the course of action taken when confronted with a foreign threat, regardless of how strong-willed a constraint-challenging leader may be. From a purely bilateral prism, a significant consideration is how the external opponent would react to escalating the conflict through forceful retaliation. Like a chess player, the political leader and their advisory team have to anticipate a series of moves and counter-moves and anticipate, gazing at all the possible scenarios up the escalatory ladder.

Escalation by using military force or symbolically threatening to unleash it is a time-tested instrument of crisis management. It conveys to the other party a willingness to accept a certain level of risk, such as broader military hostilities, to defend one's core national interests and alter the opponent's cost-benefit matrix. The Cold War-era classic theoreticians of crises, W.R. Kintner and D. Schwartz, underlined that the purpose of coercive tactics is to 'escalate a conflict to the point where either (a) a favourable position is reached, or (b) the opponent can be influenced to refrain from escalating further, or (c) negotiation is from a position of superior local or global strength.'[28] Since 'action-reaction sequences' can develop a momentum of their own and might end up in full-scale war due to misperceptions or paranoia of the other side, escalation has to be calibrated and thought through before being implemented.

Launching an all-out war in response to a brawl at the international border, for instance, would amount to a foolhardy, Rube Goldberg solution that could worsen the crisis instead of resolving it. The American scholar John Oneal has aptly described the dilemma and delicate balancing act required in opting to use force: 'National leaders must decide what degree of danger they are willing to assume to preserve values which have been endangered by the external aggressor.' He adds that 'the risks they are willing to accept should be commensurate with the importance of the values which have been engaged by the opponent's actions'.[29] The art of raising the heat just enough to sow doubt and fear in the adversary without triggering a wider conflagration is akin to threading the needle, but it is essential for success in handling national security crises.

Skilful navigation of crisis escalation also depends on the extent of a leader's knowledge and information a leader on the domestic conditions inside the rival nation. It is one thing to second-guess how the opponent will react to retaliation based on the historical behavioural pattern of that country and its elites, but such estimates have to be supplemented with intelligence about the economic and political circumstances the opponent has at home, the level of preparedness of its armed forces and their doctrines, the national mood and discourse regarding the incident which triggered the crisis in the first place. Then there is the big-picture global setting and sizing up of the moment in which the crisis is happening. Will a great power intervene on behalf of the adversary if a leader deploys coercive action against the latter? Will one's own alliances or partnerships suffer damage or be reinforced if the victim state's leader decides to hit back?

These considerations appear burdensome, especially due to the inherent uncertainty and time pressure that crises thrust upon decision-makers. They could weigh down heavily on leaders with weak wills or meek temperaments. Yet, studies show that in spite of the overload of variables and the harrowing nature of the choice confronting leaders whose territory or national interests are under threat, some individuals holding top political positions are determined to run the gauntlet and take the bull by the horns due to their self-belief and ideological hardiness. No matter the structural impediments, decisive leaders find ways to leap past them. The Israeli scholar

Keren Yarhi-Milo posits that leaders do not necessarily read the opponent in a scientific and methodically thorough manner, the way their intelligence agencies or country experts would. Instead, leaders resort to 'selective attention' techniques by relying on 'personal impressions acquired from private interactions with the adversary's leadership', 'their own individual theories and expectations about the adversary's behaviour' and 'their own pre-existing stances toward the adversary'.[30] Therefore, it is necessary to reiterate that the wealth of nationalism, passion and inner conviction that leaders possess are absolutely critical elements in determining how a country deals with a crisis. As former US President Richard Nixon wrote, 'Reaction and response to crisis is uniquely personal in the sense that it depends on what the individual brings to bear on the situation— his own traits of personality and character, his training and religious background, his strengths and weaknesses.'[31]

Even though the American presidential system of government privileges the occupant of the White House with enormous decision-making powers, and it differs from the Westminster parliamentary system, there is no gainsaying the centrality of the president or the prime minister during a national emergency. This book is about the pivotal role of political leadership when the chips are down, and the country and the world are looking up to the top leader for a befitting reply to the threatening external foe. It goes beyond mainstream defence and strategic affairs writings that overplay domestic and international structural constraints and downplay personalities in the study of crises. The message and running theme here are that nations can be safe from foreign predators only if they have leaders willing to defend them by taking reasonable and hitherto-untried risks and mobilizing societies with a nationalistic ethos of sacrifice and hardship for the sake of a better future.

National security crises are ultimate litmus tests of the

character of a country and of its leadership. By their sheer urgency and tension, crises demand the best out of a nation. The adage that 'when the going gets tough, the tough get going' has no better canvas for illustration than crises. This book tests India's political leadership under Prime Minister Narendra Modi's stewardship and makes the case that his assertive management of crises and of Indian politics has set a troubled nation dismissed as a 'soft state' on a path to self-redemption and self-revitalization.

'A War Against India'

Some have interpreted the abject response of the Manmohan Singh government to 26/11 as an inevitable outcome of structural constraints which tied India's hands. Singh's foreign secretary at the time, Shivshankar Menon, presented a long list of factors that dissuaded the Indian crisis response team under Singh from adopting a hard posture. Firstly, had India struck Pakistan, the fact of a terrorist attack on Mumbai, 'would have been obfuscated', and the world's attention would have shifted to preventing war between two nuclear-armed countries. Secondly, he says that a 'war scare' or a real war would have 'united Pakistan behind the Pakistan Army', and weakened a fledgling civilian government in Pakistan which preferred peace with India. Thirdly, a 'limited strike on selected terrorist targets' would have had 'limited practical utility' as the Pakistani military would be unlikely to terminate its sponsorship of jihadi terrorism from such a slight blow and groups like the LeT would not be deterred by 'controlled application of military force'. Fourthly, a war would have 'imposed costs and set back the progress of the Indian economy' just as the global economic crisis had started in November 2008. Menon mentions the 'high probability of war' ensuing from an Indian limited strike and credits India's restrained response as helpful to rally the international community around India and intensify counterterrorism cooperation with foreign partners.[32]

These convoluted and debatable rationales for inaction offer a fascinating window into leadership and thinking projected by the Manmohan Singh government. The obsession with impressing the international community and solicitousness about how the world might perceive India's conduct is in keeping with Hermann's model of 'conciliatory' leadership, which mellows itself in order to win praise from world powers and conform to their expectations. The behind-the-scenes diplomatic manoeuvring and crisis management done by American diplomats after 26/11, which came to light a few years later, leave no doubt that there was pressure from Washington on Singh's government to tone down its response and avoid escalating conflict with Pakistan. In return for this goody-goody behaviour, the US promised to get Pakistan to crack down on its jihad factories.

The outgoing US president, George W. Bush, who had been prosecuting an overly militarized 'global war on terrorism', got into the act early and hypocritically counselled both sides to show 'restraint'.[33] Bush's NSA Condoleezza Rice demanded that Pakistan give India 'absolute, total cooperation' to hold the perpetrators of 26/11 accountable, while simultaneously playing the balancing act by insisting that 'obviously they share a common enemy because extremists in any form are a threat to the Pakistanis as well as the Indians'.[34] Even though American officials and intelligence agencies knew much about the long history of the Pakistani state's umbilical links with jihadist groups like LeT, Rice certified that, 'the Pakistani government, I was told and I fully believe, is very committed to the war on terror and does not in any way want to be associated with terrorist elements'.[35]

On the ground in India and Pakistan, lower-level US diplomats coordinated with their British counterparts in several rounds of 'intense shuttle diplomacy, using diplomatic and intelligence channels to ease tensions between the two countries'. The British were petrified of the prospects of India attacking Pakistan and 'admitted their concern was driven in part by the presence of 500,000 British Pakistani citizens in Pakistani Kashmir'.[36] The American goal was not to strengthen India's hand to avenge or redress the massacre in Mumbai but to maintain 'stability' in the subcontinent so that no nuclear war or new conventional war erupted, which could complicate the US military's anti-Al Qaeda and anti-Taliban campaign in Afghanistan. The West's game plan was to assure India that Pakistan would be compelled to shut down terrorist paraphernalia, stretch out time until the immediate crisis environment dissipated, and then leave it to India to figure out what to do about the core problem of the festering jihadist menace that was continuing to amass inside Pakistan with the full complicity of its state security establishment.

Undoubtedly, the US was in its usual self-centred and double-standard elements. But Manmohan Singh and his advisors decided they could depend on Washington to get justice for 26/11, and thereby deflect the responsibility of a sovereign state's government to defend its own people and territory through its own means. As India failed to act decisively during the window to strike Pakistan right after 26/11, it slipped into a long phase of hand-wringing and agonizing over the knowledge that LeT, JeM and their ISI handlers were freely plotting their subsequent attacks. The cardinal error of relying on duplicitous American promises to get Pakistan to cooperate and moderate its sponsorship of terrorism hung heavily on Singh's record in office. Menon and other defenders of Singh have touted gains from global 'counterterrorism cooperation' that India received after 26/11, but that could neither contain the jihadi monster in Pakistan nor enable India to get closure on a grave injury to its national honour and image.

National security crises are stark instances in which a country and its leaders are alone in a very Hobbesian context of a 'nasty, brutish and short [sic]' world. Even in a globalized international order with all sorts of interdependencies and thickly institutionalized forms of cooperation, when a nation is physically brutalized with unspeakable savagery, banking on webs of multilateral cooperation and etiquettes of proper conduct validated by the international community is not a sign of leadership but of cowardice and ineptitude. While professing and pursuing a desire for peace with one's neighbours is a noble sentiment in an ideal world, raison d'état demands that leaders should bite the bullet and make hard choices during national security crises.

Manmohan Singh was not wrong in latching on to the promise issued by the US in 2005 that it would 'help India become a major world power in the twenty-first century'.[37] But entering into a strategic partnership with Washington did not mean he could transfer his basic responsibility to protect Indian lives and terrain from external intruders into the hands of a great foreign power. Singh had staked his political survival over the landmark India–United States Civil Nuclear Agreement, which almost brought down his coalition government in Parliament in July 2008. A trade economist and bureaucrat before entering politics, Singh had an extraordinary fondness for the US, an indispensable partner for India's GDP growth and modernization. In 2006, his government bent over backwards under American pressure to vote against Iran at the International Atomic Energy Agency (IAEA), an action that added momentum for the Bush administration to possibly attack Iran.[38] That compromise was seen as a necessary price to secure Indian access to western technology. But when it comes to the bargain Singh made with the US after 26/11, one is not sure what India secured at all except ignominy. American diplomats doing the firefighting to restrain India cunningly noted that 'the GOI needed a face saver' to take offensive options off the table. India emerged from 26/11 shamefaced.[39]

Besides the US, India also sought out China and Saudi Arabia, two staunch backers of Pakistan, to try and squeeze Pakistan diplomatically and apply joint pressure on it to concretely move against the perpetrators and planners of 26/11.[40] However, these efforts also visibly went in vain because, like the US and the United Kingdom (UK), these countries had their own strategic ties and needs with Pakistan's military establishment, and they too, simply joined the bandwagon of calming down bilateral tensions between the two sides instead of holding Pakistan's feet to the fire. Even though India opted for restraint and Singh's spin doctors touted it as a wise policy that reaped dividends in the form of unprecedented assistance from the international community, the objective record showed that few foreign powers that had leverage over Pakistan bought India's version or worked as India would have ideally wanted. The 26/11 attacks exposed the gross limitations of diplomacy without firepower.

Apart from hewing to a feeble diplomacy-centric approach, there were other reasons behind India's spineless response to 26/11. Conforming to Keller's model of 'constraint respecter' leadership, the Singh government seems to have been scared of the domestic political fallout of increasing tensions with Pakistan since a general election was around the corner in India just a few months later. Singh, a deferential yes-man and an 'accidental prime minister' who took his orders from his Congress party chief, Sonia Gandhi, was not a fully autonomous player in policymaking. Since he could not boast of a political base of his own and looked to Sonia Gandhi for cues, it is necessary to examine how 26/11 was spun by the 'high command' of the Congress party for partisan political ends.

Pakistan is a Muslim-majority country carved out of undivided India through a bloody partition during decolonization from Britain in 1947, and many Indian Muslims have relatives and ancestral ties to what became a separate nation state of Pakistan. As a result, 'secularist' politicians in India frequently hyphenate India–Pakistan relations with the well-being of India's Muslim minorities. The fact that Pakistan's intelligence agencies infiltrate and prop up radical indigenous terrorist organizations composed of Indian Muslims, such as the Students' Islamic Movement of India (SIMI)[41] and the Indian Mujahideen,[42] deepens this connection between bilateral ties and harmony among India's diverse religious communities. While opinion surveys among ordinary Indian Muslims during Manmohan Singh's rule did offer anecdotal evidence that they felt apprehensive 'that the taint of the India–Pakistan rivalry found there [in Kashmir] will prejudice their own standing in the larger Indian polity,' the systematic manipulation of this linkage was done for electoral politics in the name of maintaining 'vote banks' of minority communities.[43] Refracting international affairs via a domestic religious ideological prism, and connecting them to the interests and safety of Indian Muslims extends beyond Pakistan. The same has been cynically deployed by the Congress party and its allies to limit strategic ties between India and Israel,[44] and to even constrict the India–US partnership that Singh himself was trying to elevate.[45]

The Congress party's shenanigans after 26/11 came to the fore when A.R. Antulay, a veteran loyalist of the Nehru-Gandhi dynasty served as the minister of minority affairs in Singh's cabinet, courted controversy when he questioned if there was a deeper conspiracy behind the killing of the Maharashtra

Anti-Terrorism Squad (ATS) head, Hemant Karkare. Even though it was well established that the top cop fell to bullets of the LeT terrorists, Antulay insinuated that he might have been targeted owing to his previous investigations of 'non-Muslims involved in the acts of terrorism.'[46] If the ruling party of India itself sowed doubt about how an Indian officer in the line of duty died during a terrorist attack, the mixed messaging helped buttress Pakistan's denial of any involvement in 26/11 and confused segments of the Indian public about the severity of the threat posed by the LeT and the ISI. Observant American diplomats posted in India saw through the crassness behind this narrow political ploy:

> Compounding matters, the Congress party, after first distancing itself from the comments, two days later issued a contradictory statement which implicitly endorsed the conspiracy. During this time, Antulay's completely unsubstantiated claims gained support in the conspiracy-minded Indian-Muslim community...The entire episode demonstrates that the congress Party will readily stoop to the old caste/religious-based politics if it feels it is in its interest.[47]

Politicized red herrings of 'Hindu terror' amid a perilous national security crisis wrought by a foreign adversary unveiled a disunited and fragmented India in an era of muddled multiparty coalitions and weaponization of religious identities. No less than US President Barack Obama sensed the weakened and vitiated internal atmosphere in India when he recounted meeting Manmohan Singh in 2010 and heard the Indian prime minister again drawing the linkage between India's Muslim minorities, Indian secularism and his weak response to Pakistan during 26/11.

Then there was the problem of Pakistan: its continuing failure to work with India to investigate the 2008 terrorist attacks on hotels and other sites in Mumbai had significantly increased tensions between the two countries, in part because Lashkar-e-Tayyiba, the terrorist organization responsible, was believed to have links to Pakistan's intelligence service. Singh had resisted calls to retaliate against Pakistan after the attacks, but his restraint had cost him politically. He feared that rising anti-Muslim sentiment had strengthened the influence of India's main opposition party, the Hindu nationalist Bharatiya Janata Party (BJP). 'In uncertain times, Mr President,' the prime minister said, 'the call of religious and ethnic solidarity can be intoxicating. And it's not so hard for politicians to exploit that, in India or anywhere else.'[48]

In India's noisy news media discourse, the phrase 'politicization of terror' is a regular trope funnelled by politicians of all hues and backgrounds looking to score points over each other. But the politicization that happened over 26/11 had more than domestic electoral implications. It sapped the Indian state's will to respond adequately to Pakistan's outrageous deed. With Singh and Sonia Gandhi apparently having made up their mind that retaliation against Pakistan was not advisable, it is not surprising that the actual operational military options that were presented to the crisis response team in the prime minister's office (PMO) on 28 November and 2 December 2008 were all struck down as unfeasible or too risky. Here is a telling account of the defensive and predisposed nature of the crisis deliberations:

> The government was clear that a strike across the international border (at the JuD [Jama'at-ud-Da'wah, the parent institution of the LeT] headquarters in Muridke,

Lahore...) would be provocative and escalate matters...It would also be unacceptable internationally... Air strikes needed exact coordinates of camps... 'There was a very real risk of the operation killing civilians'... This last option too was discarded.[49]

Had there been a bolder and more nationalistic leadership in New Delhi, India would have surely selected one or more options without worrying excessively about the operational risks or of international opinion. The problem was not so much a shortage of intelligence or military capabilities, imperfect as they always are in the fog of most national security crises, but a submissive political leadership with other ideas. Falling for Pakistan's nuclear blackmail and assuming that Pakistan would counter-retaliate disproportionately using unconventional weapons of mass destruction were logical fallacies. During the Kargil War of 1999, India did not go as far as sending its military into Pakistani-controlled territory. But on that occasion, India did call Pakistan's nuclear bluff. The conflict remained below the nuclear threshold and led to a defeat and withdrawal of Pakistani forces from occupied Indian land following international intervention *against* Pakistan, not in its favour.

Moreover, in late 2008, around the time of the 26/11 attacks, Pakistan was in an acute economic and financial crisis and hardly in shape to dictate terms to India in any limited war. The political uncertainty following General Musharraf's fall and the onset of a new civilian government added to Pakistan's woes. Any perceptive eye could see that Indian decision-makers exaggerated Pakistan's might after 26/11 to suit their pre-existing choices. The American scholar Daniel Markey's analysis from January 2010 is worth citing here as he could see through the straw men set up by Indian leaders:

Pakistan's military response could be intentionally disproportionate to the initial Indian attack so as to compel the international community to force a ceasefire. That said, Pakistan's present government and military command also have meaningful incentives to calibrate their actions from the start, not least the desire to limit international pressure and to retain ties with partners in Beijing, Riyadh, and Washington.[50]

Even as the horror of 26/11 was unfolding in Mumbai, an outspoken politician who was seen as a rising star in India's right-wing opposition, Bharatiya Janata Party (BJP), delivered a stern speech outside one of the venues ravaged by the terrorists, the Oberoi Trident hotel. The then chief minister of Gujarat, Narendra Modi, criticized the central government's failure to avert the attack despite what he claimed were multiple intelligence warnings the Gujarat state government had given about Pakistani terrorists using stolen Indian boats to carry out nefarious terrorist activities via the coastal route of western India. He also denounced the prime minister for his 'disappointing' speech when the attacks began and demanded an effective counterterrorism strategy.[51] Once it became evident, as months passed, that India's response was a total cop-out, Modi upped the ante and laid down, in stark terms, the gravity of what had happened in Mumbai and what should have been done:

> Through these attacks, Pakistan had initiated war against India and we should have responded accordingly, but instead the Indian government went and begged before the United States of America, pleading with them to act against Pakistan.[52]

Since he was still only the chief minister of a state and not even the prime ministerial choice of the BJP at that stage, his opponents could rebut such fiery language as playing to the gallery to garner votes with a clarion call for hyper-patriotism. After all, Modi had not yet gotten into the hot seat of leading the entire country, with all its unbearable dilemmas and impossible choices. He had no experience of global diplomatic pushing and hauling nor any access to higher-level inside intelligence about the military doctrines of the Indian or Pakistani armed forces. It is always easy to turn on shrill rhetoric when in the Opposition, but the pressures and constraints an incumbent prime minister has to contend with are known only to those who make it to the summit of Indian political power.

In subsequent chapters of this book, we will see that Modi defied such belittling depictions when he ascended to the chair of prime minister of India. In spite of greater power and a much larger domain of responsibility, he did not shy away from risks and sacrifices when confronted with national security crises. The remarkable strategic consistency and clarity he has manifested whenever India or Indian security interests have been in jeopardy will come through in each crisis episode I will parse in the pages to come.

Dragon Breathing Fire

Modi's national security crises have not been limited to the perpetual menace of unconventional threats posed by Pakistan. The following chapters also discuss China, India's northern neighbour, which has progressively grown into the foremost strategic challenge in the Modi era, overshadowing Pakistan and pushing India to play out of its skin and undertake countermeasures in all three domains of crisis response—military, economic and diplomatic.

Even before the Modi-led BJP's landmark victory in the 2014 general elections, China had flashed glimpses of its new aggressive avatar in a series of mini-crises with India at the

LAC, which were the worst since the 1980s. The first stand-off happened in April 2013 at Daulat Beg Oldi (DBO) in the Depsang Valley, a historic Indian campsite in northeastern Ladakh, when dozens of Chinese People's Liberation Army (PLA) soldiers intruded as far as 20 kilometres into what India considers to be its side of the uninhabited and undemarcated border, and hunkered down in tents to claim that the stretch of land belonged to China. However, despite Indian patrols discovering the Chinese tents and expressing objections to the latter's presence there in no uncertain terms, the PLA forces refused to retreat. India then deployed an equivalent number of Indo-Tibetan Border Police (ITBP) troops just 300 metres from where the Chinese were camped, and a stand-off ensued for three weeks. Hectic diplomatic parleys and local military commanders' meetings ensued, and eventually, both sides agreed to vacate their respective perches and step back.

The icebreaker apparently centred on Chumar, 250 kilometres away from DBO in southeastern Ladakh, where China demanded that Indian military bunkers be dismantled. In 2012, PLA forces had begun intruding onto what India considered its side in Chumar via helicopter drops and made Chumar an 'epicentre of heightened activities' prior to the DBO tensions at the northern end of Ladakh.[53] The DBO row eventually ended after three weeks in May 2013, with India believed to have agreed to abandon and demolish the bunkers in Chumar and the Chinese letting Indian forces patrol as they used to in the past. Indian Defence Ministry officials were quoted as admitting that 'the deal to end the stand-off was a quid pro quo' and that 'China had also demanded India take down listening and observation posts in the Chumar area'.[54] Although the Singh government denied that it had succumbed to Chinese demands in Chumar, a lingering perception that remained from this episode was that China got the better of

India. The reader will revisit Chumar in Chapter 2 of this book, as this front was renewed in the opening salvo from China to the new Modi government.[55]

While bilateral disagreements and friction over different segments of the 'perceptive' LAC date back multiple decades, the PLA's actions at DBO and Chumar in 2012–2013 hinted at a challenging future where China would try to dictate terms to India on disputed points by virtue of its superior conventional might and a willingness to demonstrate strength to bargain from an advantageous position. In the incidents of April–May 2013, China adopted the role of demander and first-mover while India was compelled to look for military and diplomatic tactics to hang on to its perceived claims. The cat-and-mouse pattern that these face-offs indicated should have rung alarm bells in New Delhi and caused a strategic reassessment of the threat posed by China. But given Manmohan Singh's liberal outlook of enhancing economic cooperation with neighbours and weaving a thick web of intergovernmental rules and parameters to build goodwill, the two sides went on to sign a Border Defence Cooperation Agreement (BDCA) in October 2013 with the hope of institutionalizing communications and reducing tensions.

The BDCA's preamble prominently invoked the India–China Strategic and Cooperative Partnership for Peace and Prosperity, an agreement that Singh had signed with his Chinese counterpart Wen Jiabao way back in 2005. The prevailing ethos at that time in the Indian government was to believe that Sino-Indian relations were progressing positively overall and that the LAC frictions were irritants that needed to be massaged by building trust via mechanisms and treaties. Singh famously subscribed to the notion that there was 'enough space in the world for both China and India to grow,'[56] while his cabinet minister coined the neologism 'Chindia' to propose a non-zero-sum-game friendship and held that 'one side feeling threatened by the other is not caution but paranoia.'[57] India agreed to host Chinese Premier Li Keqiang in April 2013, even amid the border tensions, to show that broader bilateral ties would keep on improving and to potentially use the high-profile visit as a lever to de-escalate the LAC situation. Singh downplayed the LAC incidents as a 'localized problem', and his foreign minister, Salman Khurshid, gave the analogy of the PLA incursions as mere 'acne that can be addressed by simply applying an ointment.'[58]

What India did not realize in 2013 was that it had failed to read the tea leaves and was clinging on to hopes of peaceful coexistence with a China that was becoming more bumptious since the advent to power of Xi Jinping, the new chief of the Chinese Communist Party (CCP) and the Central Military Commission, in 2012. Although there are no publicly available primary sources proving that the new strongman Xi specifically and explicitly altered China's strategy towards India or its military doctrine, he did signal an aggressive intent early in his tenure through the conduct of the PLA in deliberately triggering the LAC incidents of 2013. China would henceforward demand more and apply incrementally greater pressure on India. The Indian scholar Srinivasan Sitaraman noted in 2013 the confusion in the Indian government about perceiving China for what it was:

> New Delhi has struggled to define its relations with China and it is shying away from treating China as 'enemy number one,' but clearly China is not a frenemy either… to India, China represents a regional power and a very real security threat…it has to be perpetually concerned about because of the outstanding territorial dispute and economic power differentials.[59]

Ordinary Indian citizens appeared to be ahead of the Singh government in reappraising the threat of China. An opinion poll conducted by Australia's Lowy Institute before the DBO and Chumar strains found that 83 per cent of surveyed Indians perceived China as a threat, and despite China becoming India's largest trading partner, only 31 per cent of Indians concurred that China's rise had been good for India.[60] The unease about India misreading China and a critique of the Singh government's handling of the LAC mini-crises also emanated from the Opposition, with BJP's senior leader, Rajnath Singh, remarking, 'when China did not even respect the Line of Actual Control, then there was no point in signing BDCA agreement with it on the issue'. He also questioned the wisdom of a provision in the BDCA, which he interpreted as meaning that, 'if Chinese forces entered into Indian side while patrolling, then India will not be able to push them back, which means that Indian forces will not be able to chase them'.[61]

The attack lines that the Manmohan Singh government was craven on national security and underestimating metastasizing foreign threats were sharpened in the wake of the upcoming general election in 2014 and the past failures of the Congress party-led coalition government to give befitting responses to Pakistan-sponsored terrorism. It was no coincidence that Modi and Rajnath were the most trenchant in slamming the Sonia–Singh combination for failing to protect national security. After the BJP's victory in May 2014, they would become prime minister and home minister (later, defence minister), respectively, and shoulder the burden of walking the talk of being uncompromising and strategically astute in managing the two perennial, but constantly morphing, threats that India faces from its west and north.

Hardening the Soft State

This book is not a treatise on Modi's foreign policy as a whole, which I covered extensively in an earlier volume.[62] My focus here is on national security crises he has had to reckon with—a subject that intrinsically requires attention to overlapping aspects of international relations, military tactics and strategy, and political leadership—during his prime ministership. My concern is about Indian land and Indian lives and how Modi has exerted himself, the Indian state and society to protect them from external threats. I am also driven by what lessons one can draw for the future from his custodianship of fundamental national interests of sovereignty, territorial integrity and safety of citizens.

For decades, commentators have bemoaned India's weak or non-existent 'strategic culture'. A former US military officer, George Tanham, alleged in 1992 that Indian elites do not think 'systematically about national strategy', do not articulate or pursue national goals 'in a coherent, disciplined fashion', are 'constantly on the defensive', vis-à-vis China and Pakistan, display 'passive or reactive tendencies in military matters', instead of initiating moves and putting pressure on rivals, and act on an 'ad hoc and pragmatic basis', instead of developing formal doctrines.[63] While many of these charges were legitimate, strategic culture is not set in stone and evolves over time. Subsequent authors have made the case that the systemic shock of the end of the Cold War and altered geopolitical conditions have brought revisions in Indian national security thinking in the form of openness to alliance-like foreign relations, expanded international ambitions and aims, enhanced faith in military power and embrace of great power politics.[64] But given the vast gap between rhetoric and practice of Realpolitik and poor institutionalization of national security structures within the Indian state, others lamented in

2010 about the entrenchment of 'continued strategic restraint' and the lack of sustained interest in the use of military force for furthering national security.[65] Following the Manmohan Singh government getting re-elected in 2009 without paying a political price for the fiasco of its non-response to 26/11, the Indian scholar Harsh Pant wrote:

> Indian grand strategy continues to be marked by its absence. Since foreign policy issues do not tend to win votes, there is little incentive for political parties to devote serious attention to them and the result is *ad hoc* responses to various crises as they emerge. Indian strategic culture will undergo a change in the coming years. If the past is any guide, then this process might take much longer than expected.[66]

The perceived absence of electoral incentives for tightening up the ship of the Indian security machine, investing in hard military power and deploying it intelligently against adversaries, has indeed been one cause for several Indian political leaders neglecting national security problems. The literature on domestic constraints on crisis decision-making we came across earlier refers to pacifying pressures on political leaders in democracies, where the voting public or other constituencies may not encourage escalation with foreign adversaries as they might prioritize other issues and not care to punch back at foreign foes. The political scientists Joshua Kertzer and Ryan Brutger have refined the theory of 'audience costs' (rulers in democratic countries have to consistently implement threats made to foreign opponents during a crisis to avoid being punished by voters) to suggest there are 'belligerence costs', i.e. some voters could punish the leader for simply threatening the use of force against a foreign foe. Citizens who are 'low in militant assertiveness', have 'high levels of international trust', are 'more sanguine about the motivations of other countries', are 'low in national chauvinism', are 'less likely to believe in the inherent inferiority of other countries', and generally liberal in outlook will look to punish a leader who wants to play hardball with international rivals during a crisis. The researchers argue that since there will be a heterogeneity of ideologies and viewpoints in a population at any given time, the leader's decision to issue or implement threats against foreign rivals 'depends on who the leader's relevant audience is'. Also, as the will of the people is not static, 'one would expect that as the composition of the public shifts, so too would the balance of considerations driving audience costs'.[67]

The caveat that 'belligerence costs' may not apply if the public mood changes to a more nationalistic or hawkish position is important to bear in mind while analysing why Indian leaders in the past preferred to respond mildly during national security crises. The Japanese scholar Akisato Suzuki has used a data set on the use of coercive diplomacy during bilateral conflicts around the world to test the hypothesis that 'under the conditions of a good economy, citizens will tolerate failure in an international crisis'. The assumption was that 'it is a risk for citizens to replace a leader who is helping the economy just because she has failed in an international crisis, as there is no guarantee that the leader who follows will be able to sustain the same economic performance'. But Suzuki could not find any empirical correlation between a healthy economy and pacifist pressures from the public on the leader. In other words, there have been many crises across the world over the last century when the public did not forgive politicians who oversaw a successful economy but failed to decisively deal with foreign adversaries. The researcher explains the possible reasoning behind this effect as follows:

...if the average citizen is a hardliner who cares about national pride much more than about economic prosperity, her leader may be able to generate audience costs better and, therefore, is likely to be more successful in coercive diplomacy *regardless of the state of the domestic economy* [emphasis in the original].[68]

To assume that the bulk of the voters always accords first priority to incumbent leaders sustaining high economic growth or managing domestic problems while tending to ignore or forgive their record on national security and foreign policy is thus not borne by evidence. What academics term as 'national pride' or 'composition of the public', and how these mass sentiments shift over time hold the key to whether or not a leader can take bold decisions during national security crises. In India, the scholar Prithvi Iyer writes that unlike in earlier eras when 'the public opinion–foreign policy linkage' was considered to be 'indirect at best' and foreign policy was seen as a 'low salience issue for the Indian public', Modi and the BJP have 'placed foreign policy debates at the centre stage of their electoral campaign and galvanized voters through key foreign policy decisions'. In the context of the surge in popularity that Modi gained in 2019 through air strikes in Pakistan's Balakot (this episode and the national security crisis preceding it are analysed in depth in Chapter 3 of this book), Iyer infers that the Indian electorate at present is 'not only concerned about domestic issues'. He adds:

Threats to national security, the government's framing of the crisis, and its means to deal with them—all have a profound impact on domestic audiences and their voting preferences. Thus, the perceived audience costs of threats to Indian national security [indicate] the power of public opinion as an intervening variable shaping foreign policy decision-making.[69]

From later chapters of this book, the reader can grasp how Modi crafted a nationalist majority in India through mass mobilization around the idea of toughness to foreign foes. If some leaders in democracies have to run scared of 'belligerence costs' during crises due to the pacifism or apathy in the voting public, Modi has inverted the scales and constructed 'belligerence benefits' by virtue of inspiring ordinary Indians to expect that the country's leader has to stand up to external bullying and aggression through forceful means. During his reign, the rise to prominence of a nationalistic news media has amplified this wave of patriotism and mass approval in Indian society for stronger national security responses. Liberal critics of Modi, especially his opponents in the Congress party and the left-wing circles, depict him as a jingoist warmonger who has recklessly provoked confrontations with China and Pakistan by escalating during crises and pushing India to the edge of the precipice.[70] But for these politicians, the writing on the wall is clear. The Indian public they used to manipulate and divide along religious and other ethnic lines before Modi arrived on the national scene no longer accepts their preferred mode of national security dovishness, hesitancy and surrender to the whims of foreign foes.

Apart from guiding the pulse of India's people in an unbending and unshakeable direction, the other positive change that Modi has attempted is to modernize India's military and security institutions and associated bureaucracy. However steely and 'constraint challenging' a political leader is, they are in charge of the ship that is the state, which has to operationalize their vision for national security. The later chapters of this book emphasize the impact that structural reforms in India's national security system, which Modi is steering, have had on the Indian government's responses to crises.

Here, I spell out a few of the standout changes he has

effected as part of a long-term revamp so that India remains up to speed with the rapidly advancing and innovative forms of aggression by China and Pakistan. The crown jewel in Modi's security overhaul efforts is creating the office of the chief of defence staff (CDS) in 2019. Modi announced his decision to establish the office of the CDS on Independence Day that year as part of his vision to improve coordination among India's army, navy and air force, and boost India's national security and power projection capabilities. This reordering of the higher military management was long due in the larger national interest and a forward-looking step for India to keep abreast of international trends in defence modernization.

The idea of CDS—the Indian equivalent of the US's chairman of the Joint Chiefs of Staff (CJCS), the UK's chief of the Defence Staff and Australia's chief of the Defence Force (CDF)— had been mooted decades ago in India, but it was stymied by bureaucratic naysaying and narrow, self-interested objections of various stakeholders. Anxieties of individual service chiefs about losing turf to their peers and the cussedness of civilian officials who feared transfer of influence to a single 'Super General', had held India back. While the entrenched tradition of bureaucratic stasis and pettiness will not vanish overnight, Modi's momentous decision to form the CDS was a welcome top-down blow to vested interests, which was buttressed by assurances from the highest levels in New Delhi that generated a broad intra-governmental coalition in favour of reform.

I spoke to Air Marshal Anil Chopra, a retired senior IAF officer, about the impact of Modi's political leadership factor on the morale and reorganization of India's military:

Modi rode to power saying 'I will be a doer'. One of the first things he told to the service chiefs after becoming prime minister was 'what could not happen in 70 years, I will make it happen and show.' Since the 1950s, there was a file going around that India must have a war memorial of its own. Once Modi took over, he brushed aside all the bureaucratic and political objections and just announced it. The next thing we saw was the whole country was running around to get the memorial done. The One Rank One Pension (OROP) reform of benefits for retired soldiers was another landmark that many politicians had contemplated before Modi, but only he could implement. The Kargil Committee Report (1999) had recommended creation of a CDS, but every government stalled until Modi came. He told the service chiefs, 'I want you to do full reform. If you plan to make theatre commands, air defence command, maritime command, etc., just do it. It's a diktat.' He said, 'You all decide the modalities, but just do it.' He pushed decisions that had been pending for years. He brought alive leadership in national security.[71]

The advantages of a CDS are myriad. For India's military to be effective in crises, deter dynamic enemies and perform the best in combat, its forces must integrate and enmesh. Inter-service rivalries over weapons acquisitions, budgets, deployment of hardware, tactics and claiming relative credit for battlefield achievements have cost many countries, including India, dearly in both war and peacetime. For example, infighting between the Indian Army and IAF during the 1999 Kargil War regarding attack helicopters and what role each wing should play in repelling Pakistani intruders caused critical delays that prolonged India's eventual victory.[72] Residual tensions between the Army Aviation Corps and the IAF, and between the Indian Navy and the Indian Army over the meagre budgets allocated to the former, had dented India's readiness to be competitive amid the advent of global military doctrines like 'AirLand Battle' and 'AirSea Battle'. Modi himself observed that the parameters and very nature of warfare were changing worldwide, and India could not afford to think in broken pieces or fragmented ways. What India needed, as he said in his 2019 Independence Day speech, was better military coordination among the three wings of the armed forces so that it could keep up with the altering global security atmosphere and trends.[73]

His reference—the manner in which established powers around the world had recognized the inadequacy of separate service commands and operational planning and undertaken structural efforts towards fusion. The US reworked its military command structure in 1986 by granting centralized power to its CJCS and forging interoperability, wherein each geographically organized command catering to a specific region of the world would include a mix of ground, naval, marine, air and special operations personnel. Chinese revolution in military affairs (RMA) concept was fast-forwarded by Xi Jinping's aggressive push to enhance 'jointness' among the wings of the PLA. It is evident that Modi has understood and wants to take a leaf from the Chinese model of reorganization through political will from above. The anomaly of India's fragmented eastern commands of the Indian Army, Indian Navy and IAF, located far apart from each other in Kolkata, Visakhapatnam and Shillong, respectively, vis-à-vis a sharp and singular western command of China, is glaring.

Having made the CDS a reality, Modi has not rested on past accomplishments but ploughed ahead and pursued joint theatre commands to become a functional reality on India's ground, air and territorial waters. Individual branches of India's military do have their own distinct sub-identities, sources of pride and philosophical characteristics, harking back to the British colonial inheritance. The task ahead is to retain those specialized attributes and affinities while bringing about a cultural and attitudinal shift in all the wings and civilian paraphernalia to serve the unified goal of securing India, and carrying it to great power status.

Another institutional innovation that the Modi government must be credited with is the creation, in April 2018, of an overarching Defence Planning Committee (DPC), chaired by the NSA and manned by the chiefs of the armed forces along with senior bureaucrats from multiple ministries. The Indian defence analyst Laxman Behera wrote that the DPC was 'arguably the boldest defence reform in decades' as it would 'clearly articulate the key national security/defence/military goals as well as prioritise defence and security requirements as per the likely available resources. [At the same time, it would provide] adequate focus on emerging security challenges, technological advancements, and establishing a strong indigenous defence manufacturing base'.[74] With the CDS joining the DPC after the former's formal advent in December 2019, and the Modi government also reconstituting the Strategic Policy Group (SPG) under the National Security Council (NSC), India is poised for the first time to have most of the relevant stakeholders of its national security gathering and deciding under collective umbrellas. The Modi government's enhanced funding for the National Security Council Secretariat (NSCS) and appointment of a third deputy NSA were also long-due investments of resources and personnel to cater to the ever-expanding workload of defending India from various quarters.

Although the National Security Strategy (NSS) has not been made public, the establishment of theatre commands of the Indian military as a logical follow-up to the CDS did not happen quickly, and India's defence expenditure on capital acquisitions has not matched its ambition to be a 'leading power' in the world, the Modi government has inched its way towards a sharper and more integrated national security system. The activation of the Defence Cyber Agency (DCA), a joint tri-service command of the armed forces to deal with internet warfare, and a Defence Space Agency (DSA) combining the three wings to operate space war and satellite intelligence, are indicators that Modi is aiming big despite the arcane intra-agency and interdepartmental bureaucratic politics that have stunted India. One can deduce a direct link between Modi's organizational reforms and his management of national security crises from the operationalization of the Armed Forces Special Operations Division (AFSOD), another tri-service body that will be responsible for carrying out joint missions against 'high-value targets, strategic installations, and to destroy the war-fighting machinery of the enemy and infrastructures of the terrorists'.[75]

Earlier, a 'Joint Indian Armed Forces Doctrine' was unveiled in April 2017 with a notable mention of special operations, which caught the attention of the whole world a year earlier when India took the battle inside Pakistan. The last phase of any national security crisis is learning from experience, assessing how the strategic equations may have shifted, and adapting the state machinery to institutionalize new practices and tactics, if not a new culture altogether. The full analysis of the 2016 national security crisis and 'surgical strikes' follow in Chapter 1 of this book.

Having inherited a tradition of strategic restraint, inertia, buck-passing and departmental silos, which left much to be desired in India's sprawled out security apparatus, Modi has tried to use crises and threats as stepping stones for integrating the multiple arms of the Indian military, intelligence and civilian security bodies into a cohesive unit. The Indian defence analyst Kapil Patil writes that Modi has 'introduced major institutional changes which are expected to bring about a structural shift in India's strategic planning and outlook', and that the net effect of his reforms is that 'India is gradually learning to harness its military resources in service of her long-term political objectives.'[76] Although the Indian defence and national security framework has miles to go before it can match the flexibility, capability and dynamism of more advanced nations, it is no exaggeration to conclude that Modi has lit the spark.

Even before rising to the level of prime minister, he had propounded a new 'philosophy of governance' based on 'silo-breaking' to reform the administration in his native state of Gujarat.[77] While it is humanly impossible for one leader to remake outmoded ways of thinking and to act in a vast national bureaucracy, the reader will see in later chapters of this book that there is a palpable 'Modi effect' on India's national security behaviour and processes, which is a hopeful sign for improved management of future crises.

According to a periodization by the Indian academician Sumit Ganguly, India's national security policies have passed through four phases, viz. Independence to the Sino-Indian War (1947–1962), marked by excessive idealism and 'neglect'; the aftermath of the China war until the end of the Cold War (1962–1991), distinguished by 'unwillingness to fully embrace the significance of material power'; the post-Cold War years (1991–2014), when there was no 'viable doctrine to deal with future terrorist attacks' and an 'inability to coerce Pakistan'; and the era of Modi (2014 onward). Ganguly describes the fourth phase as one where 'external developments in conjunction with domestic preferences are leading to changes', the Indian state has 'all but departed from the ideational rhetorical flourishes that had characterized a host of prior regimes', and has 'adopted a tougher stance toward both the PRC [China] and Pakistan'. In light of the shift in tone and substance under Modi, Ganguly asks if future Indian regimes would 'fully embrace a more neo-realist approach to the making of India's security policy', implying that they will rely more confidently on military force and also unsentimentally exploit global great power rivalries to accrue geostrategic advantages for India. Should such a denouement happen during the Modi era or under his successors, it would erase most of the deficits that Tanham and his ilk have been decrying as missing in India's national security outlook and armour.[78]

Just so that no flights of fancy arise among security buffs or howls of disapproval emerge from welfarist liberals, it is essential to clarify what the Modi effect is not doing to India. The Indian state will never become a quintessential 'national security state', a concept that the left-wing American academic Jack Nelson-Pallmeyer explicated as a persistent threat to democracy around the world.[79] This concept echoes the American sociologist Harold Lasswell's classical theory of the 'garrison state' where a politico-military elite grabs the lion's share of the public budget, erodes civil liberties, promotes unbridled militarism in society and perpetually engages in wars that generate profit and power for the elite.[80]

Pakistan fits the bill of a national security state. Like Prussia in nineteenth-century Europe or Argentina, Egypt, Turkey and Indonesia in recent times, Pakistan is 'not a country with an army but an army with a country', where the military establishment has hegemonic control over land, resources, industry, taxpayer's money and foreign and defence policies.[81] In September 2020, the ousted and exiled former Pakistani prime minister, Nawaz Sharif, deplored how the supremacy of this unelected institution had reached such heights that 'from being a state within a state, it was now a state above the state'.[82] Chapters 1 and 3 examine Pakistan's relentless hostility and hatred toward India, which keep yielding crisis after crisis. The root cause of this iterated war-like conduct is the nature of the Pakistani national security state.

Likewise, Chapters 2 and 4 of this book detail how China has pressed hard against India and many other neighbouring countries with ferocity and unswerving mind because the Chinese state has acquired facets of a national security state under Xi Jinping. Unlike Pakistan, this variant is not a military-dominated one but a Communist Party-dictated one. The Sinologist Tai Ming Cheung argues that Xi is 'building a national security Party-state', a departure from the China of his predecessors that is being implemented through a seamless correlation between a totalitarian internal security dragnet and the PLA's foreign expeditionary buildout.[83]

India, a quasi-federal democracy where power transfers from one or more civilian political parties to others regularly, and decision-making authority is diffused into the hands of elected representatives from different persuasions and regions, can seem vulnerable compared to unitary national security states such as Pakistan and China. External Affairs Minister Subrahmanyam Jaishankar has alluded to this structural disadvantage by reflecting, 'one of India's challenges is that its sense of an establishment is not fully developed'. The absence of a self-confident state establishment shielded from electoral winds, social demands and bureaucratic undermining has been a hindrance for India, especially in ably holding its ground during national security crises. To quote Jaishankar:

> It is only when a national elite has a strong and validated sense of its bottom lines that it will take a firm stand when these are challenged. So, whether it is an issue of violation of sovereignty or infringement of borders, an ability to respond categorically can come from this inherent self-belief. Asserting national interests and securing strategic goals through various means is the dharma of a state, as indeed it was of an individual warrior.[84]

What Modi has managed to do since 2014 is strive to pursue this 'dharma of a state' and gird India's loins to resist like a righteous warrior against its two principal external adversaries. In a country with a postcolonial legacy of a 'strong society' and a 'weak state', this is no mean feat.[85] Modi's India is nowhere close to being a 'hard state' or a praetorian state where national security ideology and propaganda drown out all other pursuits and priorities of government and social groups. The baseline from which Modi took over the reins of India had been so devoid of strategic culture and confidence in even limited use of military force that his impact can be accurately characterized as hardening a flabby state that has historically been stubbornly resistant to adaptation or modernization to get in sync with global trends. What has worked in favour of Modi's security reforms is his commanding political stature as an unrivalled leader with mass popularity and a huge parliamentary majority. Modi's NSA and right hand, Ajit Doval, has articulated a vision for India to become a 'hard power' and warned against the pitfalls of weak and wayward coalition governments, which had been the norm before Modi's arrival on the national scene.[86]

Not since Indira Gandhi, who was prime minister from 1966 to 1977 and again from 1980 to 1984, has India had a political leader with the charismatic weight and mass electoral mandate as Modi. In the following chapters of this book, I explain the symbiosis between Modi's forthrightness and risk-taking during national security crises and his soaring political popularity. If domestic politics had once been an insuperable obstacle to acting resolutely against external adversaries, Modi has redefined politics as an extension of a tough national security posture. Some of the spunk and the grit that India has fielded in response to crises since Modi became prime minister are unique to his personality and belief system, fulfilling the expectations of the psychological theories of crisis decision-making we referred to earlier in this Introduction. But some of it is also because India as a country, and to a lesser extent the Indian state apparatus, have transformed for the better under Modi. The fissiparous and centrifugal political and social winds that had gotten free rein under unwieldy coalition governments wedded to vote banks have been replaced by a national thinking and a national consciousness that had eluded India for decades. When there are governments with thumping legislative majorities and rousing political leadership, entire countries and not just their militaries can be psychologically better prepared for dealing with the worst threats. Even now, the will and the resolve which India lacked as it has been put to the test by its hostile neighbours are not fully there. But Modi has kick-started a renaissance.

Chapter 1

Surgical Strikes on Fear

*We make our friends; we make our enemies; but God makes
our next-door neighbour. Hence he comes to us clad in all
the careless terrors of nature; he is as strange as the stars,
as reckless and indifferent as the rain. He is Man, the most
terrible of beasts.*[1]

—British philosopher G.K. Chesterton, 1905

A Wedding and a Warning

On 25 December 2015, Prime Minister Narendra Modi was
in Kabul, Afghanistan, to dedicate the new Afghan parliament
building, a gift from India to a fraternal country. Sticking to
the geopolitically effusive script of deep and affectionate India–
Afghanistan friendship and the insecurities it was generating in
an envious and meddlesome neighbour, he took aim at Pakistan,
saying, 'There are some who did not want us to be here', and
'others who were uneasy at the strength of our partnership'.[2]

Unfortunately, any and all assistance by India to stabilize
the moderate Afghan government for two decades since the US
invasion of Afghanistan in 2001 had been in vain. In August
2021, the US abandoned the weak regime of President Ashraf

Ghani, which fell to a swift Pakistan-backed Afghan Taliban military offensive.[3] Islamabad celebrated the return of its jihadist allies to power and New Delhi had little option but to prepare for the possibility of increased national security threats from emboldened terrorists, whose morale was sky-high, in both Afghanistan and Pakistan. More India–Pakistan friction and crises loomed on the horizon.

But rewinding to late 2015, there was still some optimism. After inaugurating the new Afghan parliament structure in Kabul, Modi, on the way back in the evening, suddenly and unexpectedly landed in Lahore—Pakistan's metropolis and the political bastion of Prime Minister Nawaz Sharif. The Indian leader had invited himself to Sharif's granddaughter's wedding over a phone call and was personally received by his counterpart at the airport. As images and videos went viral across the world, the news media swooned with superlatives at the rarest of rare spectacles, the Indian and Pakistani prime ministers walking in tandem on the red carpet, hands clasped and displaying a personal bonhomie, suggesting back-channel contacts much before the drama in Lahore unfolded in public glare.

No official talks or business was conducted during this optically dazzling stopover which lasted around two hours. But the symbolism of an Indian leader setting foot in Pakistan for the first time in 11 years, bonding effortlessly with counterpart Sharif and ringing in a positive tone ahead of scheduled lower-level bilateral diplomatic talks was unmissable. Modi had launched himself on the world stage by inviting the heads of all the south Asian countries, including Sharif, to his swearing-in ceremony in May 2014. He vigorously pursued a 'neighbourhood first' foreign policy from his first day in office. The personalized attention he gave to countries small and large across the subcontinent and his pragmatic intervention in resolving outstanding bilateral disputes and winning hearts on the world stage made amends for Manmohan Singh's lacklustre and aloof performance in India's immediate backyard. Modi's grand vision was (and still is) to integrate South Asia into a cooperative common space where trade, commerce and people flow smoothly across borders, and regional governance problems are resolved through trust and collective mechanisms.

Knowing individual leaders and having their confidence held the key to the fulfilment of this ambitious dream. The Indian prime minister has often elaborated the philosophy behind his personalized diplomacy. Relations between countries, he remarked, 'depend less on "full stops and commas on papers" and more on relations between leaders. How much they know each other, how is their chemistry [sic], these are very important'.[4] A believer in personal chemistry with peers, Modi genuinely sought out Sharif as someone who could be befriended and made a partner in his mission of removing obstacles to transborder economic and cultural integration and reviving the moribund South Asian Association for Regional Cooperation (SAARC). Sharif, a former businessman, without an apparent and innate hatred for India, played along in the expectation that if connectivity with India and the rest of South Asia improved, it would offer Pakistan a way out of its perpetual economic woes.[5]

What Sharif did not reckon with was yet another fierce pushback from the deep state in Pakistan against the attempted normalization of relations with its mortal enemy. He had been ousted once before in a military coup in 1999 for being a 'traitor' who came under Indian pressure to withdraw Pakistani troops during the Kargil War.[6] His camaraderie with Modi pleased moderate Pakistanis but riled the military establishment. In an uncanny déjà vu, an extended India–Pakistan crisis would commence within days of his hobnobbing with Modi and Sharif would end up suffering a 'soft coup' shortly thereafter. The Introduction of this book explains that Pakistan is a textbook case of a 'national security state' that has never seen dual power centres even during spells of directly elected 'democratic' rule. The history of Pakistan can be summarized as a Kabuki theatre where the establishment military-intelligence complex calls the shots and reins in civilian politicians who dare to marginalize them and cooperate with India.

Modi certainly knew this sordid past quite intimately. His mentor in the BJP and former prime minister, Atal Bihari Vajpayee, had ridden in a celebrated bus journey from Amritsar in India to Lahore in February 1999 and was welcomed with open arms by Prime Minister Sharif. It was an elaborate diplomatic summit, compared to the brief Modi–Sharif tête-à-tête of 2015, with official talks between the two sides, and a declaration that had the status of an international treaty to control vertical nuclear proliferation and avoid accidental use of nukes. Vajpayee had hailed it as 'a defining moment in South Asian history,'[7] but that effusive feeling vanished in just a few months when the Pakistani military encroached into Kargil without Sharif's knowledge and India had to wage a prolonged two-and-half-month quasi-war to dislodge the intruders, sacrificing over 500 of its troops in the process. In 2018, when Sharif had again been hounded and sidelined by the military, he looked back remorsefully at that seminal episode in South Asia and expressed how helpless he felt:

> Vajpayee told me he had been stabbed in the back with the Kargil misadventure because it came soon after the Lahore Declaration. I told him I would have said the same thing if I were in his place.[8]

By 2020, Sharif was in self-imposed exile. He minced no

words and identified the main barrier to peace with India as the deep state in Pakistan, whose corruption and primacy in Pakistan are facilitated by sustaining an ambience of permanent hostility toward India.[9] As an upcoming leader in the BJP and a professed disciple of Vajpayee, Modi was aware of the dynamic of civil–military imbalance in Pakistan and the risk of blowback from the military establishment against India whenever there is a momentum for bilateral cooperation. Still, after coming to power at the national level in India, he wanted to give peace a shot as part of his region-wide 'neighbourhood first' policy and conviction that he was destined to play a leadership role in the subcontinent.

Was Modi being naïve and blind to the fundamental reality of Pakistan? So alleged his critics and political opponents after the thaw unravelled and a major national security crisis arose with the Pakistani jihadi attack on an IAF base at Pathankot, in the northern state of Punjab, on New Year's Day of 2016, hardly one week after Modi had been in Lahore.[10] Subsequent investigations of the Pathankot attack, which had scalped the lives of seven Indian security forces and a civilian, found that it had been planned by the ISI and JeM commanders long *prior* to Modi's Lahore trip. The six jihadists who sneaked past the international border unchecked and breached the perimeter fence of the airbase had trained for six months in Bahawalpur, the JeM's headquarters in Pakistan, before proceeding on their holy martyrdom mission.[11] The Pakistani military may have decided the exact timing of the attack to derail the nascent Modi–Sharif peace process, but it would have been attempted nevertheless, even if Modi never went to Lahore.[12]

The American scholar Christine Fair found from her primary research in Pakistan that JeM was being revived by the ISI as part of the internecine, jihadist factional balancing games inside Pakistan. JeM terrorists, she wrote, had 'long been poised for infiltration into India' and 'the only thing surprising about this Jaish assault [on Pathankot] is that it did not happen sooner'.[13] As explained in the Introduction, even 26/11 was a diabolical by-product of the intra-jihadist churning inside Pakistan as well as the machinations of its military establishment to remain on top of its troublesome progeny. Pathankot was not caused by Modi's unclenched hand of friendship to Sharif but by the systemic design of Pakistan's national security state.

An Extended Crisis

Even if Modi's diplomacy cannot be blamed for the Pathankot attack, it did kick off his first national security crisis that consumed much of 2016. Questions arose as to how six heavily armed Pakistani jihadis dressed in Indian military fatigues could cross the international border from Pakistani Punjab into the Indian side, reach a frontline airbase 30 kilometres away, and trespass its perimeter fairly easily to unleash mayhem. A governmental inquiry set up under the former vice chief of Army Staff, Lieutenant General Philip Campose, found 'gaping holes in security arrangements at military bases', and recommended a series of overhauls to protect sensitive military installations.[14] The IAF's separate inquiry noted 'several lapses', including 'a gathering to celebrate the New Year [that] was held despite the terror alert' issued by Indian intelligence 12 hours ahead of the attack. It was also reported that 'on at least two occasions Modi spoke to commanders of the three wings of the Indian military, referred to the Pathankot attack and expressed his displeasure over the ease with which the terrorists breached security despite the alert'.[15]

Having taken a risk to overturn decades of animosity with Pakistan, the Indian prime minister was obviously embarrassed and felt let down by the internal security failures that resulted in the Pathankot attack. Before January 2016, ceasefire violations by Pakistan along the LoC and infiltration of jihadists had been dipping for a few months. The security situation in Kashmir was relatively stable. While there were small firefights and ambushes, the Indian Army had noted in December 2015 that the 'potential of militants has significantly reduced and terrorism indicators have shown a declining trend'.[16] Modi saw a window of opportunity around the time of his Lahore visit from that weakening of terrorist activity and wanted to diplomatically push Pakistan to terminate arming and financing jihadists. He did not go overboard in seeking peace but held on to a slender propitious pattern while hedging his bets by insisting that 'we will never drop our guard on security and we will continue to judge progress on their commitments on terrorism'.[17]

Sadly, for India, the guard was dropped and it weakened Modi's hand. Only by securing India's homeland better against terrorist infiltration and attacks would he be in a stronger position to conduct business with liberal-minded elements in Pakistan's polity. The ISI and its jihadi spoilers would not have been able to wreck the positive turn in relations if, despite characteristic malevolent intentions, their capacity to inflict harm on India was blunted through India's proactive internal and cross-border security measures. Modi's opening to Pakistan needed a security cushion as part and parcel of what might be called a strategy of realistic liberalism. The Pathankot attack and a worse one to follow in Uri in September 2016 yanked the India–Pakistan relationship back to a strenuous low point from which there has been no recovery. Modi did not seek or bring upon himself a crisis so early in his first term as prime minister, but got one nonetheless, due to the combination of unremitting hatred of the Pakistani military and gaps in India's internal security set-up that he has since been trying to fill.

As was the case after 26/11, much of the media attention, after the Pathankot attack, was centred on the tenacity and bravery of India's elite Black Cat commandos, and how they paired up with the IAF and other security forces to eliminate the six JeM terrorists. Unlike 26/11, the terrorists' goals of destroying priceless Indian fighter aircraft assets and taking hostages were foiled. NSA Ajit Doval, who coordinated the multi-institutional effort, observed that, 'it was a very successful operation', and exuded confidence that 'the country has got the will, the ability, the political leadership which is capable of allowing it to do what it should do to serve the national security interests'.[18] The speed with which Doval put into motion the plan to stop the terrorists in the airbase stood in contrast to the waffling after 26/11. The apex national security body, the Cabinet Committee on Security (CCS), was not involved at that stage because its procedural and deliberative nature would have delayed the Indian reaction by several hours and the terrorists could have succeeded in their mission. Here is Doval's recounting of those tense hours:

> In an emergency, on-the-spot decisions need to be taken. If we do not take responsibility…when the country's vital security interest is endangered, what is the justification for us to be there [sic].[19]

The Indian journalist Nitin Gokhale learnt that the NSA had applied valuable lessons from the December 1999 Indian Airlines flight hijacking that was rerouted to Kandahar. The CCS had taken an inordinately long time to arrive at a decision, giving the terrorists sufficient room to steer the plane from Amritsar and fly it to Afghanistan. From the safety of Taliban-ruled Kandahar, they bargained with the Indian government and forced it to release the Pakistani terrorist mastermind Maulana Masood Azhar:

Many people in official positions insisted on following protocol when the need was to take urgent action. Doval was mortified to witness the release of Masood... The same Masood would then go on to form the Jaish-e-Mohammad... Clearly, Doval was not about to repeat the mistakes of 1999, convention be damned.[20]

While India's *internal* response to the Pathankot attack was indeed swifter and more decisive than in earlier such events, Doval knew and so did Modi that the crisis set off at Pathankot was not a domestic one, but one where Pakistan had drawn first blood. Indian intelligence intercepts of phone conversations of the airbase infiltrators and the leftover equipment of the killed terrorists left no doubt that this was the handiwork of JeM and the ISI. Even as many in India debated how to better secure the country's borders and bases through defensive measures, the immediate decision point was how Modi should respond to the external source of the attack, i.e. Pakistan's military and its jihadi proxies.

Sharif's early condemnation of the Pathankot attack in a commiserative phone call to Modi on 5 January 2016, and his promise to take 'prompt and decisive action' against the guilty terrorists mitigated against instant retaliatory action.[21] Pakistan seemed to be admitting its guilt instead of parroting the usual, 'We need more proof' line as was habitual. Sharif convened a high-level Pakistani government meeting which 'expressed national resolve not to allow our territory to be used for acts of terrorism anywhere'. His office announced that JeM offices in the country were 'being traced and sealed' and several of its leaders arrested.[22] Masood Azhar, the JeM chief who has been on the National Investigation Agency's Most Wanted list for decades of terrorism in Kashmir and the rest of the country, was believed to have been detained. India also convinced the

US to pressurize Pakistan with President Barack Obama calling the Pathankot attack 'inexcusable terrorism' and citing it as an opportunity for Pakistan 'to show that it is serious about delegitimizing, disrupting and dismantling terror networks'.[23]

The Modi government was sceptical if the Pakistani military establishment would allow any far-reaching crackdown on its radical Islamist force multipliers, but a decision was taken in New Delhi to give Sharif the benefit of the doubt and a chance to deliver on his vows. NSA Doval maintained communications with his Pakistani counterpart, General Nasir Janjua, and so did the foreign secretaries and foreign ministers of the two countries. In March 2016, for the first time ever, India allowed a Pakistani Joint Investigation Team (JIT) that included colonels from the ISI and Pakistan's military intelligence to visit the Pathankot airbase to gather and corroborate evidence that could help Pakistan prosecute the JeM perpetrators in Pakistan. External Affairs Minister S. Jaishankar later defended this unusual move and explained its rationale.

> The investigation that happened was to pressurize the Pakistanis so that they did not have an excuse to say that 'well, we made an offer and you did not accept it and therefore, it trailed away'. The idea was: Look, you ask me anything reasonable, I will agree and now you go and act.[24]

But as time rolled past, no far-reaching action against the JeM occurred inside Pakistan. Sharif was relegated into a corner by the military establishment and the JIT issued the fantastical claim that Pathankot was an Indian 'false flag operation fully facilitated by the Indian Army just to put the blame on Pakistan'.[25] The same old stalling and parrying tactics of Pakistan came to the fore and it was proven beyond doubt that the military establishment was incorrigible. If Sharif's early expression of sincerity carried a possibility that the crisis might subside through bilateral trust and cooperation between the two governments to join hands and crush terrorists, the erosion of Sharif's power and the reassertion of political dominance by the military in Pakistan ensured that the crisis had only just begun and would further intensify. In Kashmir, where there had been a downtick in terrorism in 2015 amid the India–Pakistan thaw, a surge of anti-India attacks and separatist 'uprisings' broke out in July 2016 after the Indian military liquidated a local Kashmiri jihadist commander with links to Pakistan, Burhan Wani. Indian intelligence found that the large-scale 'Kashmir unrest' of 2016 was financed via a massive transfusion of money from Pakistan to separatist politicians in the valley.[26] It was clear by September 2016 that the Pakistani deep state was going to step on all accelerators to continue its religious crusade against India. The more Pakistan could provoke India, the easier it would be for the generals in Rawalpindi to assume ever greater political power and knock out the bothersome Sharif.

The Middle Path

This was the context in which four heavily armed Pakistani jihadists of LeT crossed the mountainous Haji Pir Pass in PoK, slipped past the LoC and launched a blistering attack on a brigade headquarters of the Indian Army in the western Kashmiri town of Uri. In a repeat of the Pathankot tragedy, the attackers breached the heavy security of the camp in the early hours of 18 September 2016, sneaked in and went on a suicidal firing and grenade throwing spree that killed 19 Indian soldiers. It was the single deadliest attack on the Indian Army in Kashmir in 14 years and a coda to the brief India–Pakistan warmth which Modi, the statesman, had tested out. The crisis escalated to such a point with the Uri attack that the Indian prime minister had to shift gears to green-light the calibrated use of force to sustain India's credibility as a capable state and live up to his own record as a hardliner on national security. Modi reportedly told Indian Army commanders following the Uri attacks that, 'the retaliation should be immediate to send an unambiguous message'.[27] On 25 September, as the Indian security forces were readying to rattle Pakistan and Indian society and political discourse was in a nationalist uproar, Modi dropped hints of an impending retaliation at a public rally:

> Our 18 soldiers had to sacrifice their lives because of terrorists exported by our neighbouring country. And terrorists should clearly hear us, that India will never forget the Uri attack. Leaders of the neighbouring country used to say they will fight for 1,000 years against us. I accept this challenge.[28]

Unknown to Pakistan and to the world, Modi had already made up his mind on 23 September that India would dispatch special forces into PoK in a large operation and destroy terrorist infrastructure at four different sites. As per Gokhale's reconstruction, 'all options, economic, diplomatic and political were considered', just as they were done after 26/11. But Modi went beyond these anodyne and historically fruitless methods, and decided that a military response was apt. He was presented with options of targets to be hit in PoK and 'briefed on the possible retaliation/reaction by Pakistan', as well as the potential international reactions. Instead of getting paralysed by the constraint of Pakistan escalating after the special forces' raids, then defence minister, Manohar Parrikar, was tasked to go on an urgent military hardware acquisition spree. The mission of these last-minute defence purchases was to adequately prepare India for 'a possibility of a short, swift skirmish, if not a conflict, once it had been decided to order a retaliatory strike'.[29] Indian military chiefs were on high alert prior to the cross-border raids and villages in a 10-kilometre range near the international border were evacuated in advance of the special forces mission. Indian Army General Deependra Singh Hooda, who was in charge of the top-secret mission to attack jihadists in PoK, later explained how methodical the whole enterprise had been:

> We had sort of war-gamed all the contingencies of what could be the impact of the surgical strike. And one of the things that we did consider was that in case Pakistan decides to escalate, then what do we have to do.[30]

In the worst-case scenario, Modi's India would go to war rather than let foreign aggression go unanswered. But as John Oneal wrote, 'the avoidance of both war and capitulation is the aim of all nations embroiled in crises'.[31] Particularly for a democratic developing country like India, war is never the first choice no matter how serious the national security crisis on hand is. Contrary to the left-wing critics who denounce Modi as a militaristic and extremist politician, he has always carefully sought to avoid war while pursuing calibrated but tough national security policies. As further proof of the cool-headed and calculated manner in which the special forces' mission was designed to minimize the probability of war, the exact targets in PoK were meticulously chosen on the basis of collated human and spatial intelligence from the Research and Analysis Wing (R&AW) and the National Technical Research Organisation (NTRO) about movements of terrorists in PoK that could be interpreted as infiltration bids.[32] This was done so that the Indian operation could be presented to the world as a pre-emptive move to thwart fresh Pakistani attacks from terror launching pads, i.e. an act of self-defence in the wake of an imminent threat, rather than as mere revenge for Uri. According to the Indian journalist Saikat Datta, who interviewed insiders in Indian defence circles:

> The government decided that a strike would be carried out only if it detected plans to infiltrate militants…R&AW was specifically tasked…to gather actionable intelligence, which could be used to carry out pinpoint strikes with minimum casualties. A conscious decision was also taken to target militants rather that the Pakistani army to ensure that the situation did not escalate…[33]

As previously discussed, the Manmohan Singh government baulked from responding to 26/11, saying it lacked the 'exact coordinates of the camps' of LeT and other jihadist groups inside Pakistan. This deficit was overcome in the September 2016 response, which came to be known as 'surgical strikes', a phrase meant to connote that India's targets and purpose were precise, proportionate and limited. It was meant to be a display of controlled aggression to demonstrate that India had finally shed its defensive inhibitions, and was going to inflict costs and pain on terrorists on their home turf, while at the same time, avoiding a direct clash with the military of Pakistan. It is indeed remarkable that while approximately 80 fatalities were discerned from radio intercepts in PoK from the attacks by Indian special forces on the intervening night of 28–29 September 2016, the deaths and injuries of regular Pakistani military soldiers were believed to be only in single digits. An embarrassed Pakistan officially acknowledged the loss of only two soldiers, adding that it happened from routine cross-border firing from the Indian side rather than deep penetration actions of the Indian Army inside Pakistan-controlled terrain.[34] Manmohan Singh's government could not solve the dilemma of avoiding Indian retaliation from merging into a bigger and more worrisome full-scale war after 26/11.

However, the Modi government's arduous planning and execution of a mission that had the sharpness of a surgeon's scalpel proved to be a way out from this very dilemma.

Following the surgical strikes, cynics tried to downplay their impact by arguing that the Indian military had carried out similar raids across the LoC earlier and that there was nothing unique or extraordinary about what occurred in September 2019. But the scale, scalps and strategic advertising of the surgical strikes by the Modi government placed them way above previous localized initiatives taken by field-based Indian military commanders. Pakistan's denial that the strikes even happened did not negate their impact, but actually amplified how powerful the strikes had been. General Dhruv Katoch, a retired Indian Army officer and strategic thinker, explained the rationale behind Pakistan's refusal to publicly accept that India had struck in PoK:

> It was a very sensible action on the part of Pakistan to carry out this denial, because acceptance would have meant that they would have to take (counter-retaliatory) action. And they lacked the conventional capability to do so. Moreover, their nuclear bluff was called. This is why the first surgical strike by India in 2016 was a major turning point.[35]

Chapter 3 expands on the repetetive denialism by Pakistan after India struck deeper inside Pakistan proper, confirming that terrorism fortified by nuclear blackmail would no longer work. Modi had shuffled the cards and the game had new rules.

Tactically, there were many firsts to the credit of the 2016 surgical strikes, which were code-named Operation X inside the armed forces. Barring a full-scale war situation, the Indian forces had never before simultaneously crossed the LoC at different points spread across a 250-kilometre radius and obliterated six jihadist camps, that too by extricating themselves without suffering a single Indian death (out of a total of 70 to 80 commandos from two separate battalions who went on the mission).[36] The advantage of tactical surprise, which Pakistan's military and its proxies traditionally enjoyed in their low-intensity war, was reversed. Reports of terrorists in the camps being 'caught off guard', 'caught napping' and found in a dazed condition suggested that they never expected Indian soldiers to creep in undetected up to four kilometres inside Pakistani-controlled territory and carry out such a daring assault.[37]

The main ideological tropes in Pakistan's jihadist training schools and camps are that Muslims are 'allowed to kill infidels who stand in the way of Islam' and 'infidels are cowards who run away in fear and terror when a holy warrior attacks them'.[38] The Pakistani army's own worldview handed down over generations has been that 'one Muslim soldier was worth 10 Hindus' and that Islamist zeal would compensate for Pakistan's conventional inferiority to India.[39] The defensive 'strategic restraint' culture of Indian leaders before Modi buttressed such bigoted and hateful views and emboldened the Pakistani establishment to rain terror on India with impunity. The Pakistani military used to exude confidence that it could exert 'escalation dominance', wherein Pakistan would always have the military initiative at every level of conflict with India because of the latter's reluctance to fight and risk going up the ladder to nuclear war. With the surgical strikes of 2016 (and also the air strikes of 2019, which I have covered at length in Chapter 3 of this book), these myths and certainties were busted and the defensive-offensive scales were rebalanced. A country that had been painted as a gentle giant with no agility or gall to stand up to death-embracing holy martyrs emerged in a new light as a fiery hunter of its foes.

A primary objective of the surgical strikes was to shatter the long-held notion that India had no optimal options to respond to Pakistan-sponsored terrorism. Former Indian Foreign Secretary Shyam Saran stated the problem and challenge in these words:

> India's basic weakness is that its political leaders have no credible response options between the extreme choices of military retaliation and appeasement when it comes to Pakistan-sponsored terrorism. What we need is a toolkit of options, short of war, that can inflict costs and damages on Pakistan. We need to have a series of pressure points on Pakistan to contain its hostile activities against India…We may have to adopt counter-constraint policies to attempt to change the strategic calculus in Islamabad. This may include the option of inflicting pain on Pakistan if India's security is threatened.[40]

The 2016 surgical strikes were milestones in India's quest for counter-constraints because they offered a sliver of a middle path between all-out war and acquiescing to Pakistan's brazen terrorist attacks. One end of the extreme—threatening war and invasion to compel Pakistan—did not work in 2001–2002 following the LeT and JeM attack on the Indian parliament. The Vajpayee government opted for a slow and cumbersome mobilization of 500,000 Indian troops along the LoC and the international border. This mobilization, code-named Operation Parakram, took weeks for the full build-up, giving Pakistan ample time to assemble its defences and line up 300,000 of its troops, thereby raising alarms of another full India–Pakistan war. India's ultimatum that unless Pakistan ceased harbouring terrorists, it would hit jihadist camps and seize territory in PoK could not be enforced once the Pakistanis counter-mobilized on a mass scale and became ready to face any conventional offensive.

Concerned that Pakistan would be diverted from assisting the US on its western flank against the Taliban and Al Qaeda in Afghanistan, the George W. Bush administration intervened to extract a token 'commitment to the US by Musharraf to end permanently, cross-border, cross-LoC infiltration'. This left India with no alternative but to 'stand down from its war footing' without accomplishing its objectives.[41]

The reader has already seen the other end of the extreme in the Introduction of this book, when the Singh government set a sorry benchmark in inaction and vacillation after 26/11.

What the 2016 surgical strikes did was break the binary dilemma between war and appeasement, and show Pakistan and the world that India was innovating to find a third way out of its mounting national security threat environment. The same Daniel Markey, who appeared in the Introduction of this book pointing out Pakistan's vulnerabilities which Singh's India had not exploited after 26/11, observed a refreshing change under Modi. The American scholar wrote that the surgical strikes were 'a shrewd response to terrorist provocation' and certified that they 'passed the Goldilocks test':

> ...neither too hot nor too cool, too hard nor too soft, too large nor too small. It was just right. The strikes plugged a big hole in India's policy repertoire and simultaneously delivered the right messages to multiple audiences at once. Rarely has New Delhi managed such a shrewd response to terrorist provocation[42]

The raids into PoK were forward-looking steps towards a new era of deterrence driven by Modi's unique affinity for risk. Unlike previous Indian leaders who dithered in Hamlet-like dilemmas after countless Pakistan-sponsored outrages on Indian soil, Modi scripted history by daringly ordering the Indian military to cross the LoC on a clinical counter-terrorism mission. Modi presented a different India altogether—one willing to call the bluff of its adversaries and use force with precision to achieve clear and limited objectives. One vector of this transformation was Modi's Gujarati self-confidence and entrepreneurial spirit to undertake calculated gambles. The prospect of 'what if the army mission fails' may have crossed his mind before he authorized the surgical strikes. He must have harboured the thought that if it did fail and Indian soldiers were either killed or captured inside PoK, the consequences for India's honour and his own political survival could have been jeopardizing. On the eve of the third anniversary of the surgical strikes in 2019, Modi delivered a speech and offered a glimpse of those harrowing hours when the Indian PARA commandos were on the prowl inside PoK:

> Today is September 28. Three years ago, on this day, I could not sleep the whole night as I was waiting for a call. It was on this day that the Indian soldiers carried out the surgical strikes. They showed exemplary bravery while risking their lives.[43]

Sleepless he was, but he did not lack a spine. He had proceeded fearlessly due to a combination of informed and instinctive derring-do. When confronted with national security challenges, Modi does not tie himself into knots about the possibility of a fiasco that may boomerang and inflict a high political cost. On another occasion, he disclosed what was going on in his mind just before the surgical strikes:

> I gave clear orders that whether you get success or failure, don't think about that but come back before sunrise [sic]. Don't fall for the lure and prolong it (the operation). I knew it was a big risk. I never care about any political risk to me. The biggest consideration for me was the safety of our soldiers.[44]

Modi often senses an opportunity and pursues a decisive course with the earnestness of a leader who knows that without guts, there is no glory. One can glean this attitude from other non-crisis events as well. In 2016, Modi mobilized India's full diplomatic arsenal for a widely publicized shot at gaining membership of the Nuclear Suppliers Group (NSG), a multilateral export control technology forum that had, thus far, denied India access to sophisticated technology. He was advised from within the Indian government that there was a higher probability of failure than success. Yet, he chose to embark on an international quest laden with uncertainty, believing that honour accrues only to those who strive. Although India has still not managed to break into the NSG due to China's obstinate blocking, Modi can be viewed as boldly paving the way for this eventuality by emphasizing the positives of proactive behaviour and jettisoning the negatives of overcautious and pessimistic thought. In high-stakes international situations, Modi's preference is to be psychologically strong regarding the hazards of losing a battle or two so as to prevail and win the war.

Apart from his personal pluckiness, Modi can venture out far and take risks in crises because he enjoys massive public approval, and knows that Indians would empathize with him if the gamble does not pay off. A survey published by Pew Research Center on 19 September 2016, a day after the Uri attack but six days before the surgical strikes, revealed that a whopping 81 per cent of Indians had a favourable view of the manner in which Modi was governing the country.[45] The mass adulation and following he has accumulated enable Modi to have the advantage of gazing at long-term horizons and objectives such as changing the country's defensive strategic culture instead of panicking during a crisis. Modi is the least risk-averse prime minister India has had in decades because he knows that the country cannot march to the status of a 'leading power' in world affairs without demonstrating that it has the stomach for hard choices and tough calls.

Modi's gambits also build upon each other and are cumulative. The surgical strikes in PoK had a precedent in the form of an audacious Indian Army raid inside Myanmar against separatist Naga and Manipuri insurgent camps in June 2015. Seventy Indian commandos went past the forested border, trekked for five kilometres, then attacked the rebels with devastating firepower, killing 38 of them, and then exfiltrated back to the Indian side in the early hours of the day.[46] It was a 'hot pursuit' operation to teach the rebels a lesson after they had ambushed the Indian Army in India's northeastern state of Manipur and left 18 soldiers dead. The operation, overseen by Doval and approved by Modi after getting detailed confidential briefings, was 'carried out based on specific and very accurate intelligence' about the terrain and the location of the Naga hideouts.[47] The Indian Army regularly intercepted radio communications of terrorists and had conducted unmanned aerial vehicle (UAV) recces prior to the operation. As local tribes often cross the porous international border between India's northeastern states and Myanmar, human inputs about the movements and intentions of the terrorists were also obtained and cross-checked against technical intelligence.[48] It was a prelude to the surgical strikes in PoK.

The mission in the Sagaing Hills of Myanmar was pre-emptive and covert in nature. But it was widely publicized ex post facto to score psychological points with anti-India elements. Military raids could not solve the misgovernance and the accompanying socio-economic grievances of local people in India's Northeast, but they did convey that India was not a soft state that would passively absorb and condone the killings of its soldiers. The level of sophistication of that foreign mission conveyed that India's capacity to deter enemies was growing. Terrorists who sheltered outside India's boundaries used to brim with confidence that India could not pursue them outside its sovereign space. But the strikes in Myanmar sent out a loud subcontinental-sized message that India would 'choose the time and the place of hitting them'.[49] Combative comments from the Modi government after the Myanmar strikes of 2015 about attacks on Indians anywhere being 'unacceptable', and vows that 'western disturbances will also be equally dealt with' were open hints to Pakistan not to test India's patience.[50]

There were, of course, differences between striking in a weak but cooperative country like Myanmar and in a hostile nuclear-armed country like Pakistan. In the Myanmar 'hot pursuit' mission, it helped India's cause that the Myanmarese military was not fully in control in Sagaing. Indian special forces exploited a security vacuum as the regular Myanmar military was out of sight. Since there was no outcry from Myanmar after the Indian operation and bilateral relations kept improving, it looked as if New Delhi did its diplomatic homework and secured permission from Naypyidaw to operate within specified geographical and temporal limits. Could one imagine tacit political coordination from the host government when it came to dismantling jihadist camps in PoK? The risk and the potential fallouts of the 2016 surgical strikes were way higher, but so was the urgent need for India to demonstrate its strategic resolve. After the Myanmar hot pursuit action, Pakistan reacted nonchalantly and dared India. A hawkish Pakistani minister reminded India not to have misgivings:

> We are not Myanmar. Don't you know our military strength? Pakistan is a nuclear nation. India should stop day dreaming... Don't even look at us with aggressive

intent, and if you do, then you [India] are only living in a fool's paradise.[51]

With the 2016 surgical strikes and the 2019 air strikes discussed later, Modi called the nuclear bluff hanging around India's neck like an albatross whenever it contemplated an attack against cross-border terrorism. Harsh Pant has summed up the impact of the bold Indian forays as follows.

> With Pakistan, the Modi government has shifted the goalposts in significant ways—first with the 'surgical strikes' of 2016 and then with air strikes post Pulwama attack in 2019. There are important markets in India's approach to counter-terror, which has been hobbled by the Pakistani nuclear bluff. India has all but called that bluff, and Pakistan's decision to downplay these strikes underlines Islamabad's reluctance to retaliate. With these strikes, India has managed to convey to Pakistan and to other external stakeholders that Pakistan's nuclear blackmail has no legs to stand on and that India has military room to operate below the threshold that would trigger major conventional, or even nuclear, escalation.[52]

Modi's risky decision in September 2016 also paid off because he combined judicious use of military force with diplomatic manoeuvring. Unlike in the 26/11 flop show, when the Singh government was apprehensive and fearful of international reactions, the Modi government made extensive pre-raid preparations in international capitals and intergovernmental institutions before the surgical strikes were launched so as to provide political cover and justification for drastic actions. India's push for diplomatic isolation of Pakistan following the fading hopes of constructive resolution of the Pathankot attack constituted the spadework for the surgical strikes, which were not condemned at all internationally. Modi's quiver of full-spectrum diplomacy thus has soft and hard power arrows shooting in tandem. The result was a chiselled strategy where India dared to do the unthinkable after laying a credible narrative about Pakistan's insufferable shenanigans in front of the international community.

It is instructive for the study of national security crisis management to examine the continuous contact and discussions that the Modi government had with the US before and after the surgical strikes. On 28 September 2016, just before the surgical strikes, Doval spoke to his US counterpart, Susan Rice, who 'strongly condemned the 18 September cross-border attack on the Indian Army Brigade headquarters in Uri', and 'reiterated our [the US's] expectation that Pakistan take effective action to combat and delegitimize United Nations-designated terrorist individuals and entities, including Lashkar-e-Tayyiba, Jaish-e-Muhammad, and their affiliates'.[53] Once Rice learnt about the strikes the next day, she called Doval again, 'to ensure that there was no further escalation'. Doval reportedly 'assured her that New Delhi would not take any further action if Islamabad did not escalate matters', but also 'asked her to convey to Pakistan that India would be prepared to meet any eventuality'.[54] Quizzed by journalists on whether the US considered India's surgical strikes as an act of escalation, the Obama administration denied so and repeated that the actual escalation was caused by the Uri attacks, squarely blaming Pakistan. Asked if India actually coordinated with the US on carrying out the surgical strikes, spokesperson John Kirby's reply was ambiguously worded as, 'I don't talk about the specifics of military matters'.[55] On the day the strikes were publicized, India's foreign secretary briefed diplomats from the permanent members of the United Nations Security Council (UNSC) and 20 other countries to 'convey the context' and assured them that 'it was a classic counter-terrorism operation more than a military one.' And once again, the word went out that 'India has no plans for any further operation as of now' with the caveat that India's 'armed forces will not allow terrorists to carry out any attacks.'[56]

The framing of the strikes as counterterrorism rather than war was a masterstroke that ensured that global pressure and attention remained on the demonic forces inside Pakistan rather than being redirected to intervening in the Kashmir dispute or to fears of a nuclear holocaust. Unlike the post-26/11 Singh government, Modi had chalked out a public relations strategy to ward off adverse international comments and demands for 'restraint'. Two retired Indian military officers, Col Vivek Chadha and Brig. Rumel Dahiya, have labelled the post-surgical strikes media operation of the Modi government 'successful strategic communication'. As per their analysis:

> The operation stood out particularly for the clarity with which information about the surgical strike was presented in the public domain... The messaging was clear: this was a limited strike to pre-empt terrorists from entering India, the target were terrorists and not the Pakistan Army, India had acted within its rights and the Indian Army was in constant touch with its Pakistani counterpart.[57]

Buoyed by the approving responses from multiple world capitals after the surgical strikes, the Modi government also got into top gear at global multilateral forums to garner momentum to shame Pakistan and put it in the dock. At the Group of Twenty (G20) summit in Germany held in July 2017, Modi presented a '10-point agenda' to world leaders. India helped draft a joint commitment that undertook to eliminate 'safe spaces' in which terrorists take shelter and to hold to account terrorist 'financing hot-spots' through the enforcement of the Financial Action Task Force (FATF) norms and standards.[58] Due to Modi's strenuous and unremitting push, the topic of countering terrorism rose to prominence as a regular international discussion item and a global priority. Not all of this was mere talk. The noose of periodic FATF reviews began to tighten around Pakistan from 2017, starting with its referral to the Asia/Pacific Group on Money Laundering (APG) for not fully complying with curbs against UN proscribed terrorist entities. In February 2018, the US and European countries pushed Pakistan to be put back on the FATF's 'grey list', a step away from blacklisting that could deprive it of foreign investments and lead to economic sanctions. In a rarely witnessed spectacle, India and the US paired up to creatively soften China, the eternal ally of Pakistan and a FATF member, to drop its objections to the 'greylisting' in return for a higher profile for China in the multilateral body.[59] Modi had sworn to make Pakistan a pariah state after Uri, and he doggedly stuck to this mission for years after the surgical strikes, implying that the military action was not a be-all and end-all for him to consider the crisis to be over. The commandos had done their job with amazing verve, but India's political leader eyed a much longer time horizon to keep raising the costs of terrorism.

Apart from world powers, the other international constituency that the Modi government rallied around was its South Asian neighbours. On 27 September 2016, with the strikes in PoK about to be launched, India declared it would boycott the SAARC summit scheduled to be held in Islamabad that November, owing to the 'increasing cross-border terrorist attacks in the region' (a reference to Afghanistan, a member state facing similar jihadist attacks from Pakistan) and 'growing interference in the internal affairs of member states by one country' which 'created an environment that is not conducive'.[60] In near synchronous coordination, Bangladesh, Bhutan and Afghanistan too pulled out of the summit citing an 'unsuitable environment', and taking direct swipes at Pakistan for 'interference' in their internal affairs.[61] This mass refusal of members left the chairman of SAARC Nepal no option but to call off the summit, inflicting a serious loss of prestige to Pakistan. Historically, Pakistan prided itself for mounting the primary resistance to what is labelled as 'Indian hegemony' in South Asia and tried to play on insecurity complexes of smaller member states of SAARC to counterbalance Indian influence.[62] But thanks to the Modi government's reinvigorated 'neighbourhood first' policy since 2014 and Pakistan's destructive behaviour affecting, not just India, but also surrounding nations, the region as a whole stood up for New Delhi following the Uri attack and dealt a diplomatic snub to Islamabad.

Combining kinetic military measures with diplomatic isolation was a smart and holistic approach to make Pakistan pay for its terrorist habit. After Uri, the Modi government placed the formula of 'SAARC minus one' front and centre as its blueprint for the region and proceeded to deepen connectivity with the remaining member countries while Pakistan either stayed out due to suspicion of Indian motives or was kept out of the tent due to collective disgust for its anti-social doings. Key agreements for transnational passage of motor vehicles, railway linkages, air corridors, inland waterways and a shared South Asian satellite progressed without Pakistan's participation, rendering the old adage moot that India–Pakistan bilateral disputes were holding back regional integration. Ideally, having Pakistan's 220 million consumers join the regional integration process would have benefited all SAARC countries. As discussed, Modi had very much wanted Pakistan to be in the regional economic space and gain from commercial access to the populous markets of South Asia. But it takes two to tango and Pakistan's deep state spurned the hand that Modi had offered.

After Uri, Islamabad had to contend with a freeze-out in SAARC, even as New Delhi succeeded in convincing its remaining six members to march ahead on a shared path to prosperity. The increased salience of alternative pre-existing trans-regional and sub-regional institutions like the Bay of Bengal Initiative for Multi-Sectoral Technical and Economic Cooperation (BIMSTEC), headquartered in Dhaka, and the Bangladesh, Bhutan, Nepal, India (BBIN), following the surgical strikes heralded a new era where India could shape the agenda of South Asia in a constructive direction without being taken hostage by Pakistan's negativity. While much remains to be accomplished in South Asian economic and cultural integration, the exit of a troublemaking Pakistan from the picture has offered a new impetus for Indian leadership and for the interests of smaller countries to be upheld.

The Josh is 'High, Sir!'

After the surgical strikes, strategic communication and shoring up an anti-terrorist bloc were not confined to the international community but also directed at the domestic audience in India. The following chapters throw light on the disciplined and hard-hitting PR campaigns by the Modi government during other critical national security crises and turning points. This style of communication when Modi executes difficult decisions dovetails with the crisis management concept of 'meaning making' as a key task for political leaders when they are in a crunch. European experts on crises have emphasized the need for leaders to 'reduce uncertainty and provide an authoritative account of what is going on, why it is happening, and what needs to be done.' This not only assures an anxious and worked-up citizenry and international observers, but is essential to retain initiative: 'If other actors in the crisis succeed in dominating the meaning-making process, the ability of incumbent leaders to decide and manoeuvre is severely constrained.' Effective crisis leadership, the scholars aver, 'presupposes a sure-footed manipulation of symbols that shapes the views and sentiments of the political environment in ways that enhance leadership capacity to act.' The symbolic strategy includes leaders performing 'rituals' and 'publicly displaying compassion' in speeches and official state funerals of victims of an attack.[63]

Although Modi is unlikely to have ever had the time to delve into theoretical models of crisis management, as a practitioner, he spontaneously ticks each and every box of this template of successful communication during crunch time. The emotion and passion that he could generate about the 2016 surgical strikes within India were unparalleled. He offered a chance for the nation to hold its head up after feeling let down for decades. The Introduction of this book explicates that national security is essentially a socio-psychological phenomenon, a feeling of confidence among the citizenry that their state is protecting them from foreign threats. Notwithstanding Pakistan's denial that the surgical strikes happened at all and some narrow-minded politicians within India asking the government for 'proof' of their occurrence,[64] the vast majority of India's people believed the two most credible sources they trusted: the professional Indian Army which never lies to the public, and the popular prime minister whose own credibility among ordinary masses has been unmatched.

Modi declared the anniversary of the strikes as a national festival called *Parakram Parv* and his government has commemorated it every year with martial visuals, exhibits and videos celebrating the valour of the Indian military. The mass fervour generated by the strikes also translated into cultural expressions such as the Bollywood action blockbuster *Uri: The*

Surgical Strike (2019), where the protagonist, a major in the Indian Army, has a punchline for his unit before they embark on missions: 'How's the josh?', meaning 'How is your fighting-spirit?' To this, the commandos reply in unison, 'High, sir!' The dialogue went viral and Modi himself began to cite them to lift the spirit of Indians from different walks of life during speeches. While his political opponents cried foul that Modi was milking and exaggerating military operations for electoral gains, what they could not fathom was how the nationalist mobilization was a key component of the tougher security posture that India was displaying to its foreign adversaries and the wider world, which had earlier assumed that India was too divided and distracted to shed the image of a soft state.

Remaking India's national identity as a unified, capable and valiant country has been one of the central aims of Modi's political career. The surgical strikes were part of this larger project. Alluding to the baggage of 'strategic restraint' and the way it had stunted India's identity, he told an audience in Washington in 2017,

> When India conducted surgical strikes the world experienced our power and realized that India practices restraint but can show power when needed... The world did not and cannot stop us. We have succeeded in conveying to the world the deleterious effects of terrorism on India.[65]

Military power, which had been sublimated in India's recent self-conceptualization, gained currency and got mainstreamed in Indian popular imagination and in the national security discourse after the watershed 2016 surgical strikes. Having been subjected to repeated terrorist assaults from Pakistan and disallowed from retaliating in the past due to political and bureaucratic shackles, there was a surge in the morale of the Indian armed forces due to the 'go ahead' they got from Modi. As an Indian journalist put it exactly one year after Operation X:

> The surgical strike in PoK saw a surge in the respect for Indian Army. The astute planning of the surgical strike and professional execution of the plan enhanced the positive public opinion about the Indian Army. This, in turn, served as morale booster for the soldiers... The Indian Army has since looked more confident in handling difficult situations.[66]

The later chapters of this book shed light on the positive feedback loop between concrete exploits of the 2016 strikes, enabled by Modi reposing infinite faith in the military, and subsequent boldness in the way the Indian armed forces tackled other crises. If one were to pinpoint to the genesis of a proactive 'can do' josh in the military to raise their hands and go after foreign adversaries, the 2016 strikes were seminal. To quote Gokhale:

> ...the government's proactive strategic initiative has given the military a signal that it need not perpetually be bound by a defensive or reactive approach in dealing with the proxy war waged by Pakistan in J&K [Jammu and Kashmir].[67]

Some analysts deciphered the 2016 surgical strikes as a marker of India transitioning from the doctrine of 'strategic restraint (reticence in the use of force) towards strategic proactivism (a propensity for the use of force).'[68] Others insisted that the strikes did cross the rubicon of visibly 'doing nothing' militarily, but they still fell within the parameters of the 'grand strategy' of strategic restraint as India had not demonstrated an ability or will to conduct deeper punitive strikes inside Pakistan.[69] There was also plenty of debate among strategic elites about how the strikes represented a reification of Doval's doctrine of 'offensive defence' in contrast to 'defensive offence'. Since he was the prime mover in Modi's decision-making teams for the surgical strikes and other subsequent crises covered in this book, his thoughts carry more weightage than those of experts offering their own interpretations without insider knowledge of how the Indian state has been slowly but surely changing its stripes. The so-called 'Doval Doctrine' was described by the man himself in a 2014 speech as follows:

> 'You know, we engage an enemy in three modes,' he told his audience. One is 'defensive offence,' he explained, in which guards and soldiers strike only when their territory is attacked. 'The second is offensive defence, where we will go to the place from where the offence is coming. And third is the offensive mode, where you go outright.'[70]

The expectation that India could proactively deter Pakistan from infiltrating jihadists and staging spectacular terrorist attacks is the central premise of the Modi government's approach to national security. But to be clear, neither Doval nor Modi is sanguine that this can be achieved through a one-off demonstration of military skill and audacity. The 2016 surgical strikes alone did not establish deterrence, as Pakistan-abetted terrorist plots and attacks and incidents continued to plague Indian Kashmir throughout 2017 and up to now. Therefore, one must view offensive defence as a long-term pursuit of the Indian state, with the 2016 surgical strikes being an early milestone in a perilous journey that will take years, if not forever, before Pakistan can be forced to desist from its malevolent behaviour. India's military leadership has signalled publicly that while keeping open options like limited surgical strikes, it is also honing the conventional 'Cold Start' doctrine or 'proactive war strategy' to 'swiftly mobilize and strike hard across the border within 96 hours or so', and seize territory from Pakistan.[71] The mix of surgical strikes and Cold Start might be a one-two punch that could knock out the adversary in an extreme crisis situation, provided there is no escalation to the nuclear level or adverse intervention by China or the US to preserve the balance of power in South Asia. The very fact that the Modi government has brought back Cold Start to the table after the Singh government had disowned it indicates that the former intends to apply psychological pressure on Pakistan during crises with an attacking mindset.

All said and done, while pundits grapple with the technical judgements drawing upon abstract terminology and military jargon about what kind of disruption Modi has done to the India–Pakistan strategic equation or the South Asian security landscape, the broader addition to India's national psyche that Modi has made through his tough responses in crises is worth reiterating. It is not measurable in numerical values or statistics, but is omnipresent in the minds of laypeople. There used to be an epidemic of fear and hesitation which had rendered India a supine victim to countless terrorist attacks by Pakistanis and Pakistan-sponsored jihadis within India. That pall of doubt and inaction has now cleared because a different India has come to the fore, not just rhetorically but in the on-the-ground heroics of its military who have the political backing to take the battle into the adversary's turf. Here is the change in Modi's own words:

> They were thinking they can keep wounding India, wage attacks, proxy wars and India would not respond. The reason the enemies of India could think this was because of the attitude of the 'remote-controlled' government prior to 2014. That is why the enemies could nurture this attitude.[72]

The later chapters of this book offer additional insights into Modi's remoulding of Indian nationhood in a tougher vein—a still-unfinished task. Here, it is befitting to remember what the ancient Indian strategist, Kautilya (375–283 BCE), said about the value of self-discovery and self-validation when confronted with hostile foreign kingdoms or states:

> The attacker should know the comparative strengths and weaknesses of himself and of the enemy, and having ascertained the time of marching, the consequences, the loss of men and money, and profits and danger, he should march with his full force; otherwise one should keep quiet.[73]

Modi's India is not keeping quiet. It can call the bluff of state sponsors of terrorism and reclaim its inner strength and power that had been dissipated due to historical memory loss and intervening spells of colonial enslavement. The reversion of India to Bharat, its ancient Sanskritic self, is a theme very dear to Modi and his main national security decision-making team members. The surgical strikes were but one illustration of that mammoth metamorphosis. I will return to it in subsequent chapters.

Chapter 2

Defiant in Doklam

If you know the enemy and know yourself, you need not fear the result of a hundred battles. If you know yourself but not the enemy, for every victory gained you will also suffer a defeat. If you know neither the enemy nor yourself, you will succumb in every battle.[1]

—Ancient Chinese strategist, Sun Tzu, 475 BCE

An Early Test of Wills

Narendra Modi had taken over India's reins in May 2014 and was making a splash on the regional and global stages. With his magnetic presence in international forums, galvanization of the Indian diaspora and diligent efforts to polish India's image abroad, he announced himself as a force to reckon with in his early months in office. Since China and the US were the two pre-eminent powers in the world, his initial meetings with President Xi Jinping and President Barack Obama were of particular import as they would have a key bearing on how the geostrategic China–India–US triangle, which determines Asia's destiny, would play out in the Modi era. From 17 September to 19 September, Modi hosted Xi in India and then, on

30 September, he flew to meet Obama in the US. While both these diplomatic summits got wall-to-wall coverage and were memorable for atmospherics and visuals, the substance of the two events was like chalk and cheese.

With Obama, Modi jointly published an op-ed in *The Washington Post* recalling Prime Minister Vajpayee's phrase that India and the US were 'natural allies' and vowing that, as 'global partners', the two sides would 'jointly work to maintain freedom of navigation and lawful commerce across the seas'.[2] In diplomatic-speak, it meant that the India–US combine would together challenge Chinese hegemony in the 'Indo-Pacific', a term that the Obama administration began using from 2010 onward to promote a greater profile for India in what used to be traditionally called the 'Asia-Pacific' where China and the US used to be seen as the only two main powers. The US–India joint statement, after the first Modi–Obama summit, deliberately rankled China by expressing 'concern' about the South China Sea disputes, where Beijing had been militarily intimidating smaller neighbours over maritime territorial claims. It mentioned that 'the prime minister and president called on all parties to avoid the use, or threat of use, of force in advancing their claims'.[3] Another diplomatic salvo followed it in January 2015, when Modi and Obama unveiled a Joint Strategic Vision for the Asia-Pacific and Indian Ocean Region which vowed to 'increase ties among Asian powers' to 'better respond to diplomatic, economic and security challenges in the region'.[4] To China, it appeared to confirm apprehension that a coalition or bloc to counterbalance it was in the offing.

This was the Modi effect on Indian foreign policy. He started with sharp clarity and ambition about which country mattered for India's national security and which one posed the biggest challenge. Just contrast the operative sentences of the September 2014 Modi–Obama declaration with those issued a year earlier by Manmohan Singh and Obama. The latter noted that 'the Leaders expressed a desire to partner more closely with other Asia-Pacific countries, including greater coordination with Japan, China and ASEAN [Association of Southeast Asian Nations]'.[5] As a nationalistic politician who had been critical of the Singh government's inattention to security threats posed by foreign adversaries, Modi's debut in international relations sought to closely align Indian diplomacy with its national security. This was in spite of the fact that Modi, as the chief minister of Gujarat, had visited China four times with an exclusive focus on attracting Chinese foreign investment into his state. As the leader of India, he had moved from the provincial perspective to the national one, and it was evident to him even in those initial months as prime minister that China posed a threat unlike any other nation.

This assessment was confirmed while Modi hosted Xi in his native Gujarat and then Delhi with rousing public receptions and culturally enthralling performances from 17 to 19 September. A week before Xi landed in Ahmedabad, Indian troops discovered that around 300 PLA soldiers had intruded two kilometres into what India perceived as its side of the LAC in the same Chumar area of southeastern Ladakh that I have described in the Introduction of this book in the context of a 2013 bilateral face-off and a purported quid pro quo. For the Chinese, whatever concessions they may have extracted in Chumar from the Singh government were clearly insufficient. This time, they came back with road-building equipment to try and cement their claim and present India with a fait accompli. Another stand-off followed, but India displayed a firmness and unwillingness to accede or do a deal. According to Gokhale, Modi decided to 'pump in more troops in the area' to show the Chinese that India would go to any length to defend its sovereignty and host Xi without feeling psychologically pressured by his Chinese peer.[6]

The Indian journalist Uday Mahurkar has narrated a point-blank exchange between Modi and Xi on the banks of the serene Sabarmati River, where the Indian leader apparently said, 'this was not expected of your country' and asked, 'Can you tell me when the troops are withdrawing'.[7] While the exact wording of Modi's plain-speaking with Xi has not been officially declassified, the Indian leader revealed that he had not pulled punches out of any obligatory sense of hospitality, expectations of Chinese foreign direct investment (FDI) in the Indian economy, or deference to Chinese military might:

> I raised our serious concern over repeated incidents along the border. We agreed that peace and tranquillity in the border region constitutes an essential foundation for mutual trust and confidence and for realising the full potential of our relationship... Peace and stability in our relations and along our borders are essential for us to realize the enormous potential in our relations.[8]

Modi's message to Xi that 'even a little toothache can paralyse the entire body' was a show of political will and an attempt to set an assertive tone early in their relationship.[9] Modi let the Chinese strongman know that India would prioritize national security as the main parameter for judging bilateral ties. The Modi government's stark emphasis on confrontations at the LAC as inimical to the overall Sino-Indian relationship conveyed that India had changed and would no longer downplay Chinese territorial transgressions and intrusions as mere 'acne'. The China–India joint statement from the 2014 summit also stressed a commitment to 'mutual respect and sensitivities for each other's concerns and aspirations'. With no major rupture in relations yet, the old formulation of a 'strategic partnership' did continue to be in parlance, but there was also a reference to the 'early settlement of the boundary question' to be 'pursued as a strategic objective.'[10]

The dynamic of China wishing that bilateral ties would keep progressing in other areas such as trade, investment and multilateral institutional cooperation, while simultaneously expecting India to concede space at the disputed points of the LAC, came crashing down the day Modi came to power. Faced with the numerical strength of Indian military deployments and Modi's hard-line on respecting territorial integrity, the PLA began disengagement and redeployment back from Chumar on 26 September. While the status quo ante was restored there, this initial showdown would prove to be a precursor to a more nettlesome national security crisis in 2017.

The Main Obstacle

The road to the Doklam crisis passes through terrain that transcends differing perceptions of China and India at the LAC. What happened in the summer of 2017 was the product of accumulating conflicts of interest between China and India over regional influence in South Asia and global power alignments. Although the Chumar row was settled in 2014, Xi's China remained determined to keep testing India's will and resolve along the LAC and wider South Asian and Indo-Pacific regions. As a great power with an economy and military four to five times that of India, China believed that it had the upper hand and should drive home its advantage to hem in India and force it to submit to a new Chinese-favouring order in the subcontinent. Xi wanted to redraw the balance of power in South Asia and try to coerce Modi into conceding China's inevitable march into India's backyard.

In September 2014, I vividly remember sitting in the audience watching Xi deliver a speech in New Delhi to Indian opinion and policymakers during his maiden visit. The giveaway phrase that lingered in my mind was 'South Asia'. He heralded 'three billion people' of China and South Asia (not of China and India alone) breaking natural barriers through 'belt and road' (a reference to his mega transcontinental hegemonic project known as the BRI [Belt and Road Initiative, formerly known as One Belt One Road or OBOR] to revive China's historic maritime and land Silk Routes for trade and commerce), and 'becoming a new pole of economic growth in the world'. As the gathered Indians twitched in their seats, he unapologetically announced that China aimed to increase trade with South Asia to US$150 billion and raise its investment volume in South Asia to US$30 billion over the next five years. India, which was growing up to be the fastest-growing economy under Modi, not just in South Asia but globally, was assigned just US$20 billion of Chinese FDI, but the failing economy of Pakistan was pledged thrice that amount. Instead of contributing to Modi's dream of India as a manufacturing hub through FDI-fuelled 'Make in India', the Chinese leader presented himself as a saviour of the whole subcontinent. Calling China 'the biggest neighbour of South Asia' and India 'the largest country in South Asia', Xi slyly proposed that 'China is ready to work together with India and make greater contribution to the development of the region.' China–South Asia cooperation, he declared, was 'a massive treasure long-awaited to be unearthed'.[11]

Xi's unsaid inference was that India should not block or grudge China's deeper penetration of the former's historic sphere of influence. This appeal grated on Indian nerves because BRI's crown jewel was Pakistan. The China–Pakistan Economic Corridor (CPEC), worth approximately US$62 billion of promised Chinese loans to upgrade Pakistan's energy, transportation and industrial sectors, is the single biggest commitment by China to any country under the over

US$1 trillion valued BRI. Among CPEC's most controversial provisions are projects built by Chinese money and manpower in PoK and Gilgit-Baltistan, regions India considers to be under illegal Pakistani possession, which should rightfully be returned to India. The Indian government has 'conveyed its concerns to the Chinese side about their activities in areas illegally occupied by Pakistan in the union territories of Jammu and Kashmir and Ladakh and has asked them to cease such activities'. It has also refused to legitimize China's propaganda that BRI is a 'win–win cooperation' model that brings universal benefits to all countries. The Indian position, which bears similarities to those of Australia, Japan, the US and the European Union, is that international economic connectivity initiatives 'must follow principles of openness, transparency and financial responsibility and must be pursued in a manner that respects sovereignty, equality and territorial integrity of other nations'.[12]

Notwithstanding China's assurances that CPEC is 'purely an economic program' with no military or geostrategic motives, it has come to light that Chinese fighter jets, navigation systems, radar systems and on-board weapons are to be manufactured under the aegis of CPEC.[13] Pakistan would also be brought under China's BeiDou Navigation Satellite System, which has implications for missile and submarine warfare capabilities.[14] The CPEC Authority, a Pakistani governmental institution to facilitate Chinese investments, is run by Pakistan's military, using Chinese-aided projects 'as Trojan horses to claim a greater share of power back from the civilian government'.[15] One would recall from Chapter 1 that the civil–military imbalance in Pakistan directly impacts terrorism and hostility aimed at India. Another military ramification of the CPEC is the increased physical presence of PLA forces inside Pakistan in the name of security for Chinese engineers and workers engaged in infrastructure projects. Some of these Chinese troops have been sighted in PoK and close to the Indian border, ringing alarm bells among Indian intelligence agencies.[16] If China eventually turns Pakistan's Gwadar Port, a signature CPEC project, into a PLA naval base, it would give Beijing enormous military leverage in the western Indian Ocean.[17] It would also complement its pre-existing plans to project power on India's eastern flank through other BRI-funded constructions like the Kyaukpyu port in Myanmar and the Hambantota port in Sri Lanka. Xi has strutted like a colossus in Myanmar, Sri Lanka and the Maldives, announcing landmark infrastructure-building projects in these countries as part of the BRI. In the process, he has piqued India's insecurity of being hemmed in by what Indian and western strategic analysts label as the 'string of pearls' strategy.

There is also a deep and unbroken nuclear cooperation between China and Pakistan, dressed up as purely civilian-oriented to redress acute electricity shortages crippling the latter. India has always been in the crosshairs of the 'all-weather alliance' between China and Pakistan since the 1950s. The alliance encompasses conventional and non-conventional military give and take, material and diplomatic assistance to each other during Chinese and Pakistani wars against India, critical infrastructure construction such as the deep-water Gwadar Port, tacit understandings for Pakistan to help moderate Islamic extremism in China's restive Xinjiang region, and general foreign policy coordination at multilateral forums to counter India's interests and opportunities. On the eve of Xi's first visit to Pakistan in April 2015, the host government put up billboards all over Islamabad with the slogan that China–Pakistan friendship was 'higher than mountains, deeper than oceans, sweeter than honey, and stronger than steel'.[18] Such is the emotional depth and co-dependency of the State elites of both countries, cemented by mutual animus toward India.

Husain Haqqani, a former Pakistani ambassador to the US, has pithily explained the logic of the India-concentrated Beijing–Islamabad axis, 'For China, Pakistan is a low-cost secondary deterrent to India. For Pakistan, China is a high-value guarantor of security against India.'[19] The British author Andrew Small's take on why China prizes Pakistan so much is also worth citing.

> The balancing role that Pakistan plays in Beijing's India policy goes well beyond forcing India to keep a large number of its troops and military assets focused on its western frontier, though that undoubtedly helps. It also ensures that India is kept off balance, distracted, absorbing diplomatic, political and strategic energies that could otherwise be directed towards China. It puts a constant question mark over India's aspirations to transcend its own neighbourhood.[20]

Notwithstanding the tectonic shifts in global geopolitics that accompanied the end of the Cold War, and the transition from a US-led unipolar world order to an emerging multipolar one, the utility of Pakistan to China and vice versa remains entrenched to this day because of their shared animus towards India. To cover up this core reality and allay Indian fears about the Sino-Pakistan axis and BRI being instruments to counterbalance India, China's state-owned media has offered the alibi that 'Pakistan serves as a bridgehead for China to further develop friendly ties with West Asian and North African nations as well as regions situated on the Indian Ocean.'[21] The justification that Pakistan offers a pathway for China to access the Muslim world by virtue of the former's geographical proximity to the oil-rich Persian Gulf is not valid as China has wide-ranging keys apart from Pakistan to open doors and oil pipelines to Islamic countries of the Middle East. Beijing also has its own massive political clout in energy-abundant Muslim Central Asia. What is happening in the guise of CPEC and BRI is a case of old wine in a new bottle, i.e. a grand strategy to keep India under relentless strategic pressure in South Asia. As long as the Chinese play this game, they cannot expect to win trust or goodwill in India.

Over the years, the Modi government has been repeatedly propositioned by China to drop Indian objections to BRI and declare allegiance to the China-designed and China-dominated blueprint for hegemony in South Asia. In March 2016, Jaishankar, who was then the Indian foreign secretary, responded publicly to the Chinese entreaties with a rebuke that China was not respecting India's sensitivities and that the end goal of BRI was to establish Chinese hegemony in Asia.[22]

In January 2017, Modi himself spoke out about India forging deeper economic connectivity with its neighbours on principled grounds but warned obliquely that it would not endorse regional integration initiatives by China which fail to uphold India's sovereignty and territorial integrity.[23] Seeing through the national security implications of what China was advertising as a harmless commercial initiative and explicitly linking doing business with China to its commitment not to hamper India's security has been a hallmark of how Modi has dealt with the dragon. It could be categorized as a 'security first' doctrine. With countries that pose geopolitical threats to India, the overriding issue for Modi would be to address those threats rather than to do an end-run around them and carry on with business in other areas. It was a tougher and more obstinate line that bothered and frustrated China because India, with its size and regional influence, was proving to be the main obstacle for BRI.

Xi's desire of having the cake of BRI spreading unhindered across Asia while also eating the cake of counterbalancing India by ensnaring smaller countries in the region was not being obliged by Modi. Beijing was miffed and critiqued what it called New Delhi's 'cliché mentality of associating everything with geopolitics' and appealed to set aside 'geopolitical bias'.[24] The irony of one of the world's most ruthless players of geopolitics, China, conveniently asking a historically weak player, India, to stop playing geopolitics could not be missed. In May 2017, India boycotted China's grandiose inaugural launch for the BRI, known as the Belt and Road Forum (BRF), which was attended by 30 heads of government and representatives of 30 more countries. Modi was causing Xi discomfort.

Throughout 2016 and 2017, in the run-up to the Doklam crisis, while Chinese officials and state-run media outlets raked up India's non-participation in the BRI, India raised its own counterpoints where China was proving to be the principal bone in the throat. During the October 2016 meeting between Modi and Xi in Goa, on the sidelines of the BRICS (Brazil, Russia, India, China and South Africa) summit, the Indian leader sought a change in China's stance on India's admission into the NSG. A few months earlier, China had played spoilsport by insisting that it could contemplate India's entry only if its client state Pakistan, which had an atrocious record in nuclear proliferation, was also allowed a chance to come into the export control institution. When this ruse failed to convince 46 out of the 48 members of the NSG, China switched from 'linkage to blockage' and persuaded the host country of the NSG's plenary meeting in Seoul, South Korea, in June 2016, to defer India's application.[25]

Parallel to the NSG veto, China also raised hackles in India by impeding India's bid to get the JeM chief, Masood Azhar, who had directed the Uri attack, designated as a proscribed global terrorist by the UN's Sanctions Committee. Beijing echoed Islamabad's claim that New Delhi was maligning Azhar with ulterior intentions of embarrassing Pakistan and that there was still not enough proof of his complicity in terrorist attacks against India. Media leaks of a high-level meeting in Islamabad in the Pakistani prime minister's office in October 2016 revealed that Beijing was coordinating and taking its cues from Islamabad to protect Azhar at the UN.[26]

Whenever the issue of Azhar's ban appeared on the UN agenda, China did most of the heavy lifting on behalf of Pakistan. It stubbornly maintained its technical hold, much to India's chagrin, as it was in the midst of a major new national security crisis with Pakistan after the Pulwama attack by Azhar's JeM (this episode is covered in detail in Chapter 3). Various reasons have been proffered by analysts for why China put on such a brazen resistance on behalf of Azhar, including that he was 'Beijing's go-to man to ensure security of its geostrategic investments' under CPEC,[27] and that it was an affirmation of the 'strength of the China–Pakistan relationship' which is 'warmer, deeper, and more strategically vital than just about any other bilateral relationship in Asia'.[28] Notwithstanding boilerplate cliches from the Chinese government that there should be 'no double standards in the fight against terrorism', Beijing has been an unhesitant hypocrite on the issue due to its need to sustain its overall grand strategy of keeping India bogged down by Pakistan-sponsored jihad and Pakistan-triggered national security crises.[29]

Besides Pakistan, there was also the factor of great power rivalry between China and the US which was gathering momentum. It would not have gone unnoticed in Beijing that Modi overcame past hesitations of Indian foreign policy about losing 'strategic autonomy' and went ahead to sign the Logistics Exchange Memorandum of Agreement (LEMOA) with the US in August 2016. It was the first of three foundational defence pacts which would give the US and Indian militaries access to each other's bases. The enhanced military-to-military interoperability between India and the US that Modi was championing, thanks to his strategic clarity about which countries posed threats and which were true partners, was seen in China as a case of India tilting closer to its main global competitor to contain China's rise as a great power.

Xi's belief that India had been suborned as a pawn to serve the US's vested interests to pin down China appeared to gradually build as Modi embraced both Obama and his successor, Donald Trump, with gusto. The charge that Modi was implementing an American agenda was incongruous, especially with Trump's transactional and inconsistent approach, which lacked a grand strategy to counterbalance China. But the ever-suspicious Chinese communist elites reasoned that Modi was hitching India's wagon to the US and saw in it an additional reason to be wary of doing any favours to India.[30]

Kicking the can down the road and endlessly delaying India's most sought-after diplomatic prizes such as the Azhar ban, NSG membership and permanent membership on the UNSC on the pretext that no consensus had been reached in the international community became trademark practices of Chinese foreign policy under Xi. Chapter 4 of this book expands on how China continued to spitefully obstruct India's path to prominence in global forums as retribution for its unwillingness to join BRI, its furtherance of the India–US strategic partnership and its firmness in not yielding ground at the LAC. Unlike Pakistan, whose confrontations with India are driven by raw religious hatred and subcontinental grievances about the unfinished business of the partition of 1947, China's estimation of India is craftier and suffused with considerations of the China–India–US triangle and the wider international balance of power. The backgrounder in this section on the state of play of Sino-Indian relations and US–India relations until mid-2017 is hence a prerequisite to fully grasp the strategic context of Modi and Xi's descent into their first big crisis in Doklam.

Perpetual Peace and Friendship

The tiny landlocked Himalayan kingdom of Bhutan has had a precarious existence ever since Mao Zedong founded the People's Republic of China in 1949. Before the advent of communist rule in China, Bhutan enjoyed centuries of rich religious and political relations with its giant northern neighbour, Tibet, which experts characterize as equitable, independent and lacking in any hierarchical tutelage even though the sects of Buddhism followed in Tibet and Bhutan were different.[31] Once Mao's revolutionary China began invading and savagely gobbling up Tibet in the 1950s, Bhutan was confronted with a menacing new neighbour with the PLA right on its doorstep. By 1959, Bhutanese enclaves in Tibet had been occupied by the PLA and small-scale Chinese incursions into Bhutan proper began in the 1960s. In what would become a familiar pattern, China would build roads, set up military installations along or inside Bhutanese territory and then, furnish maps claiming historical sovereignty over those spaces. During the reformist era of Deng Xiaoping and his successors, when China followed a conciliatory foreign policy of 'cope with affairs calmly; hide our capacities and bide our time', Bhutan entered several rounds of boundary demarcation talks with China.[32] Bilateral agreements in 1988 and 1998 saw China promising to respect Bhutan's sovereignty and territorial integrity and to refrain from using unilateral force to alter the status quo until all remaining border disputes were mutually settled.

Unfortunately, the relative restraint that China had shown toward Bhutan under Deng and his handpicked Communist

Party protégés Jiang Zemin (CCP general secretary from 1989 to 2002) and Hu Jintao (general secretary from 2002 to 2012), was followed by the ultra-hawkish Xi. As mentioned in the Introduction, Xi has built a 'national security Party-state' with expansionist tendencies against all neighbours. In recent years, Bhutan and Nepal, both India's crucial buffer states in the north, have been subjected to relentless pressure by the PLA on their northern and western borders with Chinese-occupied Tibet. In the context of his grandiloquent 'China dream' of national rejuvenation under his personalized autocracy, Xi is resuscitating and chasing many of Mao's concepts, including the idea that Tibet is the palm of China's right hand, and China must consolidate control over it by 'liberating' the five fingers on Tibet's edges—the sovereign countries of Bhutan and Nepal, as well as India's territories of Ladakh, Sikkim and Arunachal Pradesh.[33] The same troublesome assertiveness and territorial hunger that Xi's China has displayed against Southeast Asian nations in the South China Sea is paralleled by a determined push southwards in the Himalayas to wrest Bhutan and Nepal away from India's influence, and to force them to accept China's new enlarged borders that encroach inside their lands.

The extreme military asymmetry between the small Himalayan countries Bhutan and Nepal vis-à-vis China's muscle-flexing military that is numerically and technically light-years ahead adds to the brooding sense of peril to their very existence as sovereign states. China being China, the pressure to convert Bhutan and Nepal into vassal states, if not annex them altogether into Chinese-occupied Tibet, is not merely military. Through the BRI, Beijing has offered Kathmandu massive infrastructure loans and also tried to wean Thimphu away from New Delhi with the promise of financial aid. In the previous section, I explained how the tactic of plying inferior developing countries with loans and extracting strategically valuable territorial concessions from them has already enabled Xi's southern expansionism in the Indian Ocean region in countries like Pakistan, Sri Lanka, Myanmar and the Maldives.

But Bhutan has been a tough nut to crack for China because its security and economy have been umbilically tied to India's as a guarantee against Chinese takeover. The 1949 Bhutan–India Treaty of Perpetual Peace and Friendship and the similarly named 2007 treaty, which adjusted ties to give Bhutan more initiative and autonomy, form the basis of an enduring special relationship. The unmentioned but unmissable crux of these legal arrangements is that India protects Bhutan from Chinese threat, and Bhutan does not allow its territory to be used to impair India's national security. Chinese communist propaganda often paints the Bhutan–India relationship as an unfair and unequal one designed to serve India's 'hegemonism in South Asia' and alleges that 'as a small country Bhutan is being controlled by India and it can't oppose it openly'.[34] This line became a shrill Chinese refrain during the Doklam crisis. But, scholars from Vietnam, a neighbour of China, which is coping with Xi's relentless expansionism in the South China Sea, have correctly argued that for a small state like Bhutan that faces an existential threat from China, it is 'important to have an 'alliance shelter', and India is best suited to meeting Bhutan's needs for political, economic, societal and strategic shelter'.[35]

For India, having already forfeited its main Himalayan buffer of Tibet to the invading Chinese and naively recognized Tibet as a part of China in the 1950s,[36] preserving the sovereignty of Bhutan from communist China has become an inexorable security requirement. Recognizing Bhutan's centrality in defending Indian national security, Modi made it his first destination for a foreign visit after becoming prime minister in 2014. He ensured that Bhutan remained the largest recipient of

Indian foreign development assistance and declared during his second visit in 2019 that 'no other two countries in the world understand each other so well or share so much'.[37] In the wake of the monarchy-guided democratization of Bhutan and some domestic resentment emerging there over the paternalistic relationship with India, Modi also recognized the dissent and showed that 'the current Indian leadership clearly fathomed the problem and so is trying to arrest the speedy erosion of India's credibility as well as recover from the past losses'.[38] But above all else, the Modi government kept an eagle's eye on PLA troop presence and infrastructure building on disputed points of the Bhutan–Tibet border as they impinge on securing India's Northeast and could hand China a huge geographical advantage to press for its 'five fingers' claims on the eastern sector of the LAC.

In June 2017, an inevitable crisis arose. Bhutan appealed urgently to India to come to its rescue after its small India-trained and India-equipped army found PLA patrols crossing into Bhutan's claimed Doklam plateau and unilaterally constructing a road southward that threatened to give China a clear line of sight to India's jugular vein, the Siliguri corridor or 'chicken's neck'. US-based defence analysts believe Beijing had two objectives in its offensive infrastructural thrust in Doklam.

> First, a road network would support a more entrenched Chinese presence in the region... Second, new infrastructure would allow Chinese troops to access a key ridge overlooking the Siliguri corridor. Chinese forces could use their positions on higher ground to collect intelligence on Indian military positions and, in a conflict, even threaten Indian supply routes.[39]

Some observers also argue that Chinese adventurism in Doklam was motivated by domestic strife in the PLA as it was being politically purged and brought under Xi's absolute command at that time.[40] The interpretation that PLA commanders might have acted autonomously in Doklam as part of their power struggle in domestic Chinese politics cannot be verified because of the opacity of China's authoritarian regime. Whatever the political impetus, the strategic effect of China's push to enforce its claims over Bhutan was not just a bilateral affair. Doklam lay at the tri-junction of Bhutan, Chinese-occupied Tibet, and India's northeastern state, Sikkim. The possibility that China could sever India's access to its vital northeastern region in wartime by taking over the chicken's neck had been a perennial nightmare for Indian strategists. Partly to ensure against such a catastrophe, India had signed an understanding with China in 2012 that 'the tri-junction boundary points between India, China and third countries will be finalised in consultation with the concerned countries'.[41] China's blatant disregard for consulting the other two parties, Bhutan and India, and its nonchalant bid to redraw the borders through military bullying could not be ignored as the geostrategic stakes were high. The Modi government decided to take a bold stand, coming in the way of China's hegemonic ambitions for South Asia.

India's first response to the crisis was not diplomatic pleading or demarches to China but Operation Juniper, authorized by Modi on the night of 17 June 2017, after a high-level discussion on the serious threat posed by Chinese browbeating of Bhutan. It led to the deployment of about 300 Indian troops with weapons and bulldozers to form a 'human wall' at Doklam to block the PLA from carrying out its construction plans. There was a dual message in the show of military resolve—India would proactively defend Bhutan even if it meant an escalation with China, particularly if the territorial dispute had direct bearings on India's own national security. An Indian official involved in the crisis decision-making explained why Modi shed old Indian strategic patience and took a pre-emptive stance in Doklam.

> We have been noticing it (Chinese road-building bit by
> bit in Doklam) for so many years. But we could not do
> anything because it was happening in the Bhutanese
> territory. We stepped in only in 2016 when the road
> directly threatened our strategic interest.[42]

Again, it was a calibrated and well-justified escalation by India without wanting to let the situation get out of control with the involvement of physical violence. The 'middle path' referred to in Chapter 1 was also at play. The Modi government issued 'strict instructions...to ensure that the Indian side did not engage in any scuffle and that things were handled as calmly as possible.'[43] Outnumbered and lacking in tactical superiority at the spot of the stand-off, the Chinese were genuinely surprised at India's no-nonsensical attitude. But instead of withdrawing and bowing to the Indian counter-pressure, the PLA brought in its reinforcements and hunkered down with a human wall of its own facing the Indians. Capitalizing on the fact that China's nearest garrison was 10 kilometres away and it would have to transport troops uphill, India decided not to budge one inch from the face-off location and progressively dispatched more forces to the location in tit-for-tat fashion so that India's comparative numerical lead remained intact. This resolute stand in the Himalayas was backed up by an emphatic diplomatic statement 12 days into the crisis, where India rebutted Chinese claims that Indian troops were occupying Chinese territory. The statement unambiguously expressed the bottom line that China's road-building in Bhutanese territory 'would represent a significant change of status quo with serious security implications for India.'[44] India would not retreat unless China halted construction and stepped back from the disputed tri-junction area.

Unfamiliar to being accosted and pre-empted, Xi's government decided to ratchet up the pressure through a series of military demonstrations that might force India to rethink its adamant stance at Doklam. On 17 July 2017, the PLA held live-fire exercises with anti-tank grenades and missiles in Tibet to 'test its joint strike capability on plateaus'. It was not lost on anyone that Doklam was a plateau. The drills were broadcast live on Chinese television to 'reassure the Chinese people that a strong PLA force is there, capable and determined to defend Chinese territory'. But more ominously, in the context of the Doklam face off, Chinese military commentators averred that the purpose was that 'the PLA wanted to demonstrate it could easily overpower its Indian counterparts'.[45] It was also announced that the PLA had moved tens of thousands of tonnes of military vehicles to Tibet. Chinese analysts surmised the move was 'likely related to the stand-off and could have been designed to bring India to the negotiating table' in line with the maxim that 'diplomatic talks must be backed by military preparation'.[46]

At a tactical level, the Chinese had been seeking inroads into Doklam to obviate their inferior position in the Chumbi Valley of Chinese-occupied Tibet, where the PLA forces 'fell in the line of sight and fire of Indian forces'.[47] Unable to ram its way through Doklam, Beijing fell back on trying to intimidate India with a menacing concentration in Chumbi. More than 12,000 PLA soldiers, 150 tanks and artillery guns were deployed in Chumbi, across the northern border of the Indian state of Sikkim and not far from the face-off site in Doklam. India matched this build-up but did not field troops right at the LAC in north Sikkim as it had the tactical advantage in the ridges of the Sikkim–Tibet border.[48] China had recognized Sikkim as part of India in 2003, but it warned it could 'readjust its stance on the matter', and 'support pro-independence appeals in

Sikkim' if India did not eschew 'regional hegemony', and 'rewrite southern Himalayan geopolitics'.[49] Unscrupulously reopening previously settled territorial disputes with fresh claims is a trademark Chinese characteristic to keep adversaries uncertain and guessing, and there was plenty of this kind of huffing and puffing during the Doklam crisis. But Modi held firm and did not budge.

Even as military shock-and-awe manoeuvres were failing to dislodge India from Doklam, China parallelly embarked on a cunning strategy: splitting Bhutan from India and converting this trilateral crisis into a bilateral one between Beijing and Thimphu, where China's exponential asymmetry would prevail. On 5 July 2017, China claimed that it had already obtained a 'basic consensus' with Bhutan, 'and there is no dispute between both of us that Doklam belongs to China'. It added that 'Chinese activities (road building) in the relevant area does not violate relevant agreements and does not alter the status quo. The Bhutan side also knows it clearly. We will work together with Bhutan through friendly negotiations.'[50] Indian government sources revealed to the news media in early August that China had offered Bhutan a US$10 billion economic assistance package, including a grant, low-interest loans and FDI, in return for Thimphu softening its stance on Chinese violations of Bhutanese sovereignty in Doklam.[51] Had Bhutan, an emerging economy with a gross domestic product (GDP) of less than US$3 billion, fallen for the bribe and declared that Doklam belonged to China, India would have been compelled to withdraw its forces from the face-off site. Challenging India's locus standi on Doklam and eliminating it from the equation was a scheme taken straight out of China's playbook of deception and skulduggery.

But this ploy also failed. One of the remarkable achievements of Modi's management of the Doklam crisis was that he did not allow cracks to appear in the close bond between India and Bhutan despite Chinese tricks and enticements. NSA Doval, once again Modi's ace troubleshooter like in the post-Uri attacks crisis, was not only 'the chief coordinator between the military and diplomats', but also 'constantly working to assure Bhutan about its safety and security in the crisis'. Foreign Secretary S. Jaishankar also 'handled the relations with Bhutan and its leadership', so that India's credibility and commitment to defend Bhutan were never in doubt.[52] An imperative in national security crises where third countries are at stake is to maintain alliance solidarity and loyalty to deny the adversary opportunities to divide one's coalition. The Bhutan–India 'perpetual peace and friendship' is a de facto alliance and has required enormous attention and sensitivity on the part of both countries' leaderships and people. In the Doklam crisis, Bhutan was petrified about the possibility of a Chinese invasion from its northern and western sides, and would have preferred it would not get squished in a military confrontation between China and India. Assuaging Bhutan's concerns about India's ironclad security guarantees while also not escalating with China to such an extent that war might break out at the trijunction and devastate Bhutan was the most delicate balancing act and a test of India's image as a reliable shelter.

The Australian scholar Iain Henry writes that 'the most obvious sign of a reliable ally is that it does not pose a risk of abandonment or entrapment. By contrast, an unreliable ally would be too timid or too aggressive'.[53] India had to ward off the Chinese challenge not just militarily but also through diplomatic acuity and maturity. The then Indian external affairs minister, Sushma Swaraj, who was also involved in lubricating ties with Bhutan during the Doklam crisis, coined a famous distinction in 2016 between 'big brother' and 'elder brother'. She declared to another Himalayan neighbour Nepal that India would be the latter, i.e. a brother in the Indian tradition who 'shows concern…tries to assist you in solving your problems… will never become the cause of your difficulties'.[54] Doklam was a moment for the elder brother to be tough with aggressive China but gentle and assuring to wounded Bhutan. The fact that Bhutan was the only other country apart from India to have skipped the May 2017 BRF extravaganza in Beijing and Thimphu's continued adherence to Indian guidance during and after the Doklam crisis even though Indian development aid to it pales before what China has dangled as a bait is a testament to how Modi has respected Bhutan's sensibilities and really taken care of it as part of his 'neighbourhood first' policy.

The Psychological War

With India and Bhutan standing undeterred and inseparable and the Indian military facing down the Chinese without balking at Doklam, Beijing was livid and seething with rage. The stage was set to implement the PLA's 'three warfares': psychologically scaring the adversary, manipulating domestic and global public opinion through a media blitz and raising international legal principles ('lawfare') to redraw maps in China's favour.[55] By mid-July 2017, China opened up a torrent of rhetorical abuses and threats against India that gushed out relentlessly from its officials and media mouthpieces. The language and tone were so violent that they were reminiscent of the heydays of Mao Zedong when foreign enemies would be excoriated with hateful denunciations. Leading the charge with a condescending and hectoring tone was Chinese Foreign Minister Wang Yi, who claimed that 'it is very clear who is right and who is wrong in the stand-off in Doklam' and demanded that the Indians should 'back out honestly'.[56] One state-run newspaper expressed bafflement 'that India has the courage to transgress another country on its behalf' and thundered that 'a third country can certainly enter into Kashmir, including India-controlled Kashmir, upon Pakistan's invitation. (This is not a far-fetched idea.)'[57] A favourite theme in the Chinese infowar was that 'New Delhi took the liberty to speak on Bhutan's behalf', and that 'Thimphu's passive resistance has embarrassed New Delhi' so badly that 'it's time for India's hegemony in South Asia to come to an end.'[58] Even though Bhutan was refusing to fall for the Chinese trap, Beijing's fake news machinery was in full swing, exposing Xi's core anxieties about India being the thorn in the flesh for China's expansionism in South Asia.

Apart from poking third countries and presenting China as their liberator from alleged Indian domination, Beijing also unleashed countless spiteful tirades, including a threat to militarily crush India if it did not withdraw from Doklam. It claimed that the PLA 'is powerful enough to expel Indian troops out of Chinese territory', and that 'the Indian military can choose to return to its territory with dignity, or be kicked out of the area by Chinese soldiers'. It also declared that if India 'believes that its military might can be used as leverage in the Donglang area (referred to as Dokalam or Dok La), and it is ready for a two-and-a-half front war, we have to tell India that the Chinese look down on their military power'.[59] The 'two-and-half front' was a mocking reference to the then Indian Army chief's scenario of being prepared for a simultaneous attack by China and Pakistan from the LAC and LoC respectively, plus attacks by separatists or Maoists internally within India.[60] Another Chinese editorial roared that if Indian troops do not stop trespassing into China's territory, Beijing may be left with no other option than to prepare for a military confrontation and utilize non-diplomatic measures to resolve the conflict. It went on that 'the later India withdraws troops, the greater the risk that it will face from a military counteraction and the more clout it will lose politically.'[61] By August, as the Doklam crisis entered its second month with Indian retreat nowhere in sight, the Chinese bullhorns grew louder and uglier. The ever truculent *Global Times* bellowed that 'the government of Prime Minister Narendra Modi should be aware of the PLA's overwhelming firepower and logistics' and that 'if a war spreads, the PLA is perfectly capable of annihilating all Indian troops in the border region.'[62] There were also several reminders from Chinese state-owned outlets about the debacle of the 1962 war, when a militarily unequipped and politically misguided India was roundly defeated by China and promises that a repeat performance was coming if India did not step back in Doklam. Retorting to an Indian news report that 'the Indian security establishment is reasonably sure China will not risk a war or even "a small-scale military operation" despite all its belligerent rhetoric', Beijing snorted that even after 55 years since the 1962 war, India was as naïve now as it was then. The bluster carried on: 'As the risk of war is rising, Indian public opinion has become clear that Indian troops cannot defeat the Chinese People's Liberation Army... India has lost in both the legal and moral senses. It also lacks strength compared with China.'[63]

When India's then defence minister, Arun Jaitley, calmly clarified that 'the India of 2017 is different from the India of 1962', the Chinese government media gave a rejoinder that 'India will suffer greater losses than in 1962 if it incites military conflicts' and added the bizarre allegation that 'India is humiliating the civilization of the twenty-first century.'[64] When a communist state dishes out so much vitriol in a choreographed fashion during a national security crisis, it takes off the veneer of 'South–South cooperation' and 'peaceful rise', and uncovers the true nature of the beast. Scholars noted that the anti-India propaganda in the Chinese media during

Doklam was 'an outburst of militant jingoism the kind of which would once be aimed mostly at the United States and Japan but has increasingly begun to target India as well'.[65] The increasing resort to attacking India, in particular in the Chinese communist narrative during and after Doklam, showed how incensed Xi and his comrades were at their inability to coerce Modi. S. Jaishankar, the then foreign secratary, would later testify before a parliamentary committee that 'none of us at least in recent memory have seen this kind of ratcheting up of political tensions that we saw during those 72 days' over Doklam.[66] In Chapter 4, the reader will see how China set a new benchmark in international nastiness through 'wolf warrior diplomacy' during the eastern Ladakh-Aksai Chin frontier crisis. Under Xi's totalitarian regime, China's hitherto suave and soft-spoken officials and journalists have all been transformed into venom-spewing spin masters whose poisonous anger can be switched on and off at the will of the Chinese Communist Party like a malleable instrument to try and psyche out foreign opponents.

Diplomacy for Security

During the Doklam crisis, Modi refused to engage in a race to the bottom with the Chinese in vituperative talk. He called the bluff of Chinese psy-ops and provocations, and ensured a dignified and disciplined official Indian verbal posture. During his annual Independence Day speech on 15 August 2017, with the face-off at Dokalm still on, he did not directly address China but reiterated the underlying principles guiding his strategy in the crisis. He said, 'India's security is our priority. Be it our coastline or our borders, the space or the cyberspace, India is capable of ensuring its own security and strong enough to ward off any threats against the country'.[67]

But there was little else in the public domain from the Indian leader during the crisis, even though a nationalistic outpouring happened extempore in Indian society with protests and fervent calls for boycotting Chinese-made goods.[68] Modi's 'be diplomatic but stand firm,'[69] line rested on confidence in India's military advantage at the face-off point in the tri-junction, alertness of the Indian armed forces to foil Chinese revenge intrusions in other sectors of the LAC, and self-belief in the multilateral diplomatic leverage India could press in to tame the dragon. Even as fireworks and dire threats were flying wildly from official Chinese quarters, Modi took a personal initiative on 7 July 2017, on the sidelines of the G20 summit in Hamburg, Germany, by spontaneously approaching Xi and proposing that the two countries' special representatives, NSA Doval and Chinese State Councillor Yang Jiechi resolve the Doklam crisis. Modi apparently also stunned Xi by saying, 'our strategic ties are far bigger than small tactical issues like Doklam.'[70] A long series of lower-level bilateral meetings and rounds of discussions ensued from this initiative of Modi. Indian officials haggling over the nitty-gritty of a solution at the tri-junction 'found their Chinese counterparts to be reasonable, a far cry from the warmongering media statements emanating out of Beijing.'[71]

Why were the Chinese apoplectic in public but pragmatic in private? It was due to their realization that dealing with Modi's India was not going to be a walkover. Also, they may have bowed to the reality of what Frank O'Donnell of the US-based Stimson Center has termed as India's 'key conventional advantages over China, despite the latter's superior mobilization logistics.' Although the overall military and economic balance of power is in China's favour, 'New Delhi boasts a greater force presence positioned permanently closer to the border area than China does.' India's military modernization, with more offensive formations such as the Mountain Strike Corps, and its potential to post 'an estimated 221,000 forces in the Western, Central and Eastern Army Commands close to the border' give it a leg-up over the Chinese who are located deeper inland in occupied Tibet.[72]

Moreover, as I explained earlier, the power asymmetry which Chinese communist tabloids were crowing about during the Doklam crisis was obviated by topographical and geographical conditions in the eastern sector of the LAC. The American scholar Taylor Fravel wrote that 'India's ability to intervene to halt Chinese activities in Doklam highlighted India's superiority and China's vulnerability in the area of the stand-off.'[73]

China also climbed down from its high horse of insisting that 'Indian border troops pulling out unconditionally is a pre-condition for any meaningful talks between the two countries' because of the timing of the Doklam crisis and two milestones that lay ahead in its diplomatic and political calendars—the ninth BRICS summit in Xiamen in September 2017 and the nineteenth national congress of the Communist Party in Beijing in October 2017.[74] Xi's prestige as a world leader and as the unchallenged 'core leader' of China were both at stake as the military face-off continued in Doklam. Modi grasped this situational dynamic and turned it to India's benefit. China resolved the Doklam conflict partly owing to apprehension that Modi might boycott the BRICS summit in Xiamen, an unprecedented possibility that would have poured cold water on China's desire to celebrate BRICS as a microcosm of a new world order where developing countries eschew narrow nationalistic animosities and treat each other respectfully.

Modi understood China's vulnerability and sensitivity as the host, and kept his participation in the Xiamen summit in abeyance until the Doklam deal was hashed out in late August

2017. The 'BRICS card' came in handy for India to moderate China. This is an illustration of the potential of multilateralism, which has been defined by Harvard University's John Ruggie as based on 'generalized principles of conduct' for the whole group 'without regard to particularistic interests of the parties or strategic exigencies'.[75] China prefers bilateral instruments to tackle territorial rows and contests because it has conventional military superiority over any rival claimant—India, Vietnam, the Philippines, Indonesia or Japan. But by investing its prestige in BRICS as a collective medium through which China can shape the emerging world order, Beijing has also been forced to constrain its worst jingoistic and bullying characteristics. India capitalized on this phenomenon to extract concessions in Doklam.

During the Doklam crisis, apart from direct bilateral channels, the Modi government consulted with and roped in Russia to impress upon China to step back and settle so as not to ruin the BRICS summit. One of the barbs hurled by China's provocateurs at the peak of the crisis was that Modi should not depend on the US and Japan for any support. They boastfully added that 'China does hold a lot of cards and can hit India's Achilles heel, but India has no leverage at all to have a strategic showdown with China'.[76] In the summer of 2017, China did have a point that the Americans would not jump to India's rescue in any fight with China, notwithstanding the Modi–Trump bonhomie and advancing India–US strategic relations. Unlike Japan, which did not hesitate to take India's side and admonish China, the Trump administration showed its trademark transactional attitude, and adopted an apathetic stance, urging nothing more than the clichéd dialogue between India and China to sort out the problem.[77]

While Xi was emboldened by the US's cold shoulder to India on Doklam, he also seems to have been mellowed by

Russia's intervention in the name of BRICS solidarity and Xi's own prestige as the host of the BRICS summit. This was an unexpected turn, as India had been perceived by some as distancing itself from its traditional strategic partner Russia and moving closer to the US in the years leading up to the Doklam crisis. However, the reality was far from what was perceived, as Modi had threaded the needle and continued to build trust with President Vladimir Putin. In October 2016, Modi and Putin signed the initial agreement for India to purchase the most advanced S-400 anti-missile system and other hi-tech military hardware from Russia in defiance of US warnings. This balanced, 'India first' diplomacy toward Russia paid dividends, and helped push China to concede and step away from the face-off site in Doklam.

Apart from the loss of face Xi would have had to reckon with had Modi boycotted the BRICS summit, the other consideration was the domestic quinquennial CCP congress where the former was looking to get re-elected for a second term and establish himself as the unparalleled greatest leader of China since Mao. According to Taylor Fravel, one of the reasons for China to agree to pull back its troops from the Doklam tri-junction in late August 2017 was that 'on the eve of the CCP's 19th Party Congress, Xi Jinping likely wanted to avoid any risky escalation that could affect the significant transfer of power that will occur.'[78] Andrew Small has also described the CCP Congress as crucial for de-escalation in Doklam:

> 19th Party Congress...a period that's politically delicate, when people don't want to make mistakes... There is no reason for Xi to see some further advantage to be engaged in conflict... He's on the one hand in a very strong position in the Party and on the other hand has a lot of enemies. Elements of such unpredictability would be unhelpful.[79]

Even in a closed totalitarian regime like that of China, there are audience costs to escalating in a national security crisis. Modi raised those costs for Xi by putting up a brave front and the Chinese dictator had no alternative but to relent. On 28 August 2017, the 73-day-long crisis came to a closure with mutual agreement by both sides that they would withdraw their militaries to previous positions and China would stop the road construction. The Chinese foreign ministry left little to doubt that political and diplomatic worries about the BRICS summit had mattered in the de-escalation:

> After the Indian troops pulled back, we hope that India will respect China's sovereignty and rightful concerns and work towards peaceful settlement. We hope that BRICS countries work towards peaceful resolution of issues and come to the event with a positive attitude.[80]

Offensive Defence and an Enduring Rivalry

Earlier in this book, I had covered the mini-crises over Depsang and Chumar in the western sector of the LAC to show that China has a long memory and a knack for clawing its way back to recursively seek what it considers to be sovereign Chinese territory. After the Doklam crisis was resolved, Beijing did not drop its territorial claims on Thimphu, turn its back on the tri-junction and just move on. It kept coaxing and threatening Bhutan to settle its border dispute with China and hand over Doklam Plateau in exchange for a territorial swap in north-central Bhutan's Jakurlung and Pasamlung valleys.[81] Rebuffed again on Doklam, China shifted the locus of its expansionism to the tri-junction around Sakteng Wildlife Sanctuary in eastern Bhutan, which borders India's Arunachal Pradesh and began terming it as 'disputed territory' in 2020. Meanwhile, a massive crisis was underway with India on the western sector of the

LAC. Felix Chang, a researcher at a Philadelphia-based think tank, wrote that this new front was meant to drive a wedge between Bhutan and India and apply 'indirect pressure on India, which recently has been a thorn in China's side'.[82]

As early as January 2018, Chinese helipads, observation posts, trenches and troop presence were reported to have been ramped up in north Doklam to establish a more permanent presence inside Bhutanese territory, and overcome the tactical disadvantage China had vis-à-vis India during the crisis.[83] The August 2017 China–India deal to end the crisis did hold at the exact site of the face off, but China was determined to blunt India's military edge in the surrounding region. It is not coincidental that China's strategic behaviour has been influenced by its 2,000-year-old board game of Weiqi, where the goal is to surround and control more territory than the opponent and to do it by patiently gaining a foothold and wearing down the other party. The game 'features multiple battles over a wide front, rather than a single decisive encounter' and 'emphasizes long-term planning over quick tactical advantage'.[84] Scholars Sumit Ganguly and Andrew Scobell wrote a year after the Doklam crisis ebbed that 'Beijing and New Delhi confront a chronic long-term condition rather than an acute short-term crisis'. With the 'underlying sources' of the rivalry enduring, there remained a 'possibility of escalation as the PRC continues to probe Indian preparedness along the Himalayan border'.[85]

An established Chinese pattern is chipping away at India's high-altitude defences and pressurizing it with ever-new territorial claims. Chapter 4 contains a full analysis of how this 'salami slicing' reached extreme levels at the LAC in 2020 in the midst of a global health pandemic and triggered the worst China–India national security crisis in generations. But as early as 2018, it was noticeable that China was not going to walk away from its setback in Doklam with its tail between its legs.

I remember meeting Chinese diplomats posted in New Delhi months after the Doklam crisis and saw them still smarting, wagging their fingers sternly and insisting that 'incidents like Doklam should never happen again,' as if the entire fault lay with India. The Australian scholar Lindsay Hughes has articulated why China could not forget Doklam:

> What India did...was more than merely stop China from constructing a road in disputed territory... It also demonstrated that China is not the unstoppable force that much current thinking would imply it is. On the other hand, it would be naïve not to recognize that China was... being stopped by a country it sees as being inferior to it economically and militarily...[86]

Looking back at Modi's decision-making during the Doklam crisis, it is clear that India surprised China by springing to Bhutan's aid and resolutely standing up for India's own national security on a third country's terrain. During the previous worst crisis with China in Sumdorong Chu (1986–87) on the border between Arunachal Pradesh and Chinese-occupied Tibet, the Indian military mobilized a large force to push back the PLA from occupying sovereign Indian land. However, in sharp contrast to the Sumdorong Chu stand-off, the Doklam crisis featured a more proactive India, which defended Bhutan in anticipation of a strategic threat from the Chinese occupation of Bhutanese land. The Indian academic Manjeet Pardesi has argued that India is 'upgrading its conventional military strategy from defence to deterrence (by denial) to respond to the Chinese challenge', meaning that there is an emphasis on trying to 'take the military offensive behind the Chinese front' and to 'identify and annex small chunks of strategically salient points on the Chinese side of the frontier...as bargaining chips'.[87] The Mountain Strike Corps, mooted during the Manmohan Singh government, has reached operational readiness under the Modi government, albeit on a downsized scale.[88] It is one example of this offensive Indian intent of entering Chinese- or Pakistani-controlled or claimed territory and raising the costs of aggression by the adversary.

The Singapore-based scholars Yogesh Joshi and Anit Mukherjee have employed a differently-worded formulation to buttress the same point that India has adjusted its doctrine in light of China's military modernization and pressure tactics at the LAC. According to them, India has shifted from a strategy of 'deterrence by denial' to 'deterrence by punishment'. If the plan in earlier eras was to deny China territorial gains in Indian-held land through defensive military posture, the thinking now is of 'imposing significant costs both in terms of Chinese territory in Tibet as well as in its war-making potential both on land and the high seas'. Joshi and Mukherjee add that, 'to impose such costs, India would not fight the battle only in its own territory; it would open up additional fronts' and communicate 'intentions to escalate the conflict into new areas and avenues so as to signal to the Chinese that once initiated, Beijing cannot be sure that it can fully control the process of hostilities'.[89] Stopping China on Bhutanese soil certainly fit this template and suggested that Modi dared to go where previous Indian leaders would not during national security crises.

Was India's crisis response in Doklam another illustration of the Doval Doctrine of offensive defence, which I spelt out in Chapter 1 of this book in the context of the 2016 surgical strikes? Given that India has conventional military superiority over Pakistan but is inferior when matched up against China, the meaning and content of offensive defence cannot be identical in the LoC and LAC theatres. But it does seem that Doval, who was engaged in several rounds of negotiations with the Chinese throughout the Doklam crisis, has influenced the way India approaches crises with greater self-confidence and unwillingness to sit back and let the adversary control the escalatory ladder. During the hottest phase of the Doklam crisis, Chinese state mouthpieces, which receive inputs from CCP bosses and intelligence agencies, depicted Doval as 'one of the main schemers behind the current border stand-off'.[90]

Since Doval is an operations specialist with a legend of penetrating into adversary nations as an undercover agent,[91] he has inserted a pre-emptive and proactive element in Indian national security strategy compared to earlier periods when circumspect career diplomats mostly manned the office of NSA. To quote Doval himself: 'in security, it does matter what happens to you, but what matters more is how you respond'.[92] India may not have defeated China in Doklam, but what mattered was that it showed plucky character derived from Doval's redrawing of India's response mechanisms, which in turn drew upon Modi's redefinition of Indian nationhood and mobilization of Indian society. Since no Indian soldiers or civilians were killed at Doklam, the level of nationalistic outpouring and feeling was not as intense as in the post-Pathankot and Uri crisis.

Yet, if Modi could stymie China with firmness in Bhutan, it was due to the phenomenal mass support in India for his fortitude and 'security first' method of dealing with adversaries. Subsequent to the Doklam crisis, Congress party, as the Opposition, questioned Modi's handling of the whole episode and pilloried him with a pun on the word Doklam in Hindi—'Dhoka Lam'—implying that the Indian leader had hoodwinked the public and given away concessions to China.[93] But as always, Modi's credibility among the masses as a guardian of India's national security and an executor of astute foreign policy remained high.[94] The feedback loop between Modi's boldness vis-à-vis foreign opponents and public approval of his nationalistic style was a game-changer and remains so to this day.

Given the hard-edged and touchy national security states that China and Pakistan are, it is inevitable that offensive defence by India would enrage and motivate them to up the ante of confrontation. Some observers are concerned that the Modi government's feistiness and willingness to resort to unpredictable military escalations during crises could set off an unstoppable chain reaction that ends up plunging India and its two main regional adversaries into full-scale war. But as the reader saw, in the post-Uri crisis of 2016 and the Doklam crisis, the Indian counter-measures were not indiscriminate gambles but calibrated uses of force that, iterated over multiple crises, might alter the calculus of the adversaries to avoid locking horns with India and forge new equilibria.

In Doklam, Xi got a foretaste of what could happen when his expansionist juggernaut runs into Modi's offensive defence wall. The Chinese analyst Yun Sun notes that India's assertiveness in Doklam 'forced China to reassess India's strategic capability and resolve' and 'challenged much of the previous longstanding bias that colored China's judgment, including the simplistic and static view of India's inferior status in the regional power hierarchy.'[95] With Modi at the helm, Xi could no longer take India for granted as a soft-hearted lightweight that could be elbowed out militarily or outmanoeuvred diplomatically in South Asia. The competition of Asia's nationalistic giants was truly on—a thread I will pick up again in Chapter 4.

Chapter 3

Breaking Barriers in Balakot

With the demonstration of a frontal attack [as a ruse] and making the enemy firmly believe that [thus keeping the enemy forces engaged in that direction], the Vijigishu (attacker) should employ his heroic band of soldiers to charge swiftly [to surprise] the enemy forces from the rear...Similar methods of Kutayuddha (concealed warfare) may be adopted on either flank (right or left).[1]

—Ancient Indian strategist Kamandaka, third century CE

The Praetorian Peril

In the summer of 2017, Prime Minister Nawaz Sharif was on the ropes. Although not averse to compromise with the military for his political survival, Sharif's streak of reaching out to Modi and the international community, and questioning the Pakistani deep state's continued patronage of jihadist terrorists at home and in neighbouring Afghanistan and India, appeared to have written his political death warrant. His old nemesis, the military establishment of Pakistan, had decided that it was time to cut short his five-year tenure, which had begun in 2013, and pack him off to political oblivion. Instead of launching an overt coup d'etat for the umpteenth time, one that would have invited global economic and diplomatic sanctions, the military decided to use underhanded legal means to dethrone Sharif. His ouster on corruption charges by Pakistan's Supreme Court in July 2017 was a stark reminder of how the failing country was trapped in a vicious circle of undemocratic rule, which in turn precipitated crisis after crisis with India. The sinister presence of Military Intelligence (MI) and ISI members in the JIT, which suspiciously amassed reams of evidence in a short period to nail Sharif in the Supreme Court, and the culture of political vendettas settled through ostensibly 'legal' means, left no doubt that Pakistan had been irretrievably captured by the shadowy powers that be.

Every coup de grâce handed to elected politicians by the deep state in Pakistan carries a message: the military will not brook dilution of the status quo of its lordship at home, eternal war with India, and the quest for domination of Afghanistan. Removal of popular civilian figures by hook or crook is a ritual for upholding this unwritten law. The assassination of two-time prime minister, Benazir Bhutto, in 2007, which had the unmistakable hand of the military, was a historic milestone in laying down the principle of the army's absolute domination. Benazir's father, Zulfiqar Ali Bhutto, had paid the price with his life for defiantly standing up to the men in uniforms in 1979. Sharif, who had been sentenced to life imprisonment by a military-compliant court in 2000 and escaped by a hair's breadth owing to Saudi Arabia's intervention, finally ran out of whatever little luck he had still left by 2017.

After eliminating mass politicians one by one, the road was paved for endless de facto military tyranny and jihadist mayhem. With Sharif gone, Pakistan and its neighbouring countries had to brace for a violent fallout because the last potential hurdle to the military and the ISI going berserk was removed. The next act in this choreographed drama was in July 2018, when Imran Khan's Tehreek-e-Insaf (PTI) party won a controversial general election, ringing alarm bells in New Delhi. The victory of Khan, a former cricketer and national hero who frequently bashed India during his campaign rallies, had serious security implications for New Delhi. During election rallies in 2018, he would inveigh against the disqualified Sharif and his weakened party with the slanderous slogan, '*Modi ka jo yaar hai, woh gaddar hai* [He who is a friend of Modi, is a traitor].'[2]

Khan's victory was not a democratic triumph but a win for forces most threatening to India. He had sold himself to voters as a transformative broom who would sweep Pakistan free of corruption and dynastic misrule. But that did not impress India, where he was perceived as a lackey of the deep state that had been the de facto arbiter of Pakistan's destiny. The Pakistani scholar Hasan Askari Rizvi has argued that his country was a 'praetorian state' where the military dominates all the core institutions and processes, 'including the transfer of power from one set of the elite to another'.[3] Indians extrapolate from such theses that peace with an undemocratic Pakistan is impossible as long as its State and economy are captive to the shadowy military officers, whose raison d'être is to protect their country from what they claim to be hegemonic designs of India.

Given this structural problem, India did not buy Khan's rhetoric of a 'new Pakistan'. From New Delhi's perspective, it had to contend with the same old Islamabad, where men in camouflage endowed with what the American scholar Christine Fair termed as an 'irrational' and suicidal strategic culture, focussed obsessively on wresting Kashmir from India and avenging past defeats on the battlefield with a conventionally stronger India.[4]

Terrorism was an integral component of this quest. Khan had been derided by critics as 'Taliban Khan' for teaming up with radical jihadist, sectarian and religious conservative parties and candidates in the run-up to his election victory.[5] He expressed sympathy for the Afghan Taliban as well as the mujahideen, or holy warriors, waging insurgencies in Indian Kashmir. His first speech after winning the election referred to alleged human rights abuses being committed by the Indian military in Kashmir and how Kashmir was the 'core issue' for him.[6] When the Afghan Taliban militarily overran the internationally recognized moderate government in Kabul in August 2021 following a disastrous US withdrawal, Khan heaped praise on the jihadist takeover of Afghanistan as breaking the 'shackles of slavery'.[7]

Khan's ascent represented a tipping point for India–Pakistan relations, not necessarily for the better. However ineffective mainstream civilian politicians like Benazir and Sharif, who had served multiple terms as prime ministers, had been in influencing the international attitudes of the Pakistani military, at least, they had acted as minimal checks on the anti-Indian tendencies of the deep state. With Khan in the saddle, the likelihood of any gap between the elected government and the military was lost. A unified civil-military line-up under Khan with an overall anti-India outlook deprived New Delhi of opportunities to bolster moderate elements inside the Pakistani governing edifice and politically blunt the security threat posed by extremists.

As the prime minister of a shaky coalition government, Khan knew the cost of deviating from the military's line on India and Kashmir. He was willing to give voice to and popularize what the ISI and the Pakistani military top brass could not say openly—that the state of Pakistan would never settle for peace with India unless the latter relinquishes Kashmir. South Asia was staring at a period of extended and intense acrimony as a Pakistani leader, beholden to his military, took charge. But before the descent into another big bilateral crisis, there was a surreal charade of diplomacy.

Once Bitten, Twice Shy

On 14 September 2018, Khan responded to a letter from Modi and proposed a restart of the bilateral dialogue process that had thus far been stalled. It was a trial balloon doomed to fail from the outset. The Indian government took six days before making Khan's reply public, reflecting New Delhi's wariness in getting entangled in another vain peace effort when Pakistan had hardly allayed India's serious security concerns. A brutal reminder that nothing had changed came on 20 September in the form of an inhumane abduction and killing of three Indian policemen in Kashmir's Shopian district by Pakistan-sponsored terrorists of the Hizb-ul-Mujahideen (HuM). An exasperated Modi, once bitten by his 2015 attempt to break the ice with Sharif, saw no point in investing time and energy in cosmetic reconciliation with such a double-dealing State. What followed was an explicit Indian condemnation of Pakistan's 'evil agenda' and Khan's 'true face', and the cancellation of a ministerial-level meeting scheduled in New York.[8] New Delhi later explained its coolness. 'India's strong protests with Pakistan and call for remedial action were met with outright denial' and so, 'under such circumstances, it was assessed that any conversation with Pakistan would be meaningless.'[9] Islamabad's credibility had sunk irretrievably in Indian eyes.

Notwithstanding the language in Khan's letter that he was 'ready to discuss terrorism' with Modi, India wanted concrete action instead of misleading talk on this sensitive matter.[10] Cross-border infiltration bids by jihadists from Pakistan continued unabated in 2018 and civilian casualties in Kashmir due to terrorist violence had risen. Moreover, the legacy issues of lack of justice for Pakistani terrorist masterminds of the 26/11 attacks and the absence of accountability for the 2016 Pathankot and Uri attacks had piled up into a collective cynicism in India that translated into a belief that talking to Pakistan was equivalent to dignifying an incorrigible terrorist state. Modi's expression of interest in bettering relations with Pakistan after Khan's swearing-in had stressed 'constructive and meaningful engagement', but India was experiencing only destructive engagement from Pakistan's military-intelligence complex.[11] Against such a backdrop, Khan's overambitious proposal of reconvening the long-postponed SAARC summit in Islamabad, which Modi would grace with his presence, sounded disingenuous and preposterous.

Apart from the mismatch between Pakistan's words and deeds, India doubted the motive behind Khan's missive to Modi. According to the US media, the Pakistani army chief, General Qamar Bajwa had 'quietly reached out to India' to resume peace talks months before Khan's military-orchestrated election victory to mitigate intense international pressure that Islamabad had been facing for its nefarious behaviour.[12] Cleaning up its image by extending an olive branch to India, then using this 'moderate' diplomatic turn to ease the harsh cut-off of military aid from the Trump administration and to receive a US$12 billion economic bailout from the International Monetary Fund (IMF), were the unstated objectives guiding Pakistan's rhetorical eagerness for peace. Pakistan's dire economic condition had put Khan under duress; rather than encourage any liberal transformation in foreign policy, he played nice in an opportunistic attempt to gain international sympathy.

Veteran watchers of subcontinental politics would recall several earlier instances where the hidden 'foreign hand' either directly or indirectly pushed Pakistan into half-hearted rapprochement or compromise with India. Such externally induced openings ultimately collapsed under the weight of internal contradictions in Pakistan and the violent ground realities at the LoC. At the turn of the millennium, the American scholar Jessica Stern had documented a widespread 'jihad culture' in Pakistan. It was connected to the inbuilt Pakistani nationalist narrative that Kashmir must be freed from Indian 'occupation' through a multifaceted 'freedom struggle', leaving little room for sustainable peace with India.[13] Routine invocations at international forums of India's alleged human rights abuses in Kashmir by Pakistani officials had been deeply internalized into their ideational system. Such verbal provocations worsened relations with India, but they rarely ceased since abandoning the 'Kashmir cause' was unthinkable for the military establishment in Pakistan.

Added to these obstacles was the extreme imbalance in civil–military relations in Pakistan, which was symbolized by Khan's rise to the prime ministership. In 2015, when Modi flew to Lahore and embraced Sharif, there was an instinct in New Delhi that Sharif genuinely wanted to break out from old mindsets and wished to set aside Kashmir to improve commercial and people-to-people links. Sharif's political downfall and legal persecution were understood in New Delhi to be the handiworks of a Pakistani deep state that feared peace with India.

With Khan, who was beholden to the military and appeared to be taking express instructions of his army chief in composing messages to Modi, India had a personal credibility barrier. Whether or not Khan promised anything to India, leave alone delivering on it, depended on the whims of the Pakistani military—an institution which remained unreformed, unapologetic and perpetually geared up to protect Pakistan from 'Indian hegemony'. Without a fundamental overhaul of the Pakistani state apparatus, India did not foresee big shifts in bilateral ties toward a lasting settlement. Following a spate of Pakistan-sponsored attacks, including a deadly Pathankot and Uri-like JeM raid on an Indian military camp in Sunjuwan, Jammu, in February 2018, that had killed six Indian soldiers, the national mood in India was firmly against believing Pakistan on face value.

With India's general elections approaching in a few months, Modi was cognizant of this public sentiment and cagey about entering yet another round of diplomacy with a neighbour whose purpose was hollow and whose essential make-up was unchanged. It would have been a dialogue of the deaf with considerable audience costs for Modi as he sought a second term in office. This prelude to a raging crisis was not a missed opportunity for peace but a case of Modi successfully avoiding falling into a Pakistani trap that would undoubtedly have begotten terror attacks on Indian soil parallel to a sham 'peace process.'

'The People's Blood Is Boiling'

On the afternoon of 14 February 2019 in Kashmir Valley's Pulwama district, a devastating act was carried out by a 22-year-old local youth, a hardcore believer in the ideology of the Pakistan-based JeM. He rammed a car laden with 200 kilograms of powerful explosives like RDX and ammonium nitrate into a convoy of vehicles carrying Indian paramilitary troops from the Central Reserve Police Force (CRPF) on the Jammu–Srinagar national highway. The impact of the bombing was so intense that the bus that was directly struck turned into a mangled heap of metal. Forty CRPF personnel were martyred, making it the deadliest suicide attack against Indian forces in the three-decade-long history of the Pakistan-abetted separatist insurgency in Kashmir. Both in its modus operandi and timing, it was an escalation from Islamabad with ominous signs for the Modi government.

Jihadists of the Islamic State (ISIS) and other international terrorist groups had been weaponizing cars to cause maximum destruction in Syria, Iraq, Afghanistan and the West. Indian intelligence agencies anticipated the arrival of such tactics in Kashmir before the Pulwama attack, but the young Kashmiri on a suicide mission could not be halted before he self-detonated.[14] Intelligence agencies uncovered proven linkages between JeM, the Taliban, the Haqqani network and Al Qaeda in the Pakistan–Afghanistan border region, and also obtained information that JeM and LeT had recruited the maximum number of local Kashmiris as jihadists in 2018 from Pulwama district.[15] In light of this, India's military and paramilitary forces ought to have taken precautions to separate their convoys from civilian traffic. Later inquiries revealed familiar lapses in alertness, security protocols for military transportation and joining the dots from intelligence leads.[16]

These flaws must, of course, be put in the context of the fact that local Kashmiri Muslims had collaborated with the Pakistani masterminds and helped organize the logistics of the attack.[17] Even the propaganda video of the suicide bomber rationalizing his operation and delivering the last message filled with jihadist hate, which was released by Pakistan-based JeM, had been shot in a Pulwama village at the home of local sympathizers of the terrorists who anoint themselves as heroic 'militants' in parts of the Valley.[18] No matter how fail-safe the defensive measures of the Indian forces, the collusion between Pakistani terrorist organizations and restive local Kashmiris, alienated from the idea of a multireligious and democratic India, poses unique challenges for India's national security. Pulwama demonstrated how JeM and its masters in the ISI exploited religious fundamentalism and social unrest in Indian Kashmir to wreak havoc.

The Pakistani establishment had been plotting this kind of attack since 2016. The explosives and Pakistani operatives meant to assist the suicide bomber infiltrated across the LoC many months ahead of the fateful day in February 2019.[19] Even as the Pakistani military and its puppet prime minister were writing letters to Modi and seeking a fresh start to revive SAARC, the planning for Pulwama had been parallelly proceeding in full swing. It was Janus-faced Pakistan at its worst. Although JeM brazenly owned responsibility for Pulwama and revealed the identity and the extremist ethos of the suicide bomber to the whole world immediately after the attack, Khan's first reaction came only five days later and was outrageously disingenuous.[20] He insisted that India was blaming Pakistan 'without any evidence', and since the suicide bomber was a local Kashmiri (technically an Indian citizen) and not a Pakistani, the real problem was not Pakistan-sponsored terrorism, but India's supposed oppression of Kashmiri Muslims under its control.[21]

Internationalizing Kashmir as a disputed territory and an unfortunate land that deserved 'self-determination' had been the Pakistani military establishment's unstinting objective since the partition of the subcontinent in 1947. Terrorism and proxy war were the asymmetric tools to achieve this goal. A spectacular attack like Pulwama was Pakistan's chance to draw global attention to what it alleged were Indian atrocities or genocide of Kashmiri Muslims. If Modi's strategy was of isolating Pakistan on the world stage as an incubator and sponsor of obnoxious jihadist poison, Khan and the generals writing his talking points wanted to turn the tables and put the spotlight back on the 'freedom struggle' in Indian Kashmir. It was as much a battle of narrative and framing as of identity and will.

As soon as news about the Pulwama attack broke out, a wave of anguish swept across India. With 40 paramilitary men dead, the scale of the suffering was comparable perhaps to the post-26/11 trauma, which has been recounted in Chapter 1. Funerals for the slain CRPF forces who hailed from different states of India were emotionally charged affairs. Descriptions of the televised events captured the deep passions and nationalistic spirits that had been aroused as coffins draped in the Tricolour were shown to grieving relatives, and the official tributes poured in.[22]

One of the crucial tasks of political leadership in the early phase of a crisis is 'sense-making', as the critical nature of any event is not self-evident and decision-makers have to judge its importance and prioritize it over other issues. In any country, leaders simultaneously deal with myriad problems and crises at a particular point in time. They will have to decide which one among them is so serious a danger to national interests and values that it deserves their unalloyed attention and a swift and suitable response. As European scholars put it, 'leaders will have to determine how threatening the events are, to what or whom, what their operational and strategic parameters are, and how the situation will develop in the period to come'. The onus is on leaders to separate the grain from the chaff and 'decide which signals to heed, which to ignore, and how to make sense of a threat that has already materialized and calls for an immediate response'.[23]

In the case of the national security threats faced by the Modi government, there were many incidents over the years, but only some which were picked up and responded to visibly and demonstrably, while other incidents were responded to below the radar in a low-key fashion. For example, the reader saw in Chapter 1 that India did not resort to any large-scale publicized kinetic action against Pakistan after the January

2016 Pathankot attack, but it did so following the Uri attack of September 2016. Was the former not seen as provocative enough while the latter was seen so because India lost fewer troops in Pathankot than in Uri? More than a numerical scale of fatalities, the reason why Modi made 'sense' of Pathankot and Uri differently was because of the difference in the political backdrop of India–Pakistan relations at those two moments. Whatever strategic patience or liberal expectations India's leader and the general public had were tested by Pathankot and evaporated by the time Uri happened. Chapter 1 depicted the period between Pathankot and Uri as an extended crisis to show this progressive dissipation of faith and credulity in India about Pakistan's sincerity and will. Counterfactually, suppose the Uri attack had not occurred, would India have still opted for surgical strikes in PoK? Maybe not at that point in time in September 2016.

Jihadist attacks against India by Pakistan-backed elements and Pakistan's India-based agents frequently happen as part of Islamabad's military doctrine of 'bleeding India to death through a strategy of thousand cuts'.[24] Several Pakistani plots are hatched and averted by Indian security forces before they get executed, while others slip through the cracks and are carried out. For an externally-sponsored attack or incursion to invite a concerted and resounding riposte by the Indian state, there is a threshold of not just lives lost, territory invaded or assets damaged but of the overall trajectory of relations with the foreign adversary. As discussed previously, India justified the surgical strikes of September 2016 not as revenge for Uri but as pre-emptive action to forestall further attacks from jihadist launch pads across the border in PoK. It meant that the Indian threat assessment was not a reaction to an attack that had already occurred but was in anticipation of further attacks in the wake of the worsened condition of India–Pakistan relations.

By February 2019, with the praetorian state of Pakistan in total command and Khan as its thinly disguised veneer of a civilian leader, there was no room for improvement in bilateral ties or any credible interlocutor on the other side. Although the Sunjuwan attack had taken the lives of Indian soldiers one year prior to Pulwama, the deterioration in what can be called the 'system state' of relations was a key consideration for Modi to up the ante after Pulwama. India had to act after Pulwama as a psychological and strategic limit had been reached, and India's masses were seething.

Modi recognized the gravity of the crisis and seized it to galvanize India. A day after the Pulwama tragedy, he addressed a public rally and declared his intentions:

> The amount of anger that is there in the country, people's blood is boiling [sic]. I can very well understand this... They have to pay a heavy price for this. Those guilty of the Pulwama attack and the conspirators must be punished... Security forces have been given permission to choose the timing, place and nature of their response.[25]

The CCS convened in New Delhi and announced the revocation of the most favoured nation (MFN) trade status that India had unilaterally accorded to Pakistan in 1996. Customs duties on all goods imported from Pakistan were raised to 200 per cent with immediate effect and India's tea exports to Pakistan, totalling 15.83 million kilograms, were curbed. Since the overall volume of bilateral trade was less than US\$ 3 billion, these steps were largely symbolic. Blacklisting Pakistan at the FATF would hurt Pakistan financially a lot more and tarnish its reputation. India compiled a detailed dossier listing Pakistan's complicity in financing JeM and other UN-proscribed terrorist entities and networked with France and the US to push Pakistan into the same doghouse as North Korea and Iran. While Pakistan managed to avoid blacklisting due to Chinese and Turkish backing, the FATF collectively expressed 'grave concern' and condemned 'the violent terrorist attack last week that killed at least 40 Indian security forces in the State of Jammu and Kashmir'.[26]

The Indian campaign to diplomatically isolate Pakistan also got a leg-up from the unequivocal support of the Trump administration, which had grown weary and disillusioned with Islamabad's inaction against terrorism by its proxy jihadists in Afghanistan. NSA Doval coordinated with his US counterpart John Bolton, who went public to say 'we support India's right to self-defence', and the White House called on Pakistan 'to end immediately the support and safe haven provided to all terrorist groups operating on its soil, whose only goal is to sow chaos, violence, and terror in the region'.[27] Eight days after Pulwama, with Modi and his national security team weighing different kinetic options in earnest, Trump proceeded to tell journalists that 'India is looking at something very strong. And I mean, India just lost almost 50 people with an attack. So, I could understand that also'.[28] Having already witnessed the surgical strikes of September 2016 and being cognizant of Modi's proportionate style of punching back at foreign adversaries, Washington did not appear to have applied any brakes with its usual pressure to 'exercise restraint' on Indian military planning. Since there was a precedent of the surgical strikes that did not lead to all-out war or nuclear Armageddon, Modi seemed to have the backing of much of the international community which had come to respect his determination to secure India through self-help and self-initiative instead of depending on the US or other external actors to do what India should have been doing as a State responsible for its security.

Fearing that Modi would walk his tough talk yet again and inflict damage on Pakistan, Khan tried to rekindle old fears in India and worldwide that crisis escalation would go out of control and lead to full-scale war and destabilization. He made it look as though India was the aggressor forcing Pakistan to defend itself.[29] Pakistani Foreign Minister Shah Mahmood Qureshi also sought urgent intervention of the UN secretary-general and appealed to him to 'consider asking India to refrain from further escalating the situation and enter into dialogue with Pakistan and the Kashmiris to calm the situation down'.[30] But instead of succumbing to this routine blackmail, the UNSC unanimously condemned in 'strongest terms the heinous and cowardly suicide bombing in Jammu and Kashmir', reaffirmed that 'terrorism in all its forms and manifestations constitutes one of the most serious threats to international peace and security', and reiterated 'the need for all states to combat by all means…threats to international peace and security caused by terrorist acts'.[31]

Clearly, the Modi government's briefings to the permanent members of the UNSC and dozens of other countries had put paid to Pakistani efforts to divert attention from the jihadist attack in Pulwama toward resolution of the Kashmir dispute or prevention of war. Strictly speaking, the commonly held legal standard of acts of terrorism is the deliberate targeting of civilians with a political motive. An attack on CRPF combatants may not have strictly met this criterion, but most of JeM's victims over the decades had been non-combatants. The vigour with which the Modi government lobbied world capitals kept the heat on Pakistan and laid the ground for military retaliation. The only exception was Pakistan's eternal ally China, which again refused to lift its hold on JeM chief Masood Azhar, and taking its cue from Islamabad, advised New Delhi that 'instead of simply blaming other countries, especially Pakistan and China', it should 'make more self-introspection on its anti-terrorism policy and dwell more on how to better administer the India-controlled part of Kashmir'.[32] But the China–Pakistan nexus had not deterred Modi from ordering the surgical strikes in 2016 and it did not come in the way this time either.

The Concealed Strike

In the early hours of 26 February 2019, a dozen IAF Mirage 2000 jets—escorted by four additional jets for an aerial defence to avoid being intercepted by the Pakistan Air Force (PAF)—crossed the LoC, and flew past PoK into Pakistan proper. Evading radar and anti-aircraft systems, these jets dropped six Israeli-made SPICE precision bombs on a crowded JeM terrorist camp on a hilltop in Balakot, Khyber Pakhtunkhwa province. They returned to Indian airspace unharmed, even as Indian intelligence estimated from local Pakistani sources that 250 to 280 terrorists had been liquidated on the ground from the payload the IAF pilots had released.[33]

'Operation Bandar', the IAF's code-named, top-secret mission, was a bolt from the blue which few had expected or predicted and became a milestone in India's long and bloody battle against cross-border terrorism. The deception and camouflage that put Pakistan on the wrong scent and the fear and panic it generated inside Pakistan's military establishment were the stuff of legends. While there are many tales of indomitable courage and ingenuity of the Indian military during wartime and in counter-insurgency, the Balakot air strike, which happened 80 kilometres beyond the LoC inside Pakistan, was in a league of its own. The entire air mission took just 19 minutes to execute in the dark of the night of 26 February; but the amount of meticulous planning and coordination amongst the civilian political leadership, various wings of the Indian military and multiple intelligence agencies which fed into it revealed an Indian state apparatus that had hardened and concentrated on a singular goal by combining all its capabilities.

Recalling the centrality of strategic surprise in operation and how it was conceived, Modi told a public rally a few weeks after the crisis had subsided that India had outfoxed Pakistan and played mind games.[34] Modi's decision to use air power across the LoC was historic, as no IAF jets had been deployed in Pakistani airspace since the 1971 war owing to the understanding that it would constitute a significant escalation and trigger full war. But with Modi in power, old assumptions and received wisdom were banished, and boldness was in. Even after the Uri attacks in 2016, Modi had asked his crisis management team about the possibility of 'a precise air strike on terrorist camps', but ended up endorsing a ground-based incursion by the special forces of the Indian Army as a better choice.[35] Modi and his aides evaluated the full range of military options in the tense days after the Pulwama attack, including a second round of surgical strikes in PoK. But as this had been done in 2016, the element of surprise would be missing if repeated. The Pakistan Army had cancelled its troops' leave and replaced paramilitaries with regular soldiers all along the LoC and the international border. India also had information that jihadists were evacuated from launch pads in PoK and shifted further inland to avert Indian raids. It was also wintertime in the Himalayas, with the snowfall making infiltration across the land border much harder than in September 2016.

A naval blockade of Pakistan, cashing in on India's fivefold advantage over Pakistan in combat vessels and manpower, was considered to apply a squeeze on the port city and financial centre of Karachi. But this 'idea was shot down because it could easily have spun off into an international crisis, as other countries would have got into the picture', and also because it 'could also be perceived as an act of war'.[36] Like in the post-Uri crisis, Modi, the responsible but resolute leader, had laid down the broad parameters within which kinetic action had to be mounted. The Indian journalist Rajdeep Sardesai listed the prime minister's instructions to his crisis response unit:

> The message to Doval and the armed forces chiefs was unambiguous: There must be 'visible' action against the terror groups and their handlers embedded in the Pakistani state. The focus needed to be on the terror training camps; collateral damage to civilian and military targets was to be avoided at all costs. In effect, India's response needed to be proportionate to what Pakistan had done and within range of what the international community would view as 'reasonable' action. Says India Today editorial director Raj Chengappa, 'The idea was not to prevent escalation but to get the escalation threshold just right.'[37]

The IAF turned out to be the best bet because it had been preparing for years for this kind of mission and was confident it could do the job if provided precise coordinates of the terrorist camps inside Pakistan. Air Marshal Hari Kumar, who headed the Western Command of the IAF during Operation Bandar, later narrated the nuts and bolts of the crisis decision-making and the alibis and tricks that were set up to mislead Pakistan.[38] In the lead-up to the air strike, India had also put in motion detailed decoys spanning both the land and the maritime borders with Pakistan. The Indian Army had already engaged in 'a sustained, high stakes cross-border duel along the LoC in the Rajouri–Poonch sector', and let journalists go public that 'operations to realign the LoC' might be on the cards.[39] The Indian Navy pivoted from an exercise of war games and redeployed an aircraft carrier, submarines and battleships to the northern Arabian Sea to bottle up the Pakistani navy in Karachi and 'expeditiously respond to the developing situation in synergy with the three services'.[40] The idea was to keep Pakistan on tenterhooks as to 'where and how the retribution would come' and scatter its strategic energies in different directions as the IAF jets homed in on their target.[41] It was a Kutayuddha-like operation that would have made Kamandaka or Kautilya proud.

In total, some 6,000 Indian defence forces personnel had been involved in the entire plan to execute the air strike. The synchronous coordination of the three services of the Indian military was complemented by the collaboration of the Indian spy agencies—the R&AW, the NTRO and the IB—to stake out the Balakot camp through technical and human sources. Even the Indian Space Research Organisation (ISRO), a civilian entity, played a role in what New Delhi labelled as an 'intelligence-led operation.'[42]

In the Introduction of this book, I listed major reforms in the Indian national security institutional architecture undertaken by the Modi government. The jointness with which different wings and agencies performed prior to the Balakot air strike suggested that these reforms were paying early dividends and delivering concrete results. The turf wars and disjointed bureaucratic politics which had pulled India in chaotic and uncoordinated directions during earlier crises did not vanish by 2019, but they were sufficiently subsumed to the extent that Operation Bandar was a military success. I asked Arvind Gupta, India's deputy NSA from 2014 to 2017, how the Modi effect on India's security establishment had translated into swifter and harmonized performance during the post-Pulwama crisis. He said:

> Leadership, its quality and character are the most important factors. When you have to take an action of this magnitude bearing such huge consequences, you need strong institutions to provide inputs, game scenarios and execute with all of them pulling in the same direction. If the direction is not clear or if there is ambiguity in

decision-making, if the leader himself is ambiguous, then it could lead to institutional paralysis. Like flowers in a garland, institutions have to be strung together. Since Modi came to power, the leadership has been very clear that India will have 'zero tolerance' for external threats and that we will take the battle into the enemy's terrain. So, this ethos has now percolated through all the security institutions for years through peacetime. The system has been honed in such a way by Modi and the BJP's muscular nationalism for years now that it responds as a whole with purposefulness rather than haphazardly in bits and pieces.[43]

Foreign Security Policy

While there are similarities in the way India went about implementing the 2016 surgical strikes and the 2019 Balakot air strike, the main difference between the two crises lay in Pakistan's reaction. The reader saw in Chapter 1 that Pakistan had denied Indian special forces' incursions inside PoK and played them down as a fake story spun by India. But the air strike could not be denied as Indian jets had gone far beyond PoK, evaded interdiction by Pakistani air defences and inflicted considerable damage on the JeM terrorist camp. Even before India made an official announcement, the ISI tweeted within 87 minutes of the strike that 'Indian Air Force violated Line of Control' and claimed that 'facing timely and effective response from Pakistan Air Force released payload in haste while escaping which fell near Balakot. No casualties or damage'.[44] What followed was a barrage of misinformation that the IAF did cross the LoC but was forced to beat a hasty retreat without accomplishing any of its goals. Pakistani social media was abuzz with mocking memes of how the Indian intruders could only manage to kill a crow and 'a few fallen trees'.[45]

Yet, despite putting on a brave face, the military establishment was deeply embarrassed. A foreign journalist with local sources reported that bodies were transported out of the Balakot JeM camp hours after the IAF strike and that the whole site was cordoned off by the military 'who did not even allow police to enter'.[46] Presumably having scrubbed the scene of telltale evidence, the Pakistani government took 43 days before finally giving a guided tour of the site to the media and diplomats. It explained the delay in allowing access by saying 'the unstable situation made it difficult to take people there'.[47]

Pakistan's credibility on the terrorist infrastructure entrenched in its soil was already on the thinnest of ice. The inconsistencies in explanations after the world came to know of the presence of the Al Qaeda chief Osama bin Laden in its northern city of Abbottabad for years, and Islamabad's constant flip-flopping on whether the Pakistani military assisted the US Navy Sea, Air and Land (SEALs) teams in the 2011 operation that killed him, left much wanting. Pakistan's attempt to hide the JeM's tracks and trivialize the impact of the Balakot strike was also rendered untenable by its next move. If the IAF had indeed been foiled, what was the need for Pakistan to mount a risky counter-retaliation by the PAF into Indian airspace a day after the JeM camp was struck? As the analyst Dhruva Jaishankar put it, 'it is worth asking what—beyond an air space violation—Pakistan is retaliating for if, as it claims, no significant damage was inflicted by India'.[48] The truth was that Modi had pierced the Pakistani national security state's sense of invulnerability and dented its image so badly that it was in crisis and had to do something to save face.

On the day of the Balakot air strike, Pakistan's military nonchalantly declared that 'India can never surprise us…

reiterate that it has not surprised us', and warned 'we are ready, wait for the surprise'.[49] Despite being in economic doldrums and running short on aviation fuel to sustain a long air war, Operation Swift Retort was launched the following morning for 'restoring the measure of honour lost due to the Indian strikes a day prior in public perception' and to 'convey an "impression" to India and the world community—that Pakistan was willing to escalate the crisis'.[50] Around 24 Pakistani aircraft reached the LoC with the aim of bombing Indian military installations but they were intercepted without making much headway and thwarted by Indian jets in what became a thrilling dogfight, the likes of which had not been witnessed in nearly four decades in the subcontinent.[51] Accounts of what really happened in the air battle on 27 February have been hotly contested by the PAF and the IAF, with the former initially claiming that it had shot down two Russian-made Indian aircraft, a MiG-21 and a Sukhoi-30, and the latter claiming that it had scalped a US-made F-16. Even after the dust settled on the crisis, the fog never lifted on which side 'won' the skirmish or even which particular jets were deployed in the Pakistani squadron. Islamabad denied that any F-16s had been used at all, as Washington strictly monitors the end-use of combat aircraft it supplies. Months after the crisis, the US 'admonished Pakistan for having "relocated, maintained and operated" the American-made F-16s and the AMRAAM missiles they use from forward operating bases not approved under the original terms of the sale'.[52] Yet, the US did not endorse India's version that one of the PAF's F-16 had been brought down during the cat-and-mouse game.

As Indians, Pakistanis and the rest of world watched the drama nervously amid talks that war might break out after the aerial jousting, a strange human twist occurred and shifted the locus of the crisis. Wing Commander Abhinandan Varthaman of the IAF gave a hot pursuit chase to the Pakistani jets back into Pakistani territory and his MiG-21 was shot down inside PoK, forcing a parachute landing in hostile territory. Images and videos of the wounded and bloodied Indian fighter pilot being manhandled by Pakistani civilians and interrogated under duress by the ISI were circulated virally in violation of the Geneva Conventions, raising nationalistic tempers. If the mood in India was jubilant when the Balakot air strike happened, it was indignant once Abhinandan was captured. For ordinary Indians, it was a nerve-wracking moment in a days-long roller coaster ride—pressure piled up on Modi to retrieve the detained soldier at any cost. Depending on the next steps, the crisis could terminate, or extend into unimaginable pathways.

In previous chapters of this book, I have shown how Modi combines military application of force with diplomatic offensives and, where relevant, economic leverage to handle national security crises. As Abhinandan was in Pakistani custody and the ISI was crudely exploiting it to generate global publicity to humiliate India, the Indian leader pulled up his sleeves and got down to action. He went into a huddle with Doval, the military chiefs and other top security officials, and formulated a strategy. A public demarche was given to Pakistan demanding Abhinandan's immediate return to India, along with an open threat that, 'Pakistan would be well advised to ensure that no harm comes to the Indian defence personnel in its custody.'[53] Bolder and more specific threats were made in private. Modi revealed bits of what transpired at an election rally in April 2019:

A senior American official said on the second day [of Abhinandan's detention] that Modi has kept 12 missiles ready and might attack and the situation will deteriorate. Pakistan announced return of the pilot, or else it was going to be a 'qatal ki raat' [a night of murder]. This was said by America, I have nothing to say about this now, I will speak about it when the time will come.[54]

It is plausible that US Secretary of State Mike Pompeo or US NSA John Bolton, who were in touch with Doval, conveyed the Indian missile threat to Pakistan and advised Islamabad to set Abhinandan free unconditionally. Modi had also authorized the then R&AW chief, Anil Dhasmana, to directly talk to his ISI counterpart General Syed Shah and communicate the message that 'our weapon arsenal is not for Diwali', a reference to the Indian festival of lights when revellers burst loud firecrackers. To credibly back up these verbal threats, the Modi government ordered the Indian military to 'ready mobile Prithvi ballistic missile batteries in the Rajasthan sector' near the international border with Pakistan—a move which apparently 'set alarm bells ringing in faraway Washington as well'.[55] Modi, who takes pride in having called Pakistan's nuclear bluff, reminisced about the Abhinandan episode a few months later, reconfirming this account.[56]

Was this callous brinkmanship or a well-calculated psychological game of chicken in which Modi was confident that the mentally tougher and conventionally stronger side would prevail? Having established a reputation as a doer on the national security front who had startled India's two principal adversaries in earlier rounds of crises, even a pathologically irrational actor like the Pakistani military establishment could not afford to take Modi's threats and Indian tactical manoeuvres at the border lightly. In late 2020, a former speaker of Pakistan's National Assembly, Sardar Ayaz Sadiq, disclosed that Pakistan's foreign minister had informed legislators during the crisis that 'if Pakistan did not release Abhinandan Varthaman, India would attack Pakistan that night by 9:00 p.m.'[57]

Accounts by western diplomats and an anonymous Pakistani minister suggested there had been 'a specific Indian threat to use six missiles on targets inside Pakistan', but Pakistan is said to have responded that 'if you will fire one missile, we will fire three. Whatever India will do, we will respond three times to that'. But notwithstanding Pakistan's rhetorical swagger, Modi's threat escalation was timed in such a way that it came when the ball was in Pakistan's court and the international community was scared to prevent further escalation. The Trump administration 'fully realized how dangerous it was' and 'US efforts were focused on securing the quick release of the Indian pilot by Pakistan and winning an assurance from India it would pull back from the threat to fire rockets'.[58]

Another set of mediators came from Saudi Arabia and the United Arab Emirates (UAE), whose backroom diplomacy was acknowledged by both Indian and Pakistani officials. The crown prince of Abu Dhabi, Mohamed bin Zayed Al Nahyan (MbZ), had spoken with both Modi and Khan and the crown prince of Saudi Arabia, Mohammed bin Salman (MbS) apparently took a 'keen interest in the situation' as war in South Asia would jeopardize massive foreign investments by the Gulf monarchies.[59] Thanks to Modi's personal attention and closeness to the top leaders of these kingdoms, India had even been invited as a special guest to the Organisation of Islamic Cooperation (OIC) foreign ministers' meeting just after the Pulwama attacks, leaving Pakistan squirming in discomfort. Modi had leveraged India's much bigger market and fast-growing major economy status to win the trust of several Islamic powers. India highlighted its large population of over 200 million Muslim citizens to make inroads into the OIC and dispel Pakistan's arguments that Muslims were oppressed in a Hindu-majority India. MbS actually visited India after the Pulwama attack and committed US$100 billion in investment.

This was in contrast to US$20 billion he promised to invest in Pakistan. He also applauded India for countering terrorism, although without naming Pakistan.

Modi's astute foreign policy of trying to isolate Pakistan within the comity of Muslim nations came in handy to apply additional pressure and ensure Abhinandan's return after two days in captivity. While Khan painted Pakistan's decision to release the IAF pilot as a 'peace gesture' and a sign of his country's maturity, the then BJP president and Modi's right-hand man, Amit Shah, took credit that, 'creating situation for return of pilot Abhinandan in such a short span of time is our diplomatic victory'.[60] Modi himself confirmed in a public speech that diplomacy was the prime instrument in getting Abhinandan back in one piece.[61]

The post-Pulwama crisis concretely demonstrated the linkage between national security and foreign policy which Modi had carefully constructed to India's advantage. Undoubtedly, Khan's adoption of a magnanimous posture in returning Abhinandan handed Islamabad a rare public relations win in its decades-long competition with New Delhi. Even if the 1 March 2019 move was forced on Pakistan through diplomatic pressure from the US, Saudi Arabia and the UAE, it looked good on television from a Pakistani perspective—a key consideration in the court of global opinion. The India–Pakistan conflict is not only a dispute over the territory of Kashmir, a clash of nationalisms and a military fight but also a contest for the sympathies of the international community. Running parallel to the aerial skirmishes, bombings and claims of violations of sovereignty by the two sides are diplomatic campaigns by New Delhi and Islamabad to turn opinion in their favour.

Islamabad did briefly profit from the Abhinandan episode, but India emerged from the crisis with far more aces in the

PR game. As that round of conflict wound down, it was clear that New Delhi enjoyed a much higher overall standing as a democratic power and vibrant rising economy. Also, the narrative that jihadist extremism emanating from Pakistan was a threat to international order resonated in a world fearful of Islamist terrorism of Al Qaeda, ISIS and their ilk. After Pulwama, India revived its oft-stalled diplomatic mission to get the JeM mastermind, Masood Azhar, proscribed by the UN. On 27 February 2019, the US, the UK, and France proposed designating Azhar a global terrorist, forcing Pakistan to clamp down on his jihadist operations. As was narrated in Chapter 1 of this book, China had stood by Pakistan at the UN and deployed technical arguments to stymie this effort often in the past. It did so once more after Pulwama, but not for much longer after that. Modi's foreign policy challenge was to convince Xi to shed Chinese strategic concerns about India's rise and get China on board to pressure Pakistan on terrorism. While that maximal goal was never fulfilled, lifting the Chinese technical 'hold' on Azhar's designation at the UN in April 2019 was an important breakthrough that may not have happened if not for the post-Pulwama crisis.

To the rest of the world, India proved that it had a comfortable lead over Pakistan during the crisis itself. Many nations viewed India as a vibrant democracy where civil and political rights were better protected than in military-dominated Pakistan. Countries such as France and the US, which experienced jihadist terror themselves, staunchly defended India's right to retaliate against Pakistan after Pulwama, with Washington labelling the Balakot air strike as justified 'counter-terrorism actions' rather than a violation of Pakistani sovereignty.[62] Most UN member states applauded or quietly approved India's proportionate and precise response to Pulwama—with the standard caveat that they hope India and Pakistan can avoid full-scale war and find a negotiated settlement. The worldwide abhorrence of jihadist extremism made it easier for the Modi government to convince the world that terror, rather than self-determination for Kashmir or human rights, was the root cause of instability and violence in the subcontinent.

Modi's India could move the argument away from the old relativistic view that 'one country's terrorist is another's freedom fighter', a notion which used to complicate its case against Pakistan by setting up a false equivalence between the two countries. As the notion that 'no political reason...no cause, no grievance justifies terrorism,'[63] was being mainstreamed, Modi capitalized on that new international ambience to leap over Pakistan. Even after the post-Pulwama crisis de-escalated, India was in a position to keep pushing for diplomatic isolation in its quest for permanent deterrence against the terrorist scourge across its borders. To Modi's credit, he did not reduce the pressure on Pakistan once the crisis subsided.

In the past, instead of treating Pakistan as a strategic challenge that must be countered through a full spectrum of relentless actions, Indian leaders had had the habit of reducing it to a periodic political threat to be pushed back at critical moments. With the passage of time, after each heinous attack, India forgot that the onus was on it to establish deterrence on a *continuous* basis against the terrorists and their godfathers. Prevention of future Pulwamas required commitment to a long struggle involving overhaul of internal security arrangements plus relentless pressure on Pakistan in a range of domains. Such a holistic campaign should only ever be relaxed when Pakistan's state structure is upended (civilian supremacy over the military) or it suffers a second break-up on the lines of the 1971 formation of Bangladesh.

Kinetic measures like surgical strikes, aerial and missile

bombardment, and covert sabotage missions inside Pakistan did convey toughness in the near term. They boosted India's national morale for a while. But these steps were in themselves insufficient for deterring a garrison state like Pakistan where the military controls policymaking and is ideologically predisposed to harm India at any cost. Modi understood that tactical operations were not substitutes for a broad, open-ended strategic mission of a full-court press until Pakistan's basic make-up changed. To radically restructure Pakistan into a moderate neighbour the way Canada is to the United States, India would have to bring into play a range of sustained instruments.

As a digital power with a vast lead in software and information technology, India began employing online propaganda techniques to reach out to ordinary Pakistanis and mould their opinions about the corruption and brutality of their own military establishment which has repeatedly caused ruin. India also moved to use the openness of the internet to penetrate all Pakistani provinces, and release a barrage of compromising facts and stories about the military and the ISI's shenanigans. The Modi government's opening of a Balochi language mobile phone app, website and radio bulletins in 2016, just before the surgical strikes in PoK, was a proactive move.[64] Similar information operations or info-ops would have to be developed for Pakistan's restive Pashtun minorities. As Russia demonstrated in recent years by flummoxing the West in Ukraine and elsewhere, we are in an era of 'hybrid warfare' with the shadowy weaponization of the internet to shape public perception and even overthrow regimes.

On the diplomatic front, the Modi government disseminated reams of proof of Pakistan's complicity in terrorism to foreign leaders, intelligence agencies and the news media. As victims of cross-border terrorism, Indians often assume that everyone around the world is already fully familiar with how thuggish military-run and jihadi-infested Pakistan is and how righteous secular and democratic India is. But isolating a rogue regime requires assiduous lobbying and reinforcing of the message so that no country buys Pakistan's denials of complicity in terrorism or its narrative of a 'freedom struggle' in Kashmir. The May 2018 Dhaka Declaration of the OIC had uncharacteristically omitted Kashmir and condemned India's alleged impunity. This feat was achieved thanks to India-friendly Bangladesh, the host country of the OIC foreign ministers' session.[65] As mentioned earlier, the February 2019 OIC invite to India left Pakistan red-faced, and compelled it to boycott the meet in Abu Dhabi. More such strategic interventions were necessary going forward after the Balakot strike to show Pakistan that India could fight on its turf militarily and diplomatically. With his nationalistic mantle as a chowkidar (watchman) who never slept so that India remained secure,[66] Modi awakened India to think and act systematically regarding the national security challenge posed by Pakistan. This intangible takeaway from the post-Pulwama crisis was invaluable and lasting.

A 'National Security Election'

The Pulwama attack, the Balakot air strike and Abhinandan's return to India have been portrayed by many observers as game-changers for Modi's political fortunes, as they gave the BJP a massive bump in popularity just in time before India's April 2019 general election. The Opposition, namely, the Congress party, cried foul that Modi 'exploits the valour of our jawans (soldiers) for his political gains', adopted the line that 'if the Army and Air Force carries [sic] out an action, the credit is fully theirs', and attacked Modi, terming it 'shameful that PM does not give them credit'.[67] The construction of an image of Modi by his critics as a selfish and egotistic politician who takes undue credit for the sacrifices of India's military personnel in the line of duty, or even decides on how robustly to retaliate against foreign adversaries depending on the electoral calendar, is totally devoid of merit. In fact, this argument merged into that of Pakistan, which kept insisting that Modi acted aggressively after Pulwama and conducted a 'false flag operation' in Balakot only to win votes in the Indian election.[68] As the landslide results in favour of Modi's re-election showed, these attacks did not stick but backfired on the Congress party for looking like an amplifier of Pakistani propaganda and lacking persuasiveness due to its lacklustre record on national security when it had been in power.

As was mentioned in the Introduction of this book, offensive and risky responses during crises invariably benefited Modi politically because the ground reality of 'audience costs' had been shifted by him in a nationalistic direction. A new national ethos of shedding the tag of a soft state had altered India's pulse so much under Modi in his first term that it expected a good prime minister not to take attacks by foreign adversaries lying down. During the 2019 election campaign trail, Modi skilfully referenced the inaction of the Manmohan Singh government after 26/11 and contrasted it with his deeds to demonstrate the difference to voters.

> The country can never forget the 26/11 terror attack in Mumbai. India should have responded then and the whole world would have supported the country. But that required courage… Today India works on 'nayi reeti, nayi neeti' (new methods, new policies)…after the terror attack in Uri…the country for the first time taught terrorists a lesson 'in a language they understand'…[69]

India's armed forces have a long history of feeling that their hands were tied by defensive civilian leaders. It transcends partisan political mudslinging about Modi snatching away the credit from the military. It is an indisputable fact that Modi has given a 'free hand' to India's military much more than his predecessors and there has been a marked improvement in civil-military synergy in India's national security institutions under him. For instance, in the run-up to the Balakot air strike, the service chiefs had a self-assured quality when they presented retaliatory options to Modi and Doval because they knew they had their backs. Arjun Subramaniam, a retired air vice marshal of the IAF, spoke to insiders and pointed out this sea change.

> A senior government official—who was also present when a military response was hesitantly contemplated by the Manmohan Singh government in 2008 after the Mumbai terrorist attack—was struck by the chiefs' confident response and the alacrity with which they responded to Modi's 'free hand' for planning India's punitive response. This time around, there was no such hesitation.[70]

Even as cynics accused Modi of peddling a 'politics of fear' through 'sabre rattling and the politicization of the armed forces', his consistent record in national security crises spoke for itself and was enough to convince ordinary Indians to give him another five years in office.[71] The Australian scholar Ian Hall studied the 2019 election and found that more than the impact of the Balakot air strike alone, the overall foreign policy, and proactivity in Modi's first term had impressed and inspired average voters to want him again as India's best available contemporary leader to propel its rise in the world. The so-called 'Balakot bounce' in the election was, on its own, not decisive but it added to the aura built over years of assiduously projecting India taking its place as a 'leading power' in the international arena through Modi's forceful diplomacy and defence of national honour.[72]

A popular trope in India's opposition circles is that Modi's handling of national security crises is nothing but political gimmickry and grandstanding done to fool voters with an overdose of patriotism and win elections. But such dismissive accounts run into rough weather when one evaluates India's crises under Modi's governance in totality. The 2016 surgical strikes, the 2017 resistance to China in Doklam, the 2019 revocation of Kashmir's special status (more on this in the next section), and the 2020 fightback against Chinese encroachment in eastern Ladakh—all occurred when Modi was not facing any general election on the horizon. Even in the case of the Balakot air strike, it was a necessary response to Pakistan's atrocity in Pulwama, which was timed and executed a few months before India's general election by the ISI and JeM, not by Modi. Had Pulwama occurred one or two years before or after the 2019 election, Modi would not have hesitated to resort to a similar daring response of taking the battle into the lair of the adversary. The method of the counter-attack may have varied, depending on various climatological or international diplomatic factors, but the offensive intent would have been the same irrespective of the election cycle.

The Indian scholar Harsh Pant, who previously lamented the lack of an electoral incentive to prioritize national security and foreign policy, has noted the transformed dynamic under Modi:

> It is illogical to say that the government should get no credit...when the use of the military is an inherently political decision and Modi's political leadership is one of the most important reasons for the Indian strategic shift... Modi and the BJP are articulating a national security and foreign policy framework that is more in sync with the aspirations of the majority...[73]

It is now simultaneously the 'dharma of a state' in its eternal quest for security as well as pragmatic and expedient politics to be tough and fearless against external adversaries. In November 2019, External Affairs Minister S. Jaishankar reflected on the question of whether India had 'become more Bharat', and how this deeper identity shift has impacted the way the country has responded to external adversaries.

> Our sense of who we are is beginning to get on the world stage. We have moved from the era of the argumentative Indian (elites) to the era of the authentic Indian (ordinary people), and the world recognizes it… If you ask an average Indian today, 'what bothers you?' he will tell you 'it is the Pakistani policy of terrorism.' The Indian street got it with clarity and it is smarter than Lutyens Delhi.[74]

The Modi government's handling of national security crises has been closer to the preference of the average Indian, thereby clearing the psychological baggage and vacillation of the past. Whether one calls it a populist or authentic turn, this shift goes beyond instrumental social science concepts like 'diversionary wars', which predict that 'when a government, democratic or not, is under domestic pressure it enacts an adventurous, diversionary foreign policy' so that 'if the foreign policy event overshadows domestic problems then the government avoids being removed from power.'[75] Throughout this book, I have given many examples of Modi consciously striving and planning to avoid war with foreign opponents while escalating against them. Like the 2016 surgical strikes, the Modi government presented the Balakot attack as a 'non-military pre-emptive strike', i.e. a proportionate and commensurate response to the Pulwama bombing focusing on hurting JeM terrorists rather than directly fighting the Pakistani military.[76] In the continuum between appeasement at one end and war at the other, Modi has looked for sweet spots that are optimal and which dovetail with the expectations of ordinary Indians, whose interests will never be served by a full-scale war with nuclear-armed neighbours.

Squelching Separatism

A few months after his re-election, Modi surprised Pakistan again. This time, it was not a military raid into Pakistani territory but a historic reconfiguration of internal administration in Indian Kashmir. His move to abrogate Article 370 of the Indian Constitution on 5 August 2019 was deemed a necessary measure to tackle head-on the long-festering politics of alienation and separatism in Kashmir that was being exploited by Pakistan. It was planned and executed like a military operation and involved the detentions of anti-India politicians and a security blanket all over Kashmir Valley to preclude violent unrest. The fact that the suicide bomber in Pulwama was a radicalized young Kashmiri Muslim who did not believe in being a loyal Indian citizen was conveniently used by Pakistan to claim that the JeM mission was an indigenous problem for which Pakistan was being unfairly blamed. At the root of the alienation of the Pulwama attacker and legions of other Kashmiri Muslims for generations has been Article 370, a provision to temporarily grant special rights and autonomy to residents of Jammu and Kashmir, which was inserted into the Constitution at Prime Minister Nehru's urging in 1949 to placate separatist tendencies among Kashmiri leaders in the context of India wanting to win 'the hearts and minds of men and women of J&K'.[77]

The political compromise under Articles 370 and its companion Article 35A allowed Muslim-majority Kashmir to have a parallel Constitution with a flag of its own. The state government in Kashmir had powers over law enforcement, residence and property rights. Central laws had no validity in

Kashmir unless the local legislature approved them. In effect, the autonomous status turned Kashmir into a ghetto with a mentality of uniqueness and distinctness from the rest of India. It strengthened the nearly seven million Kashmiri Muslims' feelings that they were not Indians but a different nationality who deserve to keep Indians out of their paradisiacal enclave except as visiting tourists. The armed secessionist movements in Kashmir against Indian rule from the late 1980s, which were financed and enabled by Pakistan, occurred in the context of this autonomous status.[78] Local elite Kashmiri Muslim politicians of various hues hung on to their privileges with the narrative that Kashmir is not really a part of India but an independent nation.[79] If pushed to extremes, it will resort to breaking away from India, and declare itself a new country or merge into Pakistan.

Indian leaders before Modi stuck to Nehru's tacit bargain whereby Kashmir retained its special status and, in return, stayed willy-nilly within the territorial boundaries of India. The autonomy provisions in the Constitution of India, enacted in the 1940s and 1950s, were meant to be a temporary fix to buy the loyalty of Kashmiri Muslims. However, they were extended indefinitely as part of a patronage bargain between New Delhi and Srinagar, the capital of Jammu and Kashmir. Over time, the halfway-house existence of Jammu and Kashmir as a state within India and yet a 'nation' that does not emotionally belong to India, failed to meet both India's objectives and Kashmiri Muslims' aspirations. Waves of anti-India uprisings and insurgencies, supported from across the porous LoC by Pakistan, kept Kashmir burning. Autonomy had become a slippery slope for separatism, jihadist extremism and alienation of Kashmiri Muslims from the rest of India.

Famed for taking the bull by the horns, Modi kept his cards close to his chest and then unveiled the strategic surprise which fundamentally transformed the issue at hand. His radical restructuring of the troubled state of Jammu and Kashmir by revoking its seven-decade-long separate autonomous status and converting it into a centrally administered territory was a landmark decision that changed the nature and contours of politics in Kashmir. Modi bet that by corralling Kashmir under tighter central government control, he would marginalize the secessionist politicians there, open Kashmir up for the return of Hindu Kashmiri minorities who had been ethnically cleansed by jihadists in the late 1980s, and in the longer run, make the Valley accessible to Indians of all religious and ethnic backgrounds.

The idea was to dissolve Kashmiri separatism in a sea of Indian nationalism. Modi's decision evoked opposition from some Indian political parties wedded to the old arrangement of special autonomy for Kashmir because they feared that such assimilation would deprive them of vote banks of Kashmiri Muslims and enfeeble Kashmiri elites whose parties can be alliance partners during and after elections at the state and national levels.

Cancelling autonomy for Kashmir also risked escalating civil unrest in Kashmir, where anti-India elements, like the Pakistan-supported Hurriyat Conference, feared falling under tremendous pressure if Kashmir was centrally governed. But the only opinion that mattered to Modi was the will of the general public across India, which emotionally welcomed his overturning of the Kashmir policy as necessary from the lens of national unity and security. Five months after Modi reshaped the destiny of Jammu and Kashmir, 58 per cent of Indians responded in opinion polls that 'the decision will provide a permanent solution to the Kashmir issue.'[80]

Whether Modi's momentous shift would pay off as Indian nationalists expected depends not only on how Kashmiri

Muslim elite politicians adjust to the new administrative reality Modi has created, but also on Islamabad. After all, one-third of the undivided Kashmir is in Pakistan's control and deadly terrorist groups like LeT and JeM are at the beck and call of Pakistan's military to infiltrate from PoK into Jammu and Kashmir to stoke separatist fires. Modi's slam dunk move is intended to yank the initiative away from Pakistan, which claim Muslim-majority Kashmir as its rightful territory, and usher in a new era of Indian consolidation over the contested Himalayan region.

Pakistan had long relied on stoking Kashmiri Muslim alienation in the two-thirds of Kashmir held by India. Freeing Kashmir from India's clutches had been a Holy Grail of the Pakistani military, which funded, trained and armed thousands of Kashmiri Muslims as well as jihadists from Pakistani ethnic groups like Punjabis and Pashtuns who slipped back and forth across the mountainous militarized LoC dividing Jammu and Kashmir from PoK.[81] Modi's determined push for total absorption of Indian Kashmir into India proper presented an existential challenge to the long-entrenched Pakistani strategy of fanning alienation of Kashmiri Muslims against India. If Kashmiri Muslims were reorganized and no longer grouped together as an exclusive ethnic entity, Pakistan would find it a lot harder to foment the flame of 'self-determination' in the Valley. Kashmiri Muslims might have become further alienated from India as a result of the abrogation of Article 370, but Modi calculated that, in years to come, they would no longer be brought up and brainwashed so as to stymie Indian sovereignty.

With the writing on the wall, Pakistan looked for drastic and urgent action in the near term to foil Modi's long-term blueprint. Islamabad threatened to 'exercise all possible options to counter the illegal steps' Modi had allegedly taken by scrapping Articles 370 and 35A, raising fears of a new national security crisis.[82]

Underscoring the existential crisis perceived by the Pakistani state apparatus, Imran Khan went on a shrill international propaganda tour accusing India of violating the human rights of Kashmiri Muslims and imposing a humanitarian catastrophe on them, and warning that the reaction against Modi would lead to a situation where 'two nuclear-armed countries will come face to face, like we came in February [after the Pulwama attack]'.[83] As the ISI attempted to activate its cells in Kashmir Valley to carry out protest attacks, the Pakistani prime minister unabashedly predicted that 'attacks like Pulwama will happen again' and that there would be 'a war that no one will win and the implications will be global'.[84]

The internationalization of Kashmir as a dangerous flashpoint that could explode in war and nuclear holocaust was a time-tested Pakistani ploy. However, Modi was prepared for it, and the Indian military's deployments at the LoC and in Kashmir Valley prevented any conflagration or provocation by Pakistan's regular army or its irregular jihadis. A surge in military clashes with India along the 740-kilometre-long LoC and terrorist attacks inside Indian territory would force a harsh counter-reaction from Modi, which could be grounds on which the US could be convinced to mediate—an ideal scenario for Pakistani hawks. Imran Khan kept urging the Trump administration that 'this is the time' to intervene and prevent Kashmir from blowing up into 'a regional crisis',[85] and did get verbal consolation from the maverick US president who repeatedly uttered off-the-cuff remarks that he 'would love to be a mediator'.[86] But nothing ever came of it. Modi memorably told Trump in a face-to-face meeting in June 2020, 'we don't want to bother any third country', and comfortably put an end to Pakistan's internationalization dream.[87]

The tact and foresight with which Modi foreclosed Pakistan's chances of fuelling a new crisis after the revocation of Article 370 was an unsung success. Modi dispatched diplomats to convince major powers around the world and ensure that the fallout of his 'Operation Kashmir' did not become unmanageable. If Pakistan's brief was to raise alarms about instability and human rights before the international community, India's talking points were about the dire threat posed by Islamist terrorism and the legitimate security needs of sovereign states. It was a game of rapid chess where one had to quickly anticipate what the other side was likely to do two or three moves down the line, and accordingly shuffle the pieces. If the Balakot air strike was a form of crisis response, the massive internal policy shift in Jammu and Kashmir and the resultant international pressure that Modi parried represented a crisis-averting feat.

In retrospect, the momentum which began with Pulwama and culminated in the reintegration of Jammu and Kashmir into India's mainstream was an arc in which Bharat acted courageously and converted a crisis into an opportunity. This period in 2019 marked a paradigm shift in subcontinental geopolitics. No matter how many terrorists the Balakot air strike actually killed or not, former Air Vice Marshal Subramaniam argued that it marked a strategic milestone where Modi overcame decades of political hesitation and opted to use air power 'as an effective tool of deterrence in sub-conventional operations.'[88] The IAF had been proffering Indian civilian leaders the option of aerial bombing of terrorist launch pads inside Pakistan since the 1990s, but only Modi dared to activate it and thereby crossed the Rubicon. Although Pakistan portrayed Modi as an Islamophobic fanatic who was trying to ratchet up tensions for winning elections, the air strike was inexorable if one understood the evolution of Modi's national security thought and the compulsions he was facing as a result of surging jihadist violence across the LoC.

The main message Modi delivered by green-lighting the Balakot strikes was that he had the gumption to use the conventional might of India to undertake controlled offensives against Pakistan that fall short of war. Now that the bar has been set, more such countermeasures will be on the anvil through land, air or sea if and when there are terrorist attacks or plots being hatched by Pakistan-based jihadists against India. A response matrix envisaging various crisis scenarios and suitable counters to each type of provocation is in place, and it is being practised and simulated by the wings of the Indian military in training sessions. Given India's bigger and more dynamic economy which can sustain a long war, its conventional military superiority over Pakistan (New Delhi has three to five times larger forces and weapons inventories than Islamabad), and the fact that both countries are assured of mutual destruction if they resort to their nuclear arsenals, sub-threshold military retaliation is unlikely to spiral into the worst-case scenario of total war.

Pakistan was the first mover into the sub-conventional warfare domain after it sustained a big loss in the 1971 war with India. Now, Modi has developed his own sub-conventional doctrine of pre-emption that is precise, disciplined and proportionate. India is not a hard state like Israel and can never be that ruthless and disproportionate in countering terrorism because it has ambitions of being accepted internationally as a responsible nation that would one day become a great power. Moreover, India has to contend with the much more formidable challenge that it faces from China on its northern border and tight-knit China–Pakistan 'all-weather alliance' that has grown as the power gap between India and Pakistan has widened in the former's favour. Many more India–Pakistan crises are inevitable in the future, especially due to the serious blowback from the return of the Afghan Taliban to power in Kabul in 2021. But Modi has altered the balance of initiative that hitherto used to always be in Pakistan's hands because it possessed what India lacked—jihadist proxies willing to die in the name of religion. By freeing and spurring the Indian military to undertake limited bursts of force, Modi has moved the needle and introduced the prospect of a balance of terror between two unequal rivals. His exhortation to the Indian military about the 'importance of enhancing indigenization in the national security system, not just in sourcing equipment and weapons but also in the doctrines, procedures and customs practised in the armed forces', is a pointer in the direction of Kautilya, Kamandaka and Shukracharya—ancient Indian theorists of statecraft and warfare. With Bharat rising to the fore, a new strategic culture is on the horizon.[89]

Chapter 4

Turning the Tables in Ladakh

Even when the only point of the war is to maintain the status quo, the fact remains that merely parrying a blow goes against the essential nature of war...the defender must strike back, or he will court destruction. Prudence bids him strike while the iron is hot and use the advantage to prevent a second onslaught...this transition to the counterattack must be accepted as a tendency inherent in defense.[1]

—Prussian military theorist Carl von Clausewitz, 1832 CE

Informal Management

On 27–28 April 2018, Narendra Modi walked with Xi Jinping along the picturesque East Lake in Wuhan, Central China, took a joint boat ride for 'peace, prosperity and development', toured a museum of historical Chinese artefacts, and engaged in hours of heart-to-heart conversations to improve bilateral relations and pursue a reset following the Doklam crisis of the previous year.[2] Dubbed as the first-ever 'informal summit' between the two Asian competitors, the concept was an innovation meant for the top leaders to be unencumbered by large official delegations, to 'talk freely without a fixed agenda, and for both to agree on principles rather than specific issues.'[3] Official sources billed the summit as an opportunity to form a 'new paradigm' to guide Sino-Indian relations for the coming 15 years, and to generate a 'general framework' through which each side will conduct itself vis-à-vis the other.[4]

The reader will recall from Chapter 2 of this book that Chinese diplomats had been huffing and puffing that they wanted to avoid a repeat of the Doklam border stand-off. India was equally keen to avoid incidents and transgressions by the PLA along the LAC, which had risen from 220 per year in 2011 to an alarming number of 415 by 2017.[5] The Modi government's precept that both countries should not 'let differences become disputes' was a sound one and also served a call for sobriety to isolate particular flashpoints, events and episodes from sapping the overall bilateral relationship.[6] India was also interested in a standard protocol whereby respect for geopolitical red lines of each side was reciprocally honoured, rather than unilaterally demanded. If China was sensitive to how India approached Tibet (especially the activities of the exiled Dalai Lama and his followers who were domiciled in India as refugees since the PLA's occupation of their homeland in the 1950s), Taiwan, Japan, Southeast Asia and the US, India was sensitive to how China was expanding in the Indian Ocean region and South Asia via the BRI. The Modi government's stand that India would abide by its commitment to the 'One China policy' only if China, in turn, adhered to a 'One India policy' (meaning that China should drop territorial claims on 90,000 square kilometres in Arunachal Pradesh) was, in effect, a proposal for each party to recognize where the other's prickly points were located and reciprocally accommodate them.[7]

But this sort of bargain was easier conceived than implemented. Xi's China was aggressively pursuing 'major country diplomacy with Chinese characteristics' premised on a self-understanding of China as a global power no less in stature than the US which deserved to be a player in far-flung corners of the world.[8] The sheer geographical scope and economic scale of Xi's BRI showed that China was not interested in limiting its strategic footprint. Under Modi's 'new India', New Delhi, too, was not interested in restricting its strategic choices and freedom of partnerships to appease China. Beijing wished to undermine New Delhi's alignment with Washington. The pressure that China maintained against India on the LAC and in multilateral fora like the NSG and in the UN—on matters such as designating Pakistani terrorists—was linked to how much Beijing believed New Delhi was coordinating with Washington as part of a grand conspiracy of western 'containment' of China.

Expecting informal summits to unfreeze the structural tension and the zero-sum game mindset with which elites in China and India eyed each other was wishful. But in the candid setting of Wuhan, neither side hid behind niceties. The Indian ambassador to China at that time said that Modi and Xi 'removed several misconceptions [they] may have about each other', and there was reasonable optimism that Asia's undeclared Cold War could be steered by the supremos of both countries into an orderly, predictable, non-violent and institutionalized path.[9] An informal return summit between Modi and Xi in the southern Indian seaside town of Mamallapuram on 11–12 October 2019 reiterated the consensus of the 'Wuhan spirit' and swore that 'efforts will continue to be made to ensure peace and tranquility in the border areas'.[10] Asia's number one and number two powers had longstanding conflicts of interest, but were looking for some semblance of stability through 'strategic communication' between their leaders.[11]

Prior to the Mamallapuram summit, old frictions had surfaced. Chinese objections to Indian military drills in Arunachal Pradesh (which Beijing claims as part of

'South Tibet'),[12] and China's condemnation of India's 'unilateral' administrative shake-up to abrogate Article 370 in Jammu and Kashmir (a part of which, Aksai Chin, is under Chinese control and other parts of which in Ladakh are claimed by China),[13] were two flaps that reminded everyone before the summit how edgy both countries remained regarding sovereignty and border matters.

There were also geopolitical grievances that could not be swept under the carpet. If China needed Pakistan to keep India hemmed in South Asia, India under Modi played the card of cosying up to the US and Russia to keep China under check. External Affairs Minister S. Jaishankar explicitly rejected the concept of 'containment of China' under a western umbrella in August 2019, but it did not mean that New Delhi was complacent about growing Chinese encroachments in its backyard.[14] Both China and India nursed strategic suspicions about being encircled by the other via third and fourth countries. Notwithstanding these misgivings, the fact that Xi and Modi engaged in a showy personal diplomatic summit where red lines were mentioned and frank reservations were expressed meant that Beijing and New Delhi saw value in gauging each other's intentions from the horse's mouths. Modi's comment at Mamallapuram that the two nations had 'agreed to be sensitive to each other's concerns'[15] was as realistic as it got. It was clear was that informal summitry could not usher in eternal peace, revive the old Nehru-era sentimental slogan of '*Hindi Chini, bhai bhai* [Indians and the Chinese live in harmony like brothers]', or forge a grand anti-western global alliance. Xi and Modi were only committed to predictable and stable bilateral relations which do not boil over.

In hindsight, as a grave national security crisis engulfed the two sides on the eastern Ladakh-Aksai Chin frontier from April–May 2020, the relatively convivial and constructive mood at Wuhan and Mamallapuram appeared to have been a chimera or a smokescreen. But one must not overlook the empirical reality that the agreement at Wuhan for Modi and Xi to provide 'strategic guidance' to their respective militaries to defuse confrontations at the LAC and enhance predictability in managing the border conflict did work for a while. India's defence ministry found that the number of PLA transgressions, and the percentage of face-offs and aggressive interactions at the LAC had 'considerably reduced' in 2018–2019.[16] The late General Bipin Rawat, the then Indian Army chief, credited 'the strategic guidance from the highest-level and understanding of the nuances of the working mechanism at the functional level' for enabling 'management of challenges along the LAC'.[17]

In the wake of the severe crisis that arose at the LAC in early 2020, we now know that the thaw was too good to last. But the respite in China–India strains during 2018 and 2019 is instructive to analyse because it offers a window into the evolving bilateral and global political dynamics which determine how adversarial or cordial the relationship can get. What worked in Modi's favour to moderate Xi's expansionist appetite for a couple of years after Doklam was the Trump factor. The personalized bilateral diplomacy at Wuhan and Mamallapuram had a triangular interface. Both Beijing and New Delhi have historically found it hard to view each other outside of the framework of relations with Washington.[18] For a long time, China feared that India was being lured into a US-led alliance meant to contain China and block its rise to superpower status. And while wary of a full-fledged alliance, New Delhi saw the US as a necessary strategic partner to build India's economic, technological and military muscle and to withstand Chinese expansionism.

This dynamic was in place for the last two decades since Washington and India began courting each other strategically, but Trump shook up the equation with his chaotic and unorthodox policymaking. America's volatile president became the unwitting trigger forcing China and India to rethink their core assumptions about the trilateral relationship. Since assuming office in January 2017, Trump pursued protectionist and economic nationalistic policies to heighten tensions with China. He abruptly ended an era when US presidents tolerated their nation's gigantic trade deficit with China, and the rapid erosion of their technological edge. Trump's 2017 NSS clearly labelled China as a rival and pledged that 'the United States will no longer turn a blind eye to violations, cheating, or economic aggression.'[19]

Yet, despite the unilateral economic attack Trump launched on China, he showed little interest in maintaining and oiling the multilateral US alliance system in Asia that could truly bottle up China's rise. His decision to abandon the Trans-Pacific Partnership and his failure to offer key allies in the Indo-Pacific region the generosity and magnanimity they usually expect from the US offered wiggle room to China to bring nearby nations into Beijing's sphere of influence. Still, Trump's threats to broaden the anti-Chinese economic assault and the sense in China that this was just the beginning of a possible 'new Cold War' that could imperil Xi's BRI, led Beijing to recalibrate its approach to its main Asian neighbour, India.

In the run-up to the 2018 Wuhan summit, the CCP-linked news media reissued warnings that India 'should stay clear and independent to avoid being used as a pawn' by the US.[20] They also explicitly linked the 'Wuhan spirit' of trying to patch up differences over the border and geostrategic competition to 'an era of great uncertainties featuring Trump's opportunistic maneuvers, braggadocio and threats.'[21] Explicit hostility from the US, it seems, had compelled China to diminish its tensions with India.

In India too, while the political and defence leadership still had faith in the US and Modi found a certain personal rapport with Trump, there were questions about how reliable an ally Washington would be in the event that conflict with China in the Himalayas or the Indian Ocean grew hot. Trump's narrow 'America First' ideology had sent strong signals to US treaty allies in Asia such as the Philippines, Thailand, Japan and South Korea that Washington might not stand by its commitments in a conflict. As a nationalist politician who wanted to pilot India to the status of a 'leading power' in the world, Modi would not simply cave into China's demands the way that Philippine President Rodrigo Duterte did by refusing to further press the Philippines' territorial claims in the South China Sea after its landmark victory in international court over disputed islands.[22] Still, the Indian leader was aware of India's vulnerabilities vis-à-vis a more powerful China and had no delusions that Trump would come to his aid in the event of new military face-offs with China.

Nevertheless, in spite of Trump's unreliability, the US remained one of the key players, together with Japan and ASEAN, for India to march to what Modi saw as its destined spot as a global power. Even if Trump failed to check threatened Chinese hegemony in the Indian and Pacific Oceans, Modi did not throw away the American card to pacify Xi. China barely cooperated with the US military, while US–Indian military ties grew exponentially under Modi, with joint manufacturing of weaponry and technology transfer on the cards. The hyperbole from China ahead of the Wuhan summit about a 'major shift' and a 'new course like never before' in China–India ties camouflaged many of China's fundamental strategic anxieties vis-à-vis the US. Modi attempted to cleverly harness these Chinese worries as implicit leverage in his engagements with Xi.

It was informative that despite the two informal China–India summits, Modi did not loosen the grip on India–US strategic partnership one bit. The Quadrilateral Security Dialogue or the Quad group, comprising Australia, India, Japan and the US, whose joint naval Malabar exercise had been dropped like a hot potato in 2008 by the Manmohan Singh government out of fear of offending China, was revived in 2017 and elevated to the level of an annual ministerial meeting in September 2019. The 2020 edition of the Malabar naval games brought back the Quad formation of four countries, posing a challenge to Chinese maritime expansionism. From a Chinese perspective, it may have seemed as though Modi had kept a revolver labelled 'US alliance plus' on the table when he shook hands and conversed with Xi. As a weaker power compared to China, India's strategy was to have counterbalancing chips to negotiate with China from a position of relative equality.

The crisis in eastern Ladakh, which began in April 2020, again, vividly illustrated the inescapable global factors and entailments behind the ebbs and flows in China–India relations. The actual bone of contention may have been disputed portions of land in the rugged Himalayan heights along the LAC, but the stakes touched much of Asia and affected the wider Indo-Pacific.

Seizing the Pandemic

As the third decade of the twenty-first century dawned, the oft-cited Chinese proverb, 'in every crisis there is opportunity', was thrown into sharp relief. The deadly coronavirus originated in China's Wuhan and was seemingly allowed by the CCP's secretive and negligent regime to spread throughout the country and around the planet for months before the world realized its devastating effects.[23] Approximately five million people had departed Wuhan before the travel restrictions and quarantining were implemented from 23 January 2020. As the pandemic continued to grip the world, millions of people were infected, millions died and the global economy entered a deep depression, with the US and Europe bearing the bulk of the brunt.

In the spring of 2020, China made a strategic assessment that its model of curbing the virus had been a phenomenal success while the US's failure to contain COVID-19 confirmed the Communist Party's vision of the inherent weakness of western democracies and the superiority of its form of government. State-owned Chinese outlets explained why the American model of liberal democracy was dying and losing its universal appeal.[24] A Chinese economist, Keyu Jin, reflected the confidence in Xi's regime that its time had come to overtake the US and argued that the pandemic had become an 'opportunity of the century for China' which it would cash in. Having 'seized opportunities to elevate its position during other recent economic crises, such as the financial crisis (of 2008) and through its support of the European debt market', Jin noted that China would not let this opportunity go to waste.[25]

The long-run game for China was to displace the US at the pinnacle of the global power configuration and export the Chinese model of authoritarian capitalism as a solution to the world's problems. The pandemic, which exposed the American and European fragility and torn to shreds the myths of legitimacy of democracies, must have been perceived by Xi to be the inflection point for a transition to this China-centric order. He urged CCP officials in late 2020 to 'grasp clearly the grand trend that the East is rising while the West is declining' and that 'there is a vivid contrast between the order of China and the chaos of the West'.[26]

Even western strategists could sense that the baton of global leadership might transfer from the US to China as a result of the COVID-19 calamity that rendered America comatose even as China recovered fast.[27] Many experts viewed the pandemic as a game-changer from the lenses of Chinese 'mask diplomacy' and economic resilience compared to Trump's 'America First' tight-fistedness and ham-handedness as the US economy tanked in 2020. But there was also a military dimension to this transitional moment in global power. Notwithstanding China's propaganda that its rise was peaceful and methodologically different from that of western imperialist powers of previous centuries, Xi and his advisors believe in the efficacy of military might. One of the central pillars of Xi's 'China Dream' is the 'dream of a strong armed forces' and a 'world-class' military that can beat the US, and prevail over any other peer competitor in the decades to come.[28] During the coronavirus pandemic, Xi consolidated additional control over the PLA and all security arms of the Chinese state, and expounded on how he intended to use the black swan opportunity of the virus in martial terms.

> If you want to become a general you must be able to win a battle... Even if you have the ability to win battles, you don't have battles every day, in particular not in times of peace... One can say that only if a chance should arise and you make use of it right away, you will succeed.[29]

What followed was a self-belief in China that its new great leap forward was unstoppable not only diplomatically and economically but also militarily. A retired Chinese PLA officer's comments from 2020 captured the new-found bounce in thinking: 'In this fight against the pandemic, there will be victorious powers and defeated ones. We're a victor power, while the United States is still mired and, I think, may well become a defeated power.'[30] Xi and his obedient generals in the PLA appear to have concluded that China had an upper hand

and that the obstacles to its quest for a unipolar Asia under its tutelage were lower than before. Chinese strategists were delighted by the fact that hundreds of American sailors on the aircraft carrier *USS Theodore Roosevelt* contracted coronavirus in March 2020 and the mega-ship had to be temporarily pulled out from its patrolling duties in and around maritime spaces China wanted to boss over in the Indo-Pacific.[31]

The notion that the US was losing its ability to stall China's swagger was well captured in the Chinese propagandist Hu Xijin's tweet in July 2020 that the US had 'become the place worst impacted by the pandemic' and that 'if the US is really to head for the decline, year 2020 will be seen by history as the turning point'.[32] The same Hu had mocked Trump as *Jianguo*— someone who was enabling China's rise to global supremacy by making America 'eccentric and thus hateful for the world'.[33] The more mired the US seemed in domestic strife and isolationist foreign policy, the easier Xi thought it was for China to get away with murder in Asia.

Not coincidentally, the first phase of Chinese military and foreign policy assertiveness vis-à-vis its Asian neighbours was observed around 2008–2009 before Xi Jinping's arrival on the scene. That uptick in the Chinese pushiness towards neighbours happened at a time when the global economic crisis had struck and devastated the US. Like in 2020, the Chinese assessment in 2008 was that the American model of capitalism had failed miserably. Beijing saw Washington struggling from a crisis wrought by its own Wall Street banking sharks and felt that China had gotten a window of opportunity to take advantage of America's woes by throwing around its weight in Asia. In May 2020, Xi's regime announced a 6.6 per cent increase in China's defence budget.[34] While China justified its humungous military expenditure as a safeguard against American imperialism and US's designs to stymie China's rise, in practice, all the military muscle China was accumulating was flexed not at the continental US or American naval or land bases in the Pacific, but against the territorial integrity and sovereignty of smaller neighbours in subregions of Asia.

In northeast Asia, China's military might was aimed at browbeating historic rival Japan over the Senkaku islands. In Southeast Asia, China built a chain of artificial military bases through dredging of islets and atolls and deployed its naval assets to impose its illegal claims over territorial waters of Vietnam, the Philippines, Malaysia, Taiwan and Indonesia.[35] As I have described earlier, in South Asia, China turned up periodic and progressively more forceful intrusions across the LAC with India and kept Bhutan under perpetual pressure by raising fresh territorial claims against the tiny buffer state separating Chinese-occupied Tibet from India. By March and April of 2020, Xi's China felt emboldened to simultaneously activate military fronts against every neighbour with whom it had rows. On 16 March, Taiwan's coast guard vessel was rammed by Chinese boats. PLA Navy maritime drills in the Taiwan Straits and the PLA Air Force's intrusions into Taiwanese airspace increased in frequency thereafter. On 2 April, China sank a Vietnamese fishing boat near the Paracel Islands. Indonesia, Malaysia and the Philippines were made to feel the heat with Chinese incursions into their maritime spaces. Chasing away or coming within collision distance with US naval vessels in the South China Sea grew apace. In May, China dispatched its aircraft carrier to the Miyako Strait in the East China Sea near Japan's Ryukyu Islands, ringing alarm bells in Tokyo.[36]

The pattern of taunting, poking and bullying all adversaries at once was driven by Xi's grandiose perception that China was in a commanding position to dictate terms to smaller nations, and that China would not face any united opposition to its violent provocations and sustained nibbling away of territories of adversaries. The Indian scholars Harsh Pant and Kartik Bommakanti noted in April 2020, even before the China–India tensions at the LAC snowballed into a huge crisis in eastern Ladakh, that China was cashing in on the COVID-19 vulnerabilities of its opponents by 'using its military to make creeping gains while the rest of the world remains busy in managing the life and death of its populace'.[37]

Full Spectrum Aggression

If China had decided to capitalize on the weakness of the US and several Asian neighbours with whom it had territorial disputes, India would not have been spared. COVID-19 provided the perfect background. In March 2020, India postponed the annual military exercises of its army and the Indo-Tibetan Border Police (ITBP) in eastern Ladakh after a soldier tested positive for the coronavirus. China also delayed exercises on its side in Aksai Chin, 'but when the manoeuvres were carried out, they surprised Indian troops by quick redeployment in the Galwan Valley and the Finger Area along Pangong Tso lake'. Using the 'first movers advantage', China reportedly pushed over seven thousand PLA troops at several strategic points inside what India perceived to be its side of the LAC in the western sector. India discovered the full extent of the incursions only by end of April 2020.[38] Indian intelligence agencies had been flagging the movement of PLA forces in eastern Ladakh since February, but officials felt that 'the intent of Chinese deployment was not clear' at that time.[39]

In May, China opened another front north of Pangong Tso and Galwan in Depsang. This, as the reader will recall from the Introduction, was an old lingering issue that had featured in the April 2013 mini-crisis. This time, thousands of PLA forces moved in with heavy vehicles, tanks and artillery, and began to block the Indian Army from patrolling at various points over an area of 80 to 90 square kilometres. An Indian military officer was anonymously quoted as saying that in Depsang too, 'we have not read the Chinese intentions well'.[40] As the Chinese quietly hunkered down in Depsang and began to 'swing into action to block an Indian patrol whenever they saw it approaching', worries arose that 'China could be diverting India's attention from the far more important Depsang region through its aggressive manoeuvres in the Pangong Tso-Chushul and other areas lower down along the frontier in Ladakh.'[41] Located just 35 kilometres from the strategic Karakoram Pass, which is at the tri-junction of China, Pakistan and India, Depsang had long been coveted by China. It gained urgency from Beijing's perspective because the Modi government had prioritized border infrastructure upgrades and completed the inordinately delayed Darbuk–Shyok–DBO (DSDBO) road, which connects with Depsang and would give the Indian military quicker and easier access to Karakoram and Chinese-occupied Aksai Chin. The road has been described as 'a thorn in China's flesh' as it could enable India to bolster the world's highest airstrip in DBO (16,800 feet) and enable offensive inroads into the Chinese side of the LAC.[42]

Derek Grossman, an American defence analyst at the RAND Corporation, contends that China's large-scale aggression at multiple friction points at the LAC was not driven by its perceived advantage owing to the pandemic, but rather an outcome of insecurity about being disadvantaged by India's rapid construction of strategic border infrastructure. He cites Chinese diplomats and writers insisting that 'since the beginning of this year [2020], the Indian side has continuously built facilities at or crossing the LAC...constantly changing the status quo on ground control' and that India 'had tried to stab China in the back' through its 'growing assertiveness at the LAC'.[43] But taking official Chinese explanations at face value or rationalizing them is erroneous because Chinese strategic behaviour is based on deception, stealth and blaming the victims of its expansionism or other misdemeanours. The brazenness with which China's 'wolf warrior' diplomats and mouthpieces spun conspiracy theories to blame the US for spreading the coronavirus and divert attention from the obvious culpability of Xi's regime was one instance of China justifying its indefensible acts through perfidy.[44]

Just because China's government repeatedly claimed during the Ladakh crisis that 'the root cause for the tensions between the two sides' was that 'for some time, the Indian side has been ramping up infrastructure development along the border and stepping up military deployment', it did not necessarily make it the most credible explanation for why such a tremendous escalation happened in 2020.[45] The PLA need not have done simultaneous ingressions at six friction points and deployed more than 50,000 heavily armed troops all at once if it was anxious about a one or two roads being built by India. External Affairs Minister S. Jaishankar, who had previously served as the ambassador to China, and had gained considerable experience in negotiating with Beijing, was a key protagonist in the 2020 crisis, and highlighted the disingenuity behind Chinese incursions in eastern Ladakh. Recounting the bilateral agreements signed since 1993, for both sides not to deploy large numbers of forces at the LAC, he wondered aloud, 'now for some reason, for which the Chinese have to date given us five differing explanations, the Chinese have violated it'.[46]

From all indications, the Chinese goal was much bigger than obstructing or pre-empting Indian border road construction. It was to force India to concede vital tactical terrain as part of China's salami slicing expansionism and to prove that no inferior power could halt China in the pandemic era. To parse the origins of the Ladakh crisis in granular details about who was building which road and who was patrolling at which point is to miss the strategic big picture of a China that was in top gear due to a pandemic-induced confidence and was firing on all cylinders at not just India but at many adversaries, unwilling to accede to its hegemony in Asia. As the Washington-based Hudson Institute puts it, 'in South Asia, unlike Southeast, East or Central Asia, there is a natural hegemon: India. China cannot cast it aside easily'. Hence, its objective was 'to limit any defiance from the world's largest democracy, India, and hinder its burgeoning partnership with the United States'.[47] Showing India its place and 'teaching it a lesson' has been an age-old Chinese communist purpose. There were flashes of this supremacist mentality during the 2017 Doklam crisis, which I elaborated on in Chapter 2. By 2020, with India struggling to control the pandemic and its economy going downhill, Xi may have seen it as the opportune time to strike full-spectrum and emphatically cut it down to size.

If Modi did fast-track border infrastructure building on the Indian side of the LAC, he was well within his sovereign rights to do so, irrespective of China claiming parts of eastern Ladakh to be disputed and objecting to the construction.[48] India practically could not, and did not, compel China to halt all the border modernization it undertook for decades on the Chinese side of the LAC, including railways, roads and bridges. Now that India was trying to catch up, reduce the asymmetry in China's favour along parts of the LAC and retain an ability to better defend Indian territory and repulse Chinese intrusions, China was muscling in and playing the aggrieved party with exaggerated grievances and apprehensions. History buffs would recall that China had blamed India for causing the war in 1962 as well.[49] China had ruthlessly grabbed 43,000 square kilometres from India in Aksai Chin in that conflict while expressing faux concerns that the Indians 'see China's Tibet, Xinjiang, and the Aksai Chin all as theirs'.[50]

Modi's abrogation of Article 370—which I analysed in relation to the India–Pakistan crises and jihadist separatism in the Kashmir Valley—was also one of the putative causes for the wholesale aggression of the Chinese at various friction points in eastern Ladakh. China took Pakistan's side after Modi scrapped special autonomy for Kashmir. It also repeatedly lobbied the UNSC to discuss what Beijing termed as India's 'unilateral' move to separate Ladakh from Jammu and Kashmir and grant it the status of a Union Territory that would be centrally governed by New Delhi. Thanks to India's strong strategic partnerships with other P-5 members, it could stymie the Chinese push to internationalize Kashmir thrice between August 2019 and January 2020, but China held on to the grudge.[51] In June 2020, with the crisis in Ladakh escalating, Wang Shida of the state-affiliated think tank, China Institutes of Contemporary International Relations (CICIR), claimed that 'India opened up new territory on the map, incorporated part of the areas under the local jurisdiction of Xinjiang and Tibet into its Ladakh union territory' and 'dramatically increased the difficulty in resolving the border issue between China and India'.[52] If Islamabad was livid at Modi's abrogation of Article 370 due to its anti-separatist implications, Beijing was angry that Ladakh's infrastructure and social panorama would be transformed under the direct central rule of New Delhi to such an extent that India would be in a position to better consolidate control over the border areas and overturn the PLA's tactical advantages.

Even if Modi's reorganization of Jammu and Kashmir was on China's mind as it planned its unprecedented coercive military push into eastern Ladakh, it begs the question as to why Xi and his generals believed that they had a right to allow or disallow India's internal security reforms. Was China the master of India's destiny? Did India need permission from China to strengthen its defences well within its side of the LAC? China mercilessly destroyed the social and political fabrics of Xinjiang and Tibet after occupying them, committed cultural genocide and exploited their land masses rapaciously with no concern for ecology or local Buddhist and Islamic ethos.[53] As I mentioned earlier in Chapter 2, the obliteration of Tibet as a natural buffer that separated the PLA from the Indian military was a serious strategic threat to India that could not be stopped. Having swept southwards into the Tibetan plateau and swarmed it with its troops, China wanted more territory in the form of the 'five fingers'. It was a perverse type of imperialism where territorial conquest begets the need for more conquest to secure the occupied territory. China had no locus standi over Ladakh except by dint of its military might. The PLA's synchronized incursions into eastern Ladakh in 2020 constituted a huge statement that superordinate China would impose its will on subordinate India and expose the latter's feebleness.

The message was transparent for those who could tune in: in a reprise of the ancient construct of Tianxia, China believed it was nominally the ruler of the world, and all the others must accept its superiority and pay tribute to it.[54] Those who dared to deny China its rightful place as the number one power in Asia, and soon in the world, would have to face a different China that is fierce and bullying. The Mao-era tradition of 'cartographic aggression', wherein the PLA entered into a contested domain and then presented distorted maps claiming that specific area (where the troops had entered) had belonged to China or fell under China's sphere of influence since millennia,[55] was continuing under Xi. What was new was that China's toolbox and domain of expansionism had enlarged. It had accumulated huge financial reserves by attracting western financial capital as the 'factory of the world' and dumping predatory exports of manufactured goods across the world. Xi deployed these surpluses and excess capacity as part of his 'Chinese dream' of expanded global influence under the umbrella of the BRI. Through a cut-throat debt trap strategy, China found a commercial pathway to fulfilling its aim of gaining control over vital waterways, ports and outlets to the oceans.

But the military options were not discarded. The aggression in eastern Ladakh was a stark reminder that looking at China as a purely economic juggernaut that expands in a less threatening way through trade, aid and debt was missing the full picture. There was more than BRI and chequebook diplomacy to China's rise. The less civilized side of China, which people outside Asia and the Indo-Pacific often ignored or dismissed as something too remote to bother them, was growing under Xi's hardline authoritarian rule and found an outlet during the global coronavirus health crisis. As the crisis in eastern Ladakh peaked in later June 2020, the American scholar Taylor Fravel observed that 'the pandemic appears to have increased Beijing's sensitivity to questions of sovereignty, from Hong Kong and Taiwan to the East and South China Seas—and to the rugged Himalayan border with India', as 'Chinese officials worry that moderation and restraint might signal weakness both to domestic elites...and to foreign countries embroiled in disputes with China.'[56]

History is replete with examples of 'security dilemmas', where the defensive moves by one country are interpreted as offensive provocations by the other and an escalatory spiral leads to arms races, competitive build-ups and wars. But applying this concept to the Ladakh crisis of 2020 and questioning whether the Chinese read the 'Doval Doctrine' of 'defensive offence' as an imminent threat is to give credence and cover to the Chinese hegemonic intentions of dominating the LAC, and dictating terms to India from an overall position of superiority. Reducing everything to proactive or offensive Indian military doings under Modi misses out on Xi's 'bottom-line thinking', which the Chinese scholar Jianwei Wang explains as drawing up an 'expansive and explicit definition of China's national interest' and not hesitating to use military force to defend its ever-enlarging 'legitimate rights' and red lines. In Xi's 'calculated assertiveness', China's peaceful development is 'not unconditional and is contingent upon what other countries' behavior is, implying that there is a possibility for an unpeaceful rise if other countries pursue unpeaceful policies towards China'.[57]

A Brawl and a Pushback

The Modi government's initial response to the Chinese encroachments in eastern Ladakh was a characteristic dual approach—resist them by dispatching more Indian military units and divisions to the friction points close to the PLA positions and simultaneously start negotiations with the Chinese at the diplomatic as well as ground commander levels. On 3 June 2020, Defence Minister Rajnath Singh said, 'the Doklam dispute was resolved through diplomatic and military talks. We have found solutions to similar situations in the past as well. Talks at the military and diplomatic levels were on to resolve the current issue'.[58] At that stage, India was hopeful that the crisis would devolve into the old pattern of Chinese encroachments being countered by Indian deployments, and eventually, a diplomatic settlement restoring the status quo ante without resorting to military clashes.

Although two physical scuffles had broken out between the PLA and the Indian Army in early May at the friction points in Pangong Tso and in Naku La, Sikkim, in the eastern sector of the LAC, with several troops injured on both sides, they were resolved between the commanders on the ground in line with the Modi–Xi agreement at Wuhan for differences to be 'sorted out locally and not allowed to escalate'.[59] On 6 June, the corps commanders of China and India met on the Chinese side of the LAC and 'agreed to peacefully resolve the situation in the border areas in accordance with various bilateral agreements and keeping in view the agreement between the leaders that peace and tranquility in the India–China border regions is essential for the overall development of bilateral relations'.[60] But even as the Chinese engaged in meetings and uttered niceties, they were digging in their heels in the encroached areas of Ladakh and preparing to hold on to them at all costs.

On the intervening night of 15–16 June, an Indian Army patrol led by Colonel Santosh Babu challenged the PLA's rebuilding of a military post at a bend in the Galwan River, which the Chinese had previously agreed to dismantle. Arguments flared and a fist fight began, spilling over for five hours in multiple bouts as both sides sent reinforcements to engage in mortal hand-to-hand combat. In the darkness, at a mind-boggling altitude of 14,000 feet, bodies piled up and the long spell of relative peace at the LAC with no deaths was broken. The protocol of not using firearms was respected, but that was the saving grace. India announced that it had lost 20 men, including the commanding officer, making it the worst incident at the LAC since 1975. China admitted that it had also had suffered casualties, the first of its kind in all its browbeating ventures against Asian neighbours in several decades. American intercepts of Chinese communications suggested 35 Chinese troops had been killed and injured,[61] while Russian sources believed there had been 45 Chinese deaths.[62] An Australian newspaper, citing Chinese social media sources, concluded that 'at least 38 PLA troops were washed away and drowned that night'.[63] But since admitting the true extent of losses would amount to accepting that inferior India could inflict damage on the myth of a superhuman and indomitable PLA, China hid the actual numbers it lost on that fateful night, claiming that it was withholding the information 'with the aim of not irritating public opinion in the two countries, especially in India'.[64] It was also apparently 'very sensitive' and only Xi himself could 'approve' the figures.[65] Eight months later, with the crisis ebbing in one of the theatres and the PLA retreating from encroached portions of Pangong Tso, Beijing officially announced that it had lost only four men and one colonel-rank commander had been seriously injured.[66]

The violent Galwan Valley clash proved this was not a typical border dispute or a crisis that would quickly end. Even as S. Jaishankar called out China for its 'pre-meditated and planned action that was directly responsible for the resulting violence and casualties' and protested China's 'intent to change the facts on the ground in violation of all our agreements',[67] Beijing blamed India for transgressions and claimed that 'the sovereignty of the Galwan River Valley has always been ours'.[68] It was a classic instance of Chinese communist deceit and propaganda to conceal territorial aggrandizement. In commander-level talks with Indian counterparts, China had previously agreed that it would disengage and depart from Galwan. But the gap between what China had said and what it did on the ground was vast and was part of its time-tested ploy of keeping adversaries off-balance through opening new fronts.

As Mao, the founder of communist China and Xi's idol, held, 'creating misconceptions among the enemy and springing surprise attacks on him mean transferring the uncertainties of war to the enemy while securing the greatest possible certainty for ourselves and thereby gaining superiority'.[69] While the PLA's contemporary military doctrines were drastically different from those of Mao's guerrillas, the strategic culture of communist China remained the same because the underlying philosophy of 'historical materialism' (belief that the world goes by material power, i.e. economic and military force, rather than ideals or values) still guided Xi's foreign policy. China's playbook was to exert pressure on adversaries, use brute force in limited form where necessary, establish a fait accompli on the ground or waters through quick military thrusts, and then use historical revisionism to claim more and more territory. As a cover for this skulduggery, Xi incessantly promoted diplomatic concepts like 'harmonious world', 'win-win cooperation' for economic development, 'universal love and non-aggression', and 'a new type of international relations' based on 'jointly upholding the authority and sanctity of international law'.[70]

Lurking beneath the verbose shibboleths was a menacing power that wanted to be acknowledged as the greatest and which was inherently expansionist and perpetually dissatisfied with the status quo. Prior to the PLA's ingress into Galwan Valley in 2020, China had not asserted claims on it and India was under the impression that this particular inhospitable stretch in the Himalayas was not contested. What the PLA did in its savage assault with nail-studded rods and stones against Colonel Babu's party in Galwan was to show China's true colours—an uncompromising hegemon that sought to extract as much land and leverage to pressurize States like India which stand in the way of Chinese domination. States that were substantially weaker than China or did not resist Chinese supremacy were rewarded with a final resolution of territorial disputes. Communist China settled border disagreements with 17 countries since its inception in 1949, and in 15 out of these 17, it actually made concessions and gave up territory. But when it came to India, Bhutan (viewed by Chinese elites as an Indian proxy), Japan and Southeast Asian countries, China was unwilling to compromise on land or sea borders and was pressing forward with claims to apply geopolitical pressure during the pandemic.

For Modi, the Galwan incident showed that Xi was dropping all pretensions and acting in a far cruder and belligerent manner than before. Chinese force had to be met with proportionate counterforce. The alternative was subjugation. The Indian leader had to rally the country as it mourned the 20 martyrs of Galwan and also chalk out a multipronged strategy to push back the PLA intruders. His first briefing to other political parties after the Galwan violence stressed that 'sovereignty is most important' and assured that 'neither anyone has intruded into our territory nor taken over any post'.[71] This statement was misrepresented by opposition parties and critics in India as a sign of Modi covering up his failure to prevent multiple Chinese encroachments in Ladakh and surrendering to the PLA's diktats. Chinese propagandists and social media hawks pounced on the raucous Indian political debate to ironically ask why there was so much nationalist outpouring in India when Modi himself was saying that China had not occupied any Indian land.

A clarification emerged from the prime minister's office that what he meant was there was no Chinese presence at Galwan 'as a consequence of the bravery of our armed forces' and that the Indian Army had 'foiled the attempt of the Chinese side to erect structures and also cleared the attempted transgression at this point of the LAC on that day'.[72] Modi implicitly communicated that with the blood and sacrifice of India's soldiers, China had been repelled in Galwan, and that the same could be done unless the PLA retreated from all the friction points. Even as the political fracas in India about Modi's supposed kowtowing to China went overboard, much to the delight of China, he issued orders to beef up military presence at the friction points and modify the 'rules of engagement' that had previously prevented usage of firearms at the LAC. Defence Minister Rajnath Singh went on the offensive where public relations were concerned, to sound out Beijing and assure an anxious Indian public that 'the government has given "full freedom" to the local commanders to give a "befitting" response to any Chinese misadventure'.[73] Modi's vow that 'whenever the time has come, we have demonstrated our power, proving our capabilities in protecting the integrity and sovereignty of the country', was a clear signal that India would escalate in response to the Chinese aggression and not rest until restoring the LAC positions prior to April 2020.[74]

The crisis was Modi's most challenging and testing one. Unlike Pakistan, which could only cause injury through terrorist attacks or shelling at the LoC, China had the manpower and the border infrastructure to inflict casualties on Indian troops as well as invade Indian territory. The economic and military asymmetry in China's favour meant that war could never be a rational choice for India. Throughout this book, the reader has seen that Modi's crisis management preference is to save national honour and sovereignty through a mix of kinetic and diplomatic options below the threshold of war. Kautilya's advice to the weaker king could not have gotten a better canvas than this crisis: 'One should *neither submit spinelessly nor sacrifice oneself in foolhardy valour* [emphasis added]. It is better to adopt such policies as would enable one to survive and live to fight another day.'[75]

To repel a marauding imperialistic power like China, India had to show a spine of steel. The Modi government decided to go for 'mirror deployment' at the friction points, meaning India would have an equivalent or more troops with heavy artillery, tanks and missile defence systems in close proximity to the PLA. This meant 50,000 Indian troops, many at a proximity of just 300 metres from their Chinese counterparts.[76] It was the largest troop mobilization that India had managed in record time. When opposing armies are at such close quarters and are backed by reinforcements a few kilometres away in the 'depth areas', small incidents of shooting or confusing movements at one location could proliferate and engulf nations in all-out war. Until then, no country except the US had shown the will to match China man for man and weapon for weapon. India's demonstration of endurance and ability to handle the high-altitude environment in eastern Ladakh put some pressure back on China, whose forces lacked the experience of being posted to fight in such unforgiving Himalayan heights. Still, after losing PLA lives in Galwan, Xi could not afford to lose his nerve or face and maintained his hard line.

The crisis dragged on month after month with China not budging and India not relenting. Soon, it became a non-violent version of the trench warfare of World War I, where opposing armies dug themselves into nearly permanent trenches in the ground at close quarters and conducted attacks and counter-attacks from the relative safety of those fortified positions without any side gaining much territorially. In January 2021, as winter temperatures at the LAC hovered around -40°C, Indian Army Chief General Manoj Mukund Naravane cited the example of the 1986 Sumdorong Chu stand-off in the eastern sector of the LAC and vowed that India would do whatever it took to not yield in the long-drawn stand-off. He said, 'we will ensure that we reach a solution that is acceptable and not detrimental to our interests. If talks get prolonged, so be it. We are prepared to hold our ground'.[77] Staring down China indefinitely by sustaining weapons and supplies, with regular troop rotations in and out of the confrontation points to avoid fatalities from frost, was a superhuman logistical feat for India, especially as its border infrastructure was not as advanced as what the Chinese enjoyed on their side of the LAC.

But persistence was a key feature of the Modi government's response as it had to convince China that it could not outlast India and render its encroachments permanent. Even though the Indian economy was in a recessionary funk due to the pandemic, enormous additional sums were allocated to sustain the LAC mirror deployment come rain, hail or shine. If China had launched the aggression believing it had the upper hand as India was mired in the coronavirus pandemic and the related economic collapse, Modi once again put national security above everything else and committed resources beyond the annual defence budget to meet China with an unflinching and unflappable force posture. Lifting all caps on defence expenditure, India spent ₹20,776 crore (approximately US$2.86 billion) on 'emergency and unbudgeted defence expenses' in 2020 'as the armed forces went on a global hunt for equipment and stores to respond to the China challenge on the Ladakh border'.[78] Purchases from the US, Russia, France and Israel bolstered India's military hardware and showed China, which is barred from buying weapons from western countries, that there were limits to the asymmetry it enjoyed. For instance, when the French Rafale 4.5th generation combat aircraft arrived in India in July 2020, they were compared with China's premier J-20 5th generation jet in the patriotic Indian media and defence circles, and Beijing was notified that the superior French jets were going to be doing sorties in eastern Ladakh by scanning the airspace. Modi welcomed the Rafale jets with a tweet quoting a stirring Sanskrit verse:

> There is no greater blessing than protecting the nation, protecting the nation is a virtuous deed and protecting the nation is the best yagna (sacrifice). There is nothing beyond this.[79]

One of the unique attributes of Modi's responses to national security crises, which the reader would have noted in earlier chapters, is to harness the 'jointness' of the Indian military to present a unified front to the external adversary. In the Ladakh crisis, even though it was primarily a land-based conflict, the Modi government opted to deploy 'total combat potential' and got the IAF working in tandem with the Indian Army to move frontline fighter jets and surface-to-air missiles to forward air bases.[80] Air Chief Marshal R.K.S. Bhadauria publicly asserted during the crisis that deployment of offensive air power in Ladakh was 'strong posturing' that was 'instrumental in dissuading the adversary to a large extent.'[81]

The reader would recall from the Introduction that Modi's historic defence management reforms had created the office of the CDS by this time. The first CDS, the late General Bipin Rawat, coordinated with the three service chiefs and encouraged the much-desired formal coordination among the Indian Army, Navy and IAF during the Ladakh crisis. He got the three services to defer all peacetime activities and adopt supportive roles by redeploying to sharper China-centric missions. For instance, the Indian Navy was 'asked to focus on the Andaman and Nicobar Islands to monitor Chinese warship activity in the Indian Ocean rather than get concerned about PLA Navy deployments off the coast of Africa.'[82] Since China could shift the theatre of the conflict to the oceans to pile up additional pressure via the Arabian Sea or the Bay of Bengal, the Indian Navy adopted a 'forward posture' in the extended Indian Ocean region during the Ladakh crisis. It was reported that the Navy's proactive massing of assets 'ensured that three PLA Navy warships have taken to safe waters in Gulf of Aden, off the coast of Djibouti, and three other warships have exited through Malacca Straits to home base [sic].'[83] As mentioned earlier in this chapter, the Indian Navy had also paired up with the Quad group and had conducted the Malabar joint military exercises in November–December 2020 in the Bay of Bengal and the Arabian Sea thereby sending a loud message to China. The Indian Navy's MARCOS (marine commandos) were also notably deployed in the Pangong lake friction points alongside the Indian Army's PARA (Special Forces) and the IAF'S Garud force 'to enhance the integration of the three services' and to demonstrate combined power to China.[84]

Apart from the regular wings of the Indian military, the Modi government also brought to the fore the secretive Special Frontier Force (SFF), composed of Tibetan refugees living in India. The SFF was publicly recognized and honoured as being 'at the forefront part of operations against Chinese belligerence'.[85] A senior functionary of Modi's ruling BJP, Ram Madhav, attended the funeral of an SFF soldier who had died in Pangong Tso because of stepping on a landmine. His tweet paying tribute to the slain Tibetan warrior referred to 'the Indo-Tibetan border' rather than the India–China border. While it was deleted, an unmistakable volley went out to China that if it claimed Ladakh as Chinese territory and poached on it, then India could withdraw its seven-decade-old recognition of Tibet as a part of China and let loose Tibetan fighters itching to retake their China-occupied motherland.[86] Another bold step taken by India was to realign the offensive MSC, which are capable of carrying out transborder actions inside the adversary's terrain, from the Pakistan front to the western and eastern sectors of the LAC, with one division of a corps assigned even to the central sector of the LAC (least disputed with China) to strengthen offensive options 'in case of any protracted conflict with China'.[87] If China cited the pretext of Indian offensive posturing for its incursions into Ladakh, Modi's strategy was to keep China guessing that it might become a self-fulfilling prophecy.

Game Reversal

So aggravating and existentially threatening was the Chinese conduct during the Ladakh crisis that it gave the Modi government a rare window of opportunity to cross India's self-imposed limitations and taboos. Xi started the fight, assuming he could convert the pandemic's health and economic crises into a strategic opportunity. But Modi took the fight back to him through a daring mission code named 'Operation Snow Leopard', which proved to be a seminal blow to China's hegemonic designs. On the night of 28–29 August 2020, units of the MSC, the SFF and the Indian Army's PARA (Special Forces) undertook a stealthy offensive operation and occupied strategic heights on the south bank of the Pangong Tso. They also occupied Rechin La and Rezang La in the Kailash Range, overlooking the PLA's encroached positions on the lake's north bank and China's pivotal Moldo garrison. As per the Chinese versions of the map, some of these heights fell several kilometres inside China's claimed alignment of the LAC, i.e. in Aksai Chin. India officially did not insist that the heights were in Chinese-controlled territory and publicly held that the operation was to pre-empt the PLA from taking Indian territory on the south bank, but the fact that it was dubbed an offensive mission left no doubt that it was a tit-for-tat for the Chinese ingression on the north bank. NSA Doval, then CDS Rawat and the Army Chief Naravane had 'planned and managed' the mission with the objective of giving the Indian negotiating position 'a great boost'.[88] It was a 'counter-offensive' tactic by India, wherein mountain warfare specialists, tanks and armoured personnel carriers climbed up the heights and set up a sustainable supply line while bamboozling the Chinese with 'false flag manoeuvring' and 'unorthodox deployment' techniques that led their satellites and spotters astray.[89]

Modi's 'free hand' to the military had achieved noteworthy success. Operation Snow Leopard had been in the making since the start of the crisis because the Indian negotiators at the military and diplomatic levels had sensed that China would not retreat unless it suffered territorial setbacks, felt the pinch and was compelled. The mirror deployments blocked the path for China to intrude further at the LAC or launch a full-scale invasion, but they were in themselves insufficient to restore the status quo ante because Xi understood only one language—that of force and pressure rather than diplomatic goodwill. India 'initially waited for China to move back but when that did not happen...cleared the crucial operation' as a necessary bargaining chip to push the PLA back to its pre-April 2020 positions.[90] There was strategic patience at the outset when Modi dealt with the crisis but also a keen realization that diplomacy or defensive troop mobilization alone would not change the Chinese calculus. Mao's dictum that 'power flows from the barrel of a gun' continued to guide Xi's strategy and it was necessary to pay him back in his own coin. China, which was used to making the first move and establishing the fait accompli, did not expect India to apply counter-pressure like this.

Once India was in control of the Kailash Range and could not be dislodged despite gunshot warnings and threats by nearby PLA units, China began demanding, in commander-level talks, that India first vacate the occupied heights before proceeding with broader disengagement at the LAC. India could then lay down preconditions for it to vacate the heights and thus move the previously immovable PLA back. General Y.K. Joshi of the Indian Army's Northern Command revealed that 'after India's action on 29–30 August China was forced to bow down. After this, when the next round of talks took place, India had an upper hand.'[91] The first phase of the crisis had China calling the shots due to its surprise push at various friction points. But from September 2020 onward, the second phase was defined by India holding leverage and increasing Xi's unease which had started mounting since the Galwan Valley violence. After the game was reversed, a Modi government official said that 'unlike previous undetected attempts of incursions, this time, we have surprised China'.[92] The reader will recall from Chapter 2 that Modi had surprised Xi in the 2017 Doklam crisis as well and nullified the asymmetric power advantage that China had over India with tactical and diplomatic astuteness. According to Gordon Chang, a critic of the CCP, Xi's aggression in Ladakh 'unexpectedly flopped' because 'India's troops are displaying new-found boldness' and 'the failure to push around the Indian military means Xi's ability to intimidate anyone is much reduced'.[93] Modi's counter-offensive was not just defending India but also offering hope to Vietnam, Indonesia, the Philippines, Australia, Japan and Taiwan, all of which were eagerly watching how India was mobilizing to repel Chinese intrusions. For these regional powers which had been subjected to constant harassment and salami slicing by China, the Indian response in the Ladakh crisis offered lessons, and optimism. I remember being told by officers in the Vietnam Military Science Academy in late 2020 that 'we salute India's resistance and are studying the way it is taking on the might of China'.[94]

Apart from the military counter-offensive, Modi also opened an economic front against China that added to Xi's discomfiture in this crisis. His June 2020 'digital strike' of banning dozens of Chinese mobile phone apps, including China's first global social media sensation TikTok, deprived the company of no less than 300 million users in India and inflicted US$6 billion worth of losses.[95] The ban put China on notice that it cannot enjoy unfettered access to India's vast market and profit from it if the Chinese military continues its expansionist spree. Barriers to trade and investment were also brought into the picture. Chinese communist mouthpieces lamented that India's imports from China had fallen by 13 per cent in 2020, partly due to what they complained as 'rising "prejudicial attitude" from the Indian government toward China'.[96] India had leverage with China on trade. Indian exports to China were limited, and since India's GDP growth was not export-dependent, it was China that would hurt more from tariff and non-tariff barriers to its exports. A decline in Indian consumer welfare was possible in the event of a trade war with China, but the hit that China's economy would take from the loss of a big export market like India was comparatively more significant.

Earlier in mid-April 2020, as the Chinese incursions into Ladakh were beginning, the Modi government closed the 'automatic route' for FDI from China, citing the threat of 'opportunistic takeovers' of Indian companies in the context of the pandemic devastating them and leaving many vulnerable for easy foreign pickings.[97] In August 2020, India moved to push Chinese 5G network providers like Huawei out of its vast telecom market, another hit to Xi's ambition of global informational and commercial hegemony.[98] As an export-driven and capital-surplus economic machine, China's GDP rebound depended on the openness of global markets in the pandemic era. India's trade measures had the potential to compound China's goal of a sustained recovery from the coronavirus-induced slowdown. Economic strikes by India, the US and other prime destinations of Chinese goods and capital might have forced a rethink in Xi's policy advisory circles about the wisdom of forfeiting business for the sake of geopolitical pre-eminence. This reassessment came through during talks to de-escalate the Ladakh crisis between foreign ministers S. Jaishankar and Wang Yi, with the latter repeatedly insisting that the border dispute 'is not the whole of China–India relations, and it should be put at a proper place in the overall bilateral relations'.[99] The former's consistent rebuttal was that 'I can't have friction, coercion, intimidation, and bloodshed on the border, and then say let us have a good relationship in other domains. It's not realistic'.[100]

Once again, the Modi government's 'security first' motto and strategic use of India's power as a consumer demand paradise were on display. It peeved China no end because India was retaliating in many dimensions and refusing to take the LAC incursions lightly or trade them away for potential economic benefits from China. The problem for China was compounded by the spontaneous nationalistic angst across India as the PLA's LAC ingressions came to light. Even before the watershed Galwan Valley clash, the patriotic Confederation of All India Traders (CAIT) declared a mass boycott of thousands of Chinese products without any explicit prompt by the Indian government. They pledged to 'not only motivate traders not to sell Chinese goods but also urge Indian consumers to buy indigenous products in place of Chinese goods and in this way Prime Minister Narendra Modi's call "Vocal for Local" will also be fructified'.[101] Indian society was so profoundly galvanized by the Chinese threat and PLA brutality that opinion polls after the Galwan violence found that, '87 per cent of Indians want to boycott Chinese products for a year and a large majority also want Indian government to at least give a level playing field to products manufactured domestically'.[102] Eventually, this trend did not sustain as the crisis stopped making newspaper headlines and media attention shifted to other topics. Indian imports from China rose again in subsequent years, but the memory of the post-Galwan boycotts showed that India could retaliate in a variety of ways.

As the confrontation at the LAC was on, Modi raised

a clarion call for a 'self-reliant India' to respond to the vulnerabilities caused by the pandemic and excessive concentration of manufacturing abilities in China, which was handing it the authority to blackmail the rest of the world. This dovetailed with the Trump administration's diversification agenda to reduce American dependence on China for essential medical and other consumer goods. The LAC crisis was intersecting with the larger global coronavirus crisis, and the Modi government was alert to make the strategic linkages between the global inward-looking nationalistic turn, business concepts like 'supply chain resilience' and China's respect for India's territorial integrity.

Throughout the crisis in eastern Ladakh, China was aggrieved by the spirited wave of patriotism in Indian society and the news media, which suggested to Beijing that Modi could not compromise and that Indian citizens wholeheartedly and passionately backed him. Wang Yi even brought up the issue in talks with Doval, saying, 'we hope India can work with China to guide public opinion in the right direction.'[103] But since India had been the injured party that was trying to push China back from the encroached territory and which had publicly acknowledged the loss of 20 of its soldiers in the Galwan encounter, the anti-China sentiment was understandable and natural. For Chinese communists, who applied maximum censorship and thought control on the Chinese people, the way Indians came out on the streets and burnt effigies of Xi and stomped on Chinese flags was alien due to their undemocratic political culture.[104]

Modi did not outrightly whip up anti-China feelings, but he did play the essential role of the leader during a mammoth national security crisis by rallying the public to raise the morale of the Indian military and sternly remind China that it could not trample over India. The speech that Modi, dressed in military fatigues, delivered to an audience of Indian soldiers in the capital of Ladakh, Leh, on 3 July 2020, was a televised highlight of the crisis. It established beyond doubt India's strategic resolve to yield not even an inch to China:

> We have been paying a lot of attention to all the modern weapons for the armies or the equipment needed by you… the expenditure on border infrastructure has been almost tripled. This has also led to the development of border area and construction of roads and bridges along the border at a rapid pace…the era of colonial expansion is over… The whole world now has made up its mind against the policy of expansion.[105]

Modi's mention of the expedited border infrastructure enhancements and weapons acquisitions was intended to transmit clearly this message to China: whatever its grievances were in driving the LAC incursions, its wishes would not be complied with by India. Not since Indira Gandhi had an Indian leader taunted and rebuffed China like this. The unbending messaging also percolated down the Indian hierarchy. External Affairs Minister S. Jaishankar did some plain speaking to China as well when he warned, 'If you extend your hand, we will extend our hand but if you point a gun at us, we will do the same.'[106] Defence Minister Rajnath Singh, the man in charge of the Indian military pushback in Ladakh, was asked if India was still stuck in its old persona of a soft state in responding to Chinese aggression. He replied point-blank that, 'India will not tolerate anything that hurts its self-respect. Soft does not mean that anyone can attack our pride and we sit and watch silently. India will not compromise on its pride.'[107]

All this was not cheap talk to just play to the nationalist gallery or pacify a restive public in India. In October 2020, Modi inaugurated a new all-weather, year-round tunnel connecting

Manali to Leh which would reduce transport time by many hours for the Indian military to send reinforcements to eastern Ladakh. The event occurred even as bilateral negotiations on disengagement and de-escalation with China reached a deadlock, and both sides were testing each other's endurance and determination. His comments at the launch were directed at the external adversary:

> Security of the country is of prime importance for the Union government and the creation of border infrastructure is one of its top priorities...development of border infrastructure will not only benefit the common man but also help the military. Connectivity in border areas is directly related to security-related issues of the country.[108]

The 'Quad Plus' Counter

If China's military adventurism was aimed at rolling back India's border infrastructure growth, it would have to contend with the opposite outcome. And if China wanted to forcibly compel India to distance itself from the US, it would reap the obverse. Modi's response to Xi's massive incursions at the LAC included not only military and economic ripostes but also diplomatic retaliation that would raise the costs of Chinese aggression. Unlike the 2017 Doklam crisis, when Trump was indifferent to India and in a deal-making mood with China, the 2020 Ladakh crisis unfolded as the US was turning decisively and aggressively anti-China due to the pandemic, China's browbeating of Japan, Taiwan and rivals in the South China Sea, its crackdown on Hong Kong, Xinjiang and Tibet, and Trump's re-election politics. Before 2020, the 'new Cold War' was one out of three to four different pathways for China–US relations. But in a year mired with the COVID-19 pandemic, it became the defining feature each passing day, so much so that by July 2020, Beijing admitted that its ties with Washington were 'facing the most serious challenges since the establishment of diplomatic relations [in 1979]'.[109]

The Modi government was alert to the great power discord and not averse to utilizing it in a Realpolitik manner for India's national security. S. Jaishankar's strategic clarity that India should be 'advancing national interests by identifying and exploiting opportunities created by global contradictions', made sense after the Galwan clash.[110] As China's discarded decades-long restraint and violently pushed to attain tactical territorial advantages at the LAC, which was mirrored by similar bouts of aggression against other Asian neighbours with whom China had outstanding maritime disputes, Jaishankar's approach threw the old playbook of 'competition-cum-cooperation' out of the window. The new reality was that with a power-hungry totalitarian like Xi in command, conflict rather than coexistence with China would define the horizon for countries that were unwilling to accept its hegemony and 'bandwagon' under Chinese hegemony. New Delhi's old habit of 'hedging' between Beijing and Washington in the name of 'Nonalignment 2.0' and remaining equidistant between the two great powers was illogical when China was provoking and threatening India's sovereignty.

While the Ladakh stand-off was simmering, China's state-owned media issued formulaic warnings that India should avoid a 'trap' and steer clear of the US, to whom 'India is a pawn, even a cannon folder' that would be used and thrown away.[111] To rub it in for China, and raise the costs of its aggression at the LAC, Modi did the converse and opted for closer alignment with the US, particularly through deeper military interoperability. In October 2020, New Delhi and Washington fast-forwarded negotiations and signed the Basic Exchange and

Cooperation Agreement (BECA) for geo-spatial cooperation the last foundational agreement that brought the two sides close to be de facto allies. On that occasion, the visiting US Secretary of State Mike Pompeo and Secretary of Defense Mark Esper stood beside S. Jaishankar and Rajnath Singh, and delivered hard-hitting critiques of 'increasing aggression and destabilizing activities by China' and swore that 'the US would stand with the people of India to confront threats to their sovereignty'.[112] American surveillance gear, satellite footage and intelligence-sharing to monitor and track PLA movements along the LAC increased manifold during the Ladakh crisis, helping India plug gaps in its capabilities to read and interpret Chinese operational tactics and respond appropriately.[113]

India and the US recombined with Japan and Australia to make the 2020 Malabar naval exercises a potent deterrent signal to China in the maritime domain. In earlier periods, the value of the Quad used to be more like a tactical bargaining chip for India to convey to China that if it did not respect India's national security red lines, India could enter into an alliance-like formation to counterbalance China. Now, all that signalling business was over. It was obvious to India that China did not respect India's security and sensitivities. So, holding back on the fuller strategic blossoming of the Quad and hedging on operationalizing it was no longer sensible. India wanted more 'jointness' in the Quad without any qualms as a result of the Ladakh crisis. All four Quad members realized that the only way to have leverage over China at that stage was not to play nice and talk cooperation with it, but to show that expansionism would be met with a unified countervailing force.

Xi would have realized by the end of 2020 that China had brought it upon itself with its reckless militaristic threats and interventions. Instead of dividing the Quad and keeping its members limited to halfway measures, China unintentionally gave a new strategic fillip to the grouping. The future for the Quad lay not only in making Malabar-type joint naval activity more permanent and continuous, but also in conceiving non-military instruments to match China's BRI in the Indo-Pacific. Quad-financed infrastructure projects and economic connectivity missions in developing nations along the vast maritime rim of the Indo-Pacific would be effective alternatives to Chinese 'debt trap' diplomacy. By early 2021, with the advent of the more multilateral Joe Biden administration in Washington, the Quad even held its first heads of government summit and announced pooling of finances to beef up India's vaccine production capacities so that it could maintain its lead against China in the race to rid the world of COVID-19 and shape the post-pandemic international order.[114] Chinese state-owned media were so irked by the upgrading of the Quad from ministerial to summit that they openly charged India of carrying out a kind of strategic blackmail against China.'[115] Coming from a regime that routinely blackmails its adversaries and plays hard-nosed Realpolitik, it was a backhanded compliment to the biting proactiveness of Modi's foreign policy.

Even before the Ladakh crisis, Modi knew that the Quad would be a principal determinant of India's foreign policy destiny. Once the bloody Galwan clash occurred, he seemed to have made up his mind that China would not get any liberty to take Asia for granted. His 'new India' would show zero hesitation in making hard choices for national security. John Oneal wrote that foreign policy crises helped countries clarify their minds, review their national goals and policies, and remove doubt. He added, 'A sudden adverse development may be useful in overcoming the psychological conservatism and bureaucratic inertia which impede innovation.'[116] India, whose intelligentsia and bureaucracy had not been able to fully shed the past baggage of non-alignment and hedging despite Modi's proactive efforts since 2014, leapt out of that halfway house and went full hog toward a brave new horizon due to the crisis in Ladakh. Naysayers opposing a closer relationship with the US and a reactivated Quad were isolated and marginalized as the dread of the Chinese shadow lengthened over India. It was Xi's unwitting gift to unify India around a new consensus.

By overreaching and overdoing his aggression during the pandemic, Xi also managed the self-goal of unifying many countries around the shared threat of a menacing China. Conscious that India's strategy should not be confined to the US or the Quad alone, the Modi government reached out to the Europeans to invite them into the Indo-Pacific rubric. Germany announced a new 'Indo-Pacific strategy' in September 2020, France appointed a full-time ambassador to the Indo-Pacific in October, and the UK announced a new 'Indo-Pacific tilt' in December—all upon India's urging and convincing.

Even Russia, which refused to adopt the term 'Indo-Pacific' out of deference to China, was courted by the Modi government to revive its naval presence in Asia as a subtle counter to Chinese plans to monopolize the maritime waters of the continent. Rajnath Singh's visit to Moscow days after the Galwan clash and his statement that 'ongoing contracts will be maintained and not just maintained, in a number of cases will be taken forward in a shorter time,' were reassuring to India amid the LAC crisis.[117] While Russia could not openly oppose China due to their shared animus toward the West, multibillion-dollar deals for more hi-tech weaponry from Russia to India and timely delivery of Russian spare parts for Indian fighter jets, tanks and submarines to counter China at the LAC did not go unnoticed in Beijing. Modi was signalling Xi in no uncertain terms that India had a lot of powerful allies.

India also courted an array of Asian middle power partners who, while being economically dependent on China, detested Chinese territorial expansionism and bullying. Their survival as sovereign states was in peril due to Xi's drive for maximizing Chinese power. For these regional actors, whether or not the US found the will to deter China, a 'soft balancing' coalition of countries within Asia that could draw red lines for China and diversify partnership options beyond China was a necessity. In the past, India had demurred from initiating any anti-China bloc so as not to draw Chinese ire. But after the Ladakh crisis, the onus fell on it to take the bull by the horns, skilfully convince partners and forge a loose 'minilateral' grouping. Fearless regional leadership, which was ready to absorb Chinese anger and aggregate the interests of ASEAN and Pacific Island nations, was much needed. Modi appeared to grasp this requirement and momentum during the Ladakh crisis, although much work remained to be done to forge a genuine balance of power in Asia. China's entrenchment as the go-to economic power for every Asian country and its Machiavellian carrot-and-stick policies meant that this was a task for the long haul.

One Step Backward

Thanks to the multidimensional counterbalancing pressures that Modi exerted on Xi, China implemented complete disengagement and de-escalation of the PLA from the north bank of Pangong Tso in February 2021. Notably, China had agreed, in principle, to disengage from the frictions points as early as June 2020 after the Galwan clash, but since Xi wanted to test India's fortitude and forbearance and believed that China had the advantage to press home, the actual drawdown was postponed many times throughout the year due to Beijing's foot-dragging and expectation that New Delhi would throw in the towel and cave in at some point. India kept asking but ran into a brick wall. On 27 August 2020, India reminded China that it must walk the talk and 'implement agreed actions', but to no avail.[118]

Once the Indian special forces hoisted China by its own petard through Operation Snow Leopard, the scales were upturned and China was no longer sitting pretty to dictate the outcome of the crisis. But even then, for Xi to pull back the PLA immediately after India's counter-offensive would have been to acknowledge a loss of prestige and a setback to his ego and his projection of China as an unassailable superpower. So, China continued the charade of holding back on withdrawing while its propaganda outlets bellowed threats that 'if India wants to engage in competition, China has more tools and capability than India' and that 'if India would like a military showdown, the PLA is bound to make the Indian army suffer much more severe losses than it did in 1962'.[119] As it dawned on Xi that the PLA could not cause further damage to India or occupy additional disputed stretches along the LAC, and with more frost casualties occurring to the PLA in the harsh Himalayan winter, he would have decided that withdrawal from some frictions points was inevitable but delayed it simply to prove to the world that China cannot be pressured by anyone.

The outcome of the US presidential election in November 2020 may have also played a part in prolonging the LAC crisis. When Biden won, Chinese strategists let out a sigh of relief that he would be the proverbial known devil with a mainstream approach and China would get time to anticipate and dodge his foreign policy. A reset in relations or at least a diplomatic thaw under a Biden presidency may have been wishful thinking, but Beijing was not off the mark in believing that the seasoned Biden would be 'smoother' and less volatile than Trump.[120] Biden's steady hand and rules-based foreign policy approach, and his line that China must be made to 'play by the international rules' sounded softer than Trump's trade war, technology war and the 'China virus' tirade. Beijing reckoned it could easily handle the staple liberal foreign policy that staged a comeback with Biden's win.

Chinese elites prized certainty in international relations, something that Trump denied them either by design or due to his fickle electoral calculations. The Biden administration, representing liberal and career bureaucratic interests, was expected to give China breathing room to recalibrate its own posture toward the US and the rest of the world. The strategic calculation was that if Biden moderated the 'new Cold War', China would have to worry less about being attacked by the US over Taiwan or the South China Sea and could concentrate all its military on intimidating and extracting concessions from neighbours like India. Come early February 2021, when the Biden administration hit the ground running and quickly took aim at China, warning it of 'extreme competition', criticizing its human rights violations and ramping up multilateral coalition-building with China's Asian rivals, the die was cast.[121] China could not count on getting a breather from the US on its eastern seaboard and have a free hand to ride roughshod over India and other adversaries in the Indo-Pacific.

The Indian journalist Indrani Bagchi noted perceptively that the PLA's withdrawal from occupied tracts in Pangong Tso had to do with India's resolve and pluck but also the global US context.

> A more accommodative stance of China by the new US administration may have impelled the Chinese to keep the stand-off going on. But it's clear now that Biden will take an equally tough approach to China. That may have tilted the balance for Beijing to finally settle this particular border confrontation.[122]

While the crisis did not end with the PLA's pullback from Pangong Tso alone, the sight of Chinese forces dismantling tents, bunkers, helipads and other structures erected in April 2020 and soldiers boarding trucks and tanks receding by 'more than 100 kilometres in a span of merely eight hours' was something to behold.[123] At one point, it was feared that China would never retreat unless forced otherwise by war. Modi had achieved the objective of restoring the April 2020 status quo ante in Galwan and Pangong Tso without having to go as far as war because the counter-offensive operations gave India leverage. Indian forces did vacate the Kailash Range as a reciprocal action for the PLA stepping back from the north bank of Pangong Tso, drawing critiques from maximalist security hawks and opposition politicians that Modi should not have given up the strategic heights until the PLA withdrew from all the friction points.

But these arguments are unfair. It was not a minor accomplishment to restore no man's land in Pangong Tso and also recreate a distancing buffer between the two militaries. When the crisis was at its peak, many fretted that the LAC was 'LOCized' or 'Siachenized', which implied that the Indian forces would have no option but to permanently show presence right at the border to avoid further encroachments by the Chinese.[124] Sustaining buffers and getting the Chinese to respect them are challenging but necessary for India's security. Secondly, Army Chief Naravane's pointed remark that 'we have our strategies in place to resolve some issues that remain' was an unqualified assertion that India had more offensive counter-attack options to force China back elsewhere if diplomacy did not yield desired results. He added that 'China has been in the habit of creeping power' and 'what we have achieved is to show that this strategy will not work with us. And every move will be met resolutely'.[125] The Indian Army also conveyed that while its stance of 'punitive deterrence' was to punish inferior Pakistan with 'overwhelmingly higher military power', its new approach to handle the superior adversary China was of 'credible deterrence'. This meant that the 'the opposite side should know that India has the ability for a counter operation and to inflict damage', and China had to realize that 'India won't [sic] budge and can actually hit back'.[126] China's decision to disengage from another LAC friction point, Gogra, in August 2021, was another positive development owing to this credible Indian deterrence.

Xi's strategy to humiliate India when it was in the throes of the COVID-19 crisis did not quite work out as he had intended. Modi once again put the brakes on Chinese expansionism. Jonathan Roberts has listed two schools of thought on successful crisis management. According to the first, the objective is to make the adversary back down, gain concessions and further one's ambitions. The second view is that the objective is to avoid war, control the situation and dampen down the conflict as the alternative to a settlement is catastrophic if both parties are nuclear-armed. Roberts concludes that 'good crisis management strikes a balance between the two concerns; it is an effort to coerce prudently, or accommodate cheaply (or a combination of both)'.[127] The Modi government has found the middle path between coercion and accommodation so that China's asymmetry is negated.

Given the kind of insatiable quest for power that China has acquired under Xi, India is bound to face more crises with it in the future. The 2021 Global Trends report of the US National Intelligence Council warned that 'India and China may slip into a conflict that neither government intends, especially if military forces escalate a conflict quickly to challenge each other on a critical part of the contested border'.[128] In the neo-Maoist worldview of Xi, China may occasionally take one step back but has to stay two steps forward regionally. China's adversaries may find it making tactical pauses now and then but cannot bet on a complete stop. As the global geopolitical scenario evolves, if Xi again construes the US and its alliance system as weak or paralysed, PLA hordes will stir up trouble for India in some sector or the other of the LAC or the Indo-Pacific. The Modi effect on national security is that India is better prepared to thwart them.

Epilogue
Operation Nation

We are all citizens of a brave country and we should also be 'parakrami' (valiant). A parakrami never thinks that he or she has done enough, should now rest. As a parakrami we have to work hard and take the country to even greater heights. India will fight, live, work and win as one and nobody can create hurdles in its march towards development. Our country will grow with new 'niti' (policies) and 'riti' (methods). We have full faith in our (military) forces.[1]

—Prime Minister Narendra Modi, 28 February 2019

What is common among Operation X, Operation Juniper, Operation Bandar and Operation Snow Leopard? They are signposts in the evolution of a new strategic culture in India. From an era when politicians were coy about using military force or even considering the military as an essential instrument of foreign policy, Modi has brought India a long way. He has led responses to national security crises audaciously and skilfully, ensuring that India overcomes the tag of a soft state mired in self-doubt and trapped in a defeatist culture of strategic restraint. As India's de facto commander-in-chief (the president of the republic is the nominal head of state and the de jure commander) during critical national security crises, Modi proved that leadership is a distinguishing factor in determining how a country tackles persistent threats to the lives of its citizens and to its borders from external adversaries. Counterfactually, had Modi not become the prime minister, it is difficult to imagine India responding as robustly and tactfully to China and Pakistan as it has done since 2014.

Throughout this book, I have elaborated on the trademark principles and methods that Modi has adopted in responding to crises and the reformative mindset with which he has pursued the structural transformation of India's national security apparatus. First, Modi has defied set precedents of how earlier political leaders handled crises. He has looked to do something different and unique to save national honour and surprise foreign adversaries. Under Modi, there have been numerous operational innovations during actual crisis episodes and institutional alterations in the relatively peaceful periods. This book has elucidated how they startled India's two hostile neighbours and remade India's image in the world as a tough nut to crack. I spoke to General B.K. Sharma, a retired Indian Army officer and part of a think-tank, about the paradigmatic shifts under Modi:

> I was a commander at the LAC in the past and we used to be told to be very cautious with China. There was a thing that we should not provoke them, things should not escalate to war, 'if and what' kind of scary scenarios. From 2014, we made a high gear shift from strategic restraint to strategic assertion. The dynamism came from Modi's leadership which told the military, 'You do it, and I will take political ownership for your action.' Modi has revived our offensive capabilities which are in a state of

recoil but can be quickly unleashed into enemy territory so that tomorrow, when there are negotiations with the Chinese, they will be on the basis of parity. We are now on the lookout for Chinese vulnerabilities where we can embarrass them. With [the] passage of time, China may forgo the option of changing the status quo on the LAC through force because India is building permanent capacities to show them counter-force.[2]

Second, when confronted with a crisis, Modi does not allow himself to be bogged down in contortions about how the rest of the world might perceive India if it took strong retaliatory postures toward its opponents. He knows the importance of getting the world on India's side and frames his responses in crisis situations so that the international community applauds India no matter how it deals with China or Pakistan. As shown in every chapter of this book, Modi converted international constraints into international assets through smart diplomacy and alacritous exploitation of alignments and alliance patterns. Self-awareness of India as a 'leading power' and wanting to consciously behave like a great power in the making explains this fearless attitude.

According to the American scholar Michael Mandelbaum, strong States have an inherent tendency to expand and 'exert influence on foreigners'. On the other hand, a weak State has to strike a 'balance between security and independence', meaning it has to hitch its wagon to a superior power for protection from a menacing adversary. A middle power that is neither very strong nor weak but is ambitious is better off pursuing a strategy of making itself stronger and responding firmly even if it is seen as provocative by the world, because it is 'better to err on the side of being too powerful than not being powerful enough'.[3] Modi instinctively follows the rising middle power template. I talked to Air Vice Marshal Arjun Subramaniam, a former IAF officer and military historian, about why Modi is not afraid of what the world might say or how it would react when it comes to defending India, and how he has inverted the previously feared costs of upsetting this country or that:

> When I was a serving officer, I used to always feel that India's strategic culture was excessively diffident, there was too much of an aura around 'responsibility and restraint', there was a typical desire to be appreciated by the world for being restrained. What we had not understood then was that in the broader comity of nations, it is strength and power that earns you respect. Particularly with China and Pakistan, strength has to be the principal currency. Modi has recognized that. He understands coercion and wants to demonstrate strength responsibly.[4]

Third, when security crises befall the nation, Modi utilizes them to reinforce India's identity as Bharat, an ancient civilization with a proud history of martial traditions, warfighting and jostling for power that had been erased from the country's memory due to the stultifying effects of centuries of colonialism and mental subjugation. There are direct correlations between the onset of India's reputation as a 'soft state', the projection of its freedom struggle as mostly non-violent, and the mythology of Indian people and society as soft and tolerant to foreign invaders and conquerors since millennia.[5] Emperor Ashoka (who renounced war and violence) and Mahatma Gandhi were overemphasized by post-Independence leaders as representing the quintessential age-old pacifist ethos of the country, while the power politics from the Mahabharata and writings of Kautilya, Kamandaka and Shukracharya were relegated to the realm of defence intellectuals. General A.K. Singh and Brigadier Narender Kumar, two Indian Army veterans, have faulted past Indian political leaders and diplomats for failing to understand the 'nuances of employment of military power in pursuance of national interests', and for remaining impervious to the reality that 'hard power occupies the pole position in statecraft'.[6]

Modi is responsible for normalizing power politics in Indian foreign policy and making it palatable and likeable among ordinary Indian people. From 2014, he started a new tradition of the prime minister visiting Indian military camps across different border areas of the country on the festival of Diwali. This served to remind the nation about the fiercer side of Bharat, which continues to seek peace, but if provoked by foreign adversaries will punch back in the finest traditions of ancient India, where counter-attack and strategic surprise were very much part of the idiom of governance and rulership. During the November 2020 Diwali celebration, as the Ladakh crisis had gripped the country, Modi was with the Indian soldiers in Jaisalmer near the international border with Pakistan. His speech on that occasion is worth quoting to explain how the cultural reinvention of a valorous Bharat is now being mainstreamed:

> I have not come here alone. I have also brought with me the love, affection and blessings that the country has for you (armed forces)... [T]he country is watching you, the sons and the daughters of Ma Bharati [mother India] who bring glory to my country... As long as you are there, the country will continue to light up like this on Diwali.[7]

If India's responses to national security crises are credible and honourable today, it is because Modi has woven a tapestry in which individual political leadership, its mass base in society and patriotic mobilization through cultural nationalism are welded together and form the foundation for the Indian state's readiness and proactiveness to fight back against foreign aggression. S. Jaishankar, the diplomatic articulator of Modi's vision during the crises narrated in this book, has also made a passionate plea for Indians to regain their 'intuitive feel' for forging and maintaining balances of power by harking back to Kautilya's realism and the cold-blooded manoeuvrings of the Mahabharata epic.[8] Bharat, as opposed to the modern construct of India, had the gene for hard power, and military operations were core ingredients in its statecraft. Reincarnating that part of India's heritage is a lasting contribution of Modi, whose torch will have to be carried forward by future leaders in the eternal quest for a secure nation.

Acknowledgements

The genesis of this work came just after my 2016 book, *Modi Doctrine: The Foreign Policy of India's Prime Minister,* was published. Dr Jitendra Singh, the minister of state in the prime minister's office, read my previous book with interest. At the launch event, he commented that I should write a sequel focused on the surgical strikes that India had carried out inside Pakistani territory, which had occurred just after my previous book had gone to print.

Subsequently, as the Modi government handled India's two perennial antagonists—China and Pakistan—in a series of nerve-wracking crises, I realized that something noteworthy was happening—India was changing in the way it handled provocations and threats to its national security.

The transformation was not limited to the usage of proportionate military force against foreign aggressors. It went deeper—to the very identity of India as a nation state. The more I heard Modi and his core national security and foreign policy teams articulate the idea of India as Bharat, which has an ancient tradition of statecraft and raison d'état, it was evident that a fundamental shift was underway in how India approached adversaries. The Modi effect had moved not just India's state elites but also Indian society in a different direction, one that shed past inhibitions and began to expect nationalistic self-assertion against external aggressors.

This book uses four case studies of seminal national security crisis episodes during Modi's first two prime ministerial terms to illustrate this metamorphosis. From immediate crisis response to structural reforms in the defence and security apparatus, India has come a long way since 2014. It has shed the ignominious tag of a 'soft state' and is headed to a braver organic horizon where its strategic culture matches its social values and civilizational ethos.

For writing this book, I had the distinct privilege of interviewing leading practitioners and thinkers of India's national security. The original insights I gained about multiple dimensions of the Modi impact from former Deputy National Security Advisor Arvind Gupta, Air Marshal (retd) Anil Chopra, Air Vice Marshal (retd) Arjun Subramaniam, Major General (retd) B.K. Sharma and Major General (retd) Dhruv Katoch added immense value. I remain indebted to these doyens of India's security establishment.

My special thanks also go to Lieutenant General (retd) Syed Ata Hasnain, who has written an apt curtain-raiser to the book. To get a foreword penned by a respected senior officer and noted analyst of defence and national security issues is a great honour.

This publication could not have seen the light of day without diligent spadework by a team of talented young researchers at the Jindal School of International Affairs of O.P. Jindal Global University. The assistance of Aakanksha Nehra, Megha Gupta and Mohan Sakthivel in unearthing quotes and statistics, doing summaries of publications and organizing background materials for me to write chapter after chapter was exemplary. I owe them immensely for their hard and laborious efforts in a time-sensitive context.

It happens to be my first collaboration with Rupa Publications, and I must commend its editorial and marketing teams for enabling a quality product to reach readers. Senior Commissioning Editor Yamini Chowdhury's eye for high calibre writing and her patient engagement with me at various stages of the manuscript deserve the highest praise. I wish every publishing house has someone of her capabilities. Thank you also to C. Sandhya, Rupa's developmental editor, who polished the manuscript and offered constructive suggestions to make it reader-friendly. If there are still errors in this book after her diligent interventions, they are entirely my faults.

I have often been asked what explains the prolific scale and scope of my publications. The answer has less to do with my intellectual fertility or diligent habits and more to do with a rock-solid family that has stood by me as a stabilizing sheet anchor. My wife, Usha Damerla, saw a writer in me when I was a teenager in the early 1990s. She has held me by the hand to reach the present juncture with the same infinite love as in those budding years. I hope to write many more books with her assuring presence right beside me.

My two children, Ahaana Kranti and Debarchan Vishnu have grown up missing me due to my relentless writing and media pursuits. I have to thank these innocent minds for letting me be this way and I undertake to somehow make up for my absences with them.

My parents, Chandrakala Chaulia and Prafulla Kumar Chaulia are the longest influences on me as a person and author. My mother's early introduction of classic books to me and my father's decades-long dialogue with me about current international affairs are the building blocks of my passion for reading and writing. I am a proud recipient of their unending gifts.

At O.P. Jindal Global University, I have enjoyed the luxury of a capable support team of faculty colleagues and non-teaching staff to handle responsibilities. Special mentions are due to my manager Lalit Kumar for being a superhuman man Friday. The professionalism of my school administrators, Swarnima Singh and Tanu Singh, has been a reassuring plus.

Above all, the limitless encouragement and backing I have received from our vice chancellor, C. Raj Kumar, has shaped my journey as an author. He believed in me when I was at a formative stage in life and has advised and mentored me at crucial junctures. A massive thanks to him is going to be inadequate.

This book is for readers who care about India's national security and aspire for India's rise as a Great Power in the world. The Bharat I am invoking and egging on in the previous pages can only emerge fully if the dream of Prime Minister Narendra Modi is carried forward by nationalistic Indians and legions of India's well-wishers in the international community. My sincere hope is that this book helps mobilize constituencies to see 'new India' in a new light and dedicate themselves to institutionalizing the epic changes Modi has ushered in.

Notes

Foreword

1. Malay Mishra, 'Kautilya's *Arthashastra*: Restoring its Rightful Place in the Field of International Relations', *Journal of Defence Studies*, Vol. 10, No. 2, 2016, p. 83, http://idsa.in/jds/jds_10_2_2016_kautilya-s-arthashastra. Accessed on 15 January 2022.

Introduction

1. Elizabeth Roche, 'Modi Says India Fighting Twin Challenges of Terrorism and Expansionism', *Mint*, 15 August 2020, https://bit.ly/3GFBZrH. Accessed on 3 November 2021.
2. ET, 'Mumbai Attack Shows New Sophisticated Face of Terror: Analysts', *The Economic Times*, 28 November 2008, https://bit.ly/3mF0P31. Accessed on 3 November 2021.
3. Andrew Buncombe and Omar Waraich, 'Mumbai Siege: "Kill All the Hostages, Except the Two Muslims"', *The Independent*, 8 January 2009, https://bit.ly/3GGjOSH. Accessed on 3 November 2021.
4. HT Correspondent in New York, 'Spy Agencies' Failure Resulted in 26/11 Mumbai Attacks: Report', *Hindustan Times*, 23 December 2014, https://bit.ly/3CLoq7C. Accessed on 3 November 2021.
5. Aman Sharma, 'Government Had Intelligence Inputs on 26/11 Mumbai Attacks, Says Former NSA MK Narayanan', *The Economic Times*, 21 January 2014, https://bit.ly/2ZUbM7Z. Accessed on 3 November 2021

6.   Sandeep Unnithan, *Black Tornado: The Three Sieges of Mumbai 26/11*, HarperCollins, New Delhi, 2014.

7.   Cathy Scott-Clark and Adrian Levy, *The Siege: The Attack on the Taj*, Penguin, New Delhi, 2013, p. 286.

8.   EFSAS, 'Pakistan Army and Terrorism; An Unholy Alliance', European Foundation for South Asian Studies, August 2017, https://bit.ly/3KPxZqq. Accessed on 28 January 2022.

9.   Stephen Tankel, *Storming the World Stage: The Story of Lashkar-e-Taiba*, Hurst, London, 2011, pp. 228–232.

10. Cited in Anthony Wanis-St. John, 'The National Security Council: Tool of Presidential Crisis Management', *Journal of Public and International Affairs*, Vol. 9, No. 1, 1998, p. 103, https://bit.ly/3rH7dYC. Accessed on 17 January 2022.

11. Jonathan M. Roberts, *Decision-Making during International Crises*, Macmillan, London, 1988, pp. 2, 37, 77, 81.

12. Sam Sarkesian, John Allen Williams and Stephen Cimbala, *US National Security: Policymakers, Processes, and Politics*, Lynne Rienner Publishers, Boulder, 1995, p. 4.

13. Ishaan Tharoor, 'A Rally in Mumbai: "Remember 26-11!"', *Time*, 3 December 2008, https://bit.ly/3GVMzei. Accessed on 3 November 2021.

14. IANS, 'Patil Quits Over Mumbai Terror, Chidambaram Gets Home Ministry', *India Today*, 30 November 2008, https://bit.ly/3GKgW7k. Accessed on 3 November 2021.

15. Ashley Tellis, 'Lessons from Mumbai', Committee on Homeland Security and Government Affairs, United States Senate, 28 January 2009, pp. 91–95, https://fas.org/irp/congress/2009_hr/mumbai.pdf. Accessed on 17 January 2022.

16. 'US Embassy Cables: India "Unlikely" to Deploy Cold Start Against Pakistan', *The Guardian*, 30 November 2010, https://bit.ly/305YFkc. Accessed on 8 November 2021.

17. Ibid.

18. Ibid.

19. Ibid.

20. Bruce Riedel, 'The Mumbai Massacre and Its Implications for

America and South Asia', *Journal of International Affairs*, Vol. 63, No. 1, 2009, p. 111, http://www.jstor.org/stable/24384175. Accessed on 17 January 2022.

21. Maroof Raza, '26/11 Attacks were India's 9/11 Moment', Times Now, 26 November 2020, https://bit.ly/3H3CLib. Accessed on 8 November 2021.

22. Srinivas Laxman, 'Govt. Rejected IAF Proposal to Strike Pakistan After 26/11: BS Dhanoa', *The Times of India*, 28 December 2019, https://bit.ly/3BVO8Fl. Accessed on 8 November 2021.

23. Jonathan M. Roberts, *Decision-Making during International Crises*, Macmillan, London, 1988, p. 170.

24. Jonathan W. Keller, 'Constraint Respecters, Constraint Challengers, and Crisis Decision Making in Democracies: A Case Study Analysis of Kennedy Versus Reagan', *Political Psychology*, Vol. 26, No. 6, 2005, pp. 835–843, https://doi.org/10.1111/j.1467-9221.2005.00447.x. Accessed on 17 January 2022.

25. Ibid.

26. Ibid.

27. Margaret Hermann, 'Explaining Foreign Policy Behavior Using the Personal Characteristics of Political Leaders', *International Studies Quarterly*, Vol. 24, No. 1, 1980, p. 12, https://doi.org/10.2307/2600126. Accessed on 17 January 2022.

28. Cited in Jonathan M. Roberts, *Decision-Making during International Crises*, Macmillan, London, 1988, p. 259.

29. John Oneal, *Foreign Policy Making in Times of Crisis*, Ohio State University Press, Columbus, 1982, pp. 54–55, 162.

30. Keren Yarhi-Milo, *Knowing the Adversary: Leaders, Intelligence, and Assessment of Intentions in International Relations*, Princeton University Press, Princeton, 2014, pp. 3–4.

31. Cited in Thomas Brewer, *American Foreign Policy: A Contemporary Introduction*, Prentice Hall, Hoboken, 1992, p. 151.

32. Shivshankar Menon, *Choices: Inside the Making of India's Foreign Policy*, Penguin, New Delhi, 2016, pp. 92–98.

33. Polly Nayak and Michael Krepon, 'The Unfinished Crisis: US Crisis Management after the 2008 Mumbai Attacks', The Henry L. Stimson

Center, 13 February 2012, https://bit.ly/3o8gcjR. Accessed on 8 November 2021.

34. ET Bureau, '10% Won't Do, Give 100%: Rice to Zardari Govt.', *The Economic Times*, 2 December 2008, https://bit.ly/3O1RNE2. Accessed on 8 November 2021.

35. PTI, 'Rice Lowers Pitch, Says US Believes Pak's Commitment', *The Indian Express*, 5 December 2008, https://bit.ly/3n1au49. Accessed on 8 November 2021.

36. Declan Walsh, 'WikiLeaks Cables: Britain 'Over-Reacted' in Wake of Mumbai Attacks', *The Guardian*, 1 December 2010, https://bit.ly/3O8z5ey. Accessed on 8 November 2021.

37. AFP, 'US Unveils Plans to Make India 'Major World Power', *Space War*, 26 March 2005, https://bit.ly/32J6cXK. Accessed on 28 January 2022.

38. Newswire, 'US a Factor for India to Vote against Iran at IAEA: Saran', *Outlook*, 21 March 2011, https://bit.ly/3bO66iv. Accessed on 8 November 2021.

39. Polly Nayak and Michael Krepon, 'The Unfinished Crisis: US Crisis Management after the 2008 Mumbai Attacks', The Henry L. Stimson Center, 13 February 2012, p. 29, https://bit.ly/3o8gcjR. Accessed on 8 November 2021.

40. PTI, 'India Asks US, China, Saudi Arabia to Put Pressure on Pak', India Today, 26 December 2008, https://bit.ly/3CQd56h. Accessed on 8 November 2021

41. Rashmi Saksena, 'Truth about SIMI: Hizb Ally, ISI Stooge', *Hindustan Times*, 15 July 2006, https://bit.ly/3JiFg0B. Accessed on 8 February 2022.

42. PTI, 'ISI Closely Connected with Indian Mujahideen Operatives: NIA', *The Hindu*, 2 October 2014, https://bit.ly/3LvI3p8. Accessed on 8 February 2022.

43. Amit Pandya, 'Muslim Indians: Struggle for Inclusion', The Henry L. Stimson Center, 2010, p. xiii, https://bit.ly/3qhyfqk. Accessed on 8 November 2021.

44. P.R. Kumaraswamy, 'The Muslim Factor in India's Foreign Policy', *The Japan Times*, 30 July 2008, https://bit.ly/3BUnkVX/.

Accessed on 8 November 2021.

45. Sanjaya Baru, *The Accidental Prime Minister: The Making and Unmaking of Manmohan Singh*, Penguin, New Delhi, 2014, p. 174.

46. PTI, 'Antulay Raises Doubts Over Karkare's Killing', *The Economic Times*, 17 December 2008, https://bit.ly/3mUnatf. Accessed on 8 November 2021

47. 'US embassy cables: Mumbai conspiracy allegations "outrageous"— US ambassador', The Guardian, 23 December 2008, https://bit.ly/3bRjbHI. Accessed on 8 November 2021.

48. Barack Obama, *A Promised Land*, New York, Viking, 2018, pp. 599–600.

49. Sandeep Unnithan, 'Why India Didn't Strike Pakistan after 26/11', *India Today*, 14 October 2015, https://bit.ly/3obOjYl. Accessed on 8 November 2021.

50. Daniel Markey, 'Terrorism and Indo–Pakistani Escalation', Council on Foreign Relations, January 2010, p. 2, https://bit.ly/303s8uF. Accessed on 8 November 2021.

51. PTI, 'Modi Blames Pakistan for Mumbai Terror Attack', *The Economic Times*, 28 November 2008, https://bit.ly/3057TwE. Accessed on 8 November 2021.

52. HT Correspondent, 'UPA Govt has Failed to Respond to 26/11: Modi', *Hindustan Times*, 22 February 2009, https://bit.ly/3wxarzZ. Accessed on 8 November 2021.

53. PTI, 'Stand-Off Continues: Chinese Choppers Airdrop Food for PLA in Chumar Area', *India Today*, 19 September 2014, https://bit.ly/3opViNt. Accessed on 8 November 2021.

54. DN, 'India Destroyed Bunkers in Chumar to Resolve Ladakh Row', *Defence News*, 8 May 2013, https://bit.ly/3BUtKEk. Accessed on 8 November 2021.

55. Bharti Jain, 'India to Give Up Chumar Post for Chinese Withdrawal?' *The Times of India*, 7 May 2013, https://bit.ly/309Fru0. Accessed on 9 November 2021.

56. PTI, 'Space for Both China and India to Grow', *The Hindu*, 16 December 2010, https://bit.ly/3D5BkxC. Accessed on 9 November 2021.

57. PTI, '"Chindia" Still Vibrant Idea: Jairam Ramesh', *The Economic Times*, 27 March 2014, https://bit.ly/3D35fpZ. Accessed on 9 November 2021.

58. Indrani Bagchi and Rajat Pandit, 'Ladakh Stand-Off Ends as China Agrees to Pull Out Troops', *The Times of India*, 6 May 2013, https://bit.ly/3BW476k. Accessed on 9 November 2021; Shubhajit Roy, 'Incursion Acne, Can Be Cured With Ointment, Says Khurshid', *The Indian Express*, 26 April 2013, https://bit.ly/30gI8dg. Accessed on 9 November 2021.

59. Srini Sitaraman, 'Chinese Grand Strategy and the Exacerbation of the Sino-Indian Territorial Dispute', *E-International Relations*, 21 August 2013, pp. 2–4, https://www.e-ir.info/pdf/42233. Accessed on 9 November 2021.

60. Rory Medcalf, 'India Poll 2013', Lowy Institute, 20 May 2013, https://bit.ly/30c9QYL. Accessed on 9 November 2021.

61. PTI, 'Rajnath Demands Centre's Explanation on Border Defence Pact with China', *The Indian Express*, 13 November 2013, https://bit.ly/3mXuu7G. Accessed on 9 November 2021.

62. Sreeram Chaulia, *Modi Doctrine: The Foreign Policy of India's Prime Minister*, Bloomsbury, New Delhi, 2016.

63. George Tanham, 'Indian Strategic Thought: An Interpretive Essay', The RAND Corporation, 1992, pp. v, vii, 53–54, 59, https://bit.ly/3g2f2CH. Accessed on 28 January 2022.

64. Cf. Ashley Tellis, 'India as a New Global Power: An Action Agenda for the United States', Carnegie Endowment for International Peace, 2005; Baldev Nayar and T.V. Paul, *India in the World Order: Searching for Major-Power Status*, Cambridge University Press, Cambridge, 2003.

65. Stephen Cohen and Sunil Dasgupta, *Arming Without Aiming: India's Military Modernization*, Brookings Institution Press, Washington, 2010, p. 13.

66. Harsh Pant, 'Indian Strategic Culture: The Debate and Its Consequences', in David Scott, ed., *Handbook of India's International Relations*, Routledge, London, 2011, pp. 20–21.

67. Joshua Kertzer and Ryan Brutger, 'Decomposing Audience Costs:

Bringing the Audience Back into Audience Cost Theory', *American Journal of Political Science*, Vol. 60, No. 1, 2016, pp. 239–240, 245–246, https://doi.org/10.1111/ajps.12201. Accessed on 17 January 2022.

68. Akisato Suzuki, 'Audience Costs, Domestic Economy and Coercive Diplomacy', *Research and Politics*, 2018, Vol. 1, No. 7, 2018, pp. 1, 6, https://doi.org/10.1177/2053168018787119. Accessed on 17 January 2022.

69. Prithvi Iyer, 'Understanding the Indian Public Opinion-Foreign Policy Relationship', Observer Research Foundation, November 2020, pp. 2, 4, https://bit.ly/3EVfD3C. Accessed on 9 November 2021.

70. IANS, 'PM Modi a 'Warmonger' for Getting India in War-Like Situation with Pakistan: Digvijaya Singh', *The Indian Express*, 14 October 2016, https://bit.ly/3qll6wO. Accessed on 9 November 2021.

71. Conversation with the author on 13 April 2021 in New Delhi.

72. Anit Mukherjee, 'Fighting Separately: Jointness and Civil-Military Relations in India', *Journal of Strategic Studies*, Vol. 40, No. 1, 2017, pp. 6–34, https://doi.org/10.1080/01402390.2016.1196357. Accessed on 17 January 2022.

73. IE, 'Full Text: PM Narendra Modi's 2019 Independence Day Speech', *The Indian Express*, 15 August 2019, https://bit.ly/30eiCWf. Accessed on 9 November 2021.

74. Laxman Kumar Behera, 'Creation of Defence Planning Committee: A Step towards Credible Defence Preparedness', Manohar Parrikar Institute for Defence Studies and Analyses, 19 April 2018, https://bit.ly/3xi0U04. Accessed on 9 November 2021.

75. FE Online, 'Armed Forces Special Operations Division formed: The best of the Armed Forces', *Financial Express*, 15 May 2019, https://bit.ly/3oT4SIU. Accessed on 9 November 2021.

76. Kapil Patil, 'Defence Modernisation and Production: Enduring Challenges', in Harsh Pant, ed., *India's Evolving National Security Agenda: Modi and Beyond*, Konark, New Delhi, 2019, pp. 27, 41.

77. Vivian Fernandes, *Modi: Making of a Prime Minister: Leadership, Governance and Performance*, Orient, New Delhi, 2014, pp. 36–38.

78. Sumit Ganguly, 'India's National Security: A Neo-Classical Realist Account', in Sumit Ganguly, Nicolas Blarel and Manjeet Pardesi, eds., *The Oxford Handbook of India's National Security*, Oxford University Press, New Delhi, 2018, pp. 25–38.

79. Jack Nelson-Pallmeyer, *Brave New World Order: Must We Pledge Allegiance?*, Orbis, New York, 1992, p. 35.

80. Harold Lasswell, 'The Garrison State', *American Journal of Sociology*, Vol. 46, No. 4, January 1941, pp. 455–468, https://doi.org/10.1086/218693. Accessed on 17 January 2022.

81. Isaac Chotiner, 'An Army with a Country', *The Wall Street Journal*, 14 August 2016, https://on.wsj.com/30a83Dz. Accessed on 9 November 2021.

82. Imtiaz Ahmad, 'Pak Army a State above the State, Says Nawaz Sharif as Oppn. Unites against Military Leaders', *Hindustan Times*, 20 September 2020, https://bit.ly/3HPj3ah. Accessed on 9 November 2021.

83. Tai Ming Cheung, 'The Chinese National Security State Emerges from the Shadows to Center Stage', China Leadership Monitor, 1 September 2020, https://bit.ly/3klifzR. Accessed 9 November 2021.

84. Subrahmanyam Jaishankar, *The India Way: Strategies for an Uncertain World*, HarperCollins, New Delhi, 2020, pp. 50, 58.

85. Joel Migdal, *Strong Societies and Weak States: State-Society Relations and State Capabilities in the Third World*, Princeton University Press, Princeton, 1988.

86. Krishn Kaushik, 'Need Strong Government for 10 Years, Enemies are Within: Ajit Doval', *The Indian Express*, 26 October 2018, https://bit.ly/3odum3i. Accessed on 9 November 2021.

Chapter 1. Surgical Strikes on Fear

1. Gilbert Chesterton, *Heretics*, Lulu, Morrisville, 2017, p. 61.

2. MEA, 'Speech by Prime Minister at the Parliament of Afghanistan', Ministry of External Affairs, 25 December 2015, https://bit.ly/3Db9IH2. Accessed on 9 November 2021.

3. Bruce Riedel, 'Pakistan's Problematic Victory in Afghanistan',

Brookings Institution, 24 August 2021, https://brook.gs/3H0vhMF. Accessed on 25 January 2022.

4. PTI, 'US President Barack Obama and I: PM Narendra Modi Stresses Personal Chemistry', *The Economic Times*, 25 January 2015, https://bit.ly/3C19CR7. Accessed on 9 November 2021.

5. PTI, 'SAARC Must Work to Change S. Asia's Economic Landscape: Sharif', *Business Standard*, 26 August 2016, https://bit.ly/3BXZtEW. Accessed on 9 November 2021.

6. PTI, 'Pervez Musharraf Blames Nawaz Sharif for Kargil Withdrawal', *The Economic Times*, 15 May 2018, https://bit.ly/3F2kpfY. Accessed on 9 November 2021.

7. PTI, 'Bus Ride and a Hug: How Vajpayee Gave Indo-Pak Peace a Chance Before Kargil', *Business Standard*, 16 August 2018, https://bit.ly/3bS5Ui2. Accessed on 9 November 2021.

8. TNN, 'Kargil "Misadventure", Was "Stab" in Atal Vajpayee's Back: Nawaz Sharif', *The Economic Times*, 12 July 2018, https://bit.ly/305foEB. Accessed on 9 November 2021.

9. ANI, 'Pak Soldiers Did Not Even Have Weapons during Kargil War, Claims Nawaz Sharif', *Hindustan Times*, 26 October 2020, https://bit.ly/3ESYszM. Accessed on 9 November 2021.

10. BS, 'Opps Calls Modi Govt "Total Failure" in Its Handling of Pathankot Attack', Business Standard, 5 January, 2016, https://bit.ly/3o2eFwj. Accessed on 28 January 2022.

11. IT, 'Pathankot Terror Attack Planned by ISI: The Inside Story', *India Today*, 4 January 2016, https://bit.ly/3bYHLqc. Accessed on 9 November 2021.

12. IANS, 'Pathankot Attack Should Not Derail Peace Talks, Say Experts', *Deccan Herald*, 3 January 2016, https://bit.ly/3IJCX6f. Accessed on 28 January 2022.

13. Christine Fair, 'Bringing Back the Dead: Why Pakistan Used the Jaish-e-Mohammad to Attack an Indian Airbase', *HuffPost*, 12 January 2016, https://bit.ly/30dCVTH. Accessed on 9 November 2021.

14. Harsha Kakar, 'Securing Military Camps Needs More than Funds', *The Statesman*, 20 February 2018, https://bit.ly/3F13xWD. Accessed on 10 November 2021.

15. Sudhi Ranjan Sen, 'Pathankot Attack: Commander Faces Show-Cause Notice', *Hindustan Times*, 30 January 2019, https://bit.ly/3CXUhC6. Accessed on 10 November 2021.

16. PTI, 'Terrorism Indicators Show Declining Trend in J&K: Army Official', *The Economic Times*, 28 December 2015, https://bit.ly/308SV8W. Accessed on 10 November 2021.

17. PTI, 'Talks with Pak Is to Try and Turn Course of History: Modi', *Business Standard*, 15 December 2015, https://bit.ly/3mWqKDf. Accessed on 10 November 2021.

18. HTV, 'Special Operations India: "Pathankot" English Episode', History TV18 Documentary, 25 June 2018, https://www.historyindia.com/show/special-ops-india-pathankot. Accessed on 10 November 2021.

19. Nitin Gokhale, *Securing India the Modi Way: Balakot, Anti-Satellite Missile Test and More*, Bloomsbury, New Delhi, 2019, p. 146.

20. Ibid. 147.

21. TN, 'Pathankot Attack: Sharif Calls Up Modi, Promises Prompt, Decisive Action', *Outlook*, https://bit.ly/3qmoaZg. Accessed on 10 November 2021.

22. Irfan Haider, 'Pakistan Arrests Jaish Members in Connection with India Air Base Attack', *Dawn*, 13 January 2016, https://bit.ly/305M1kX. Accessed on 10 November 2021.

23. TT, 'Obama Piles Pathankot Heat on Pak', *The Telegraph*, 25 January 2016, https://bit.ly/3qkfWB3. Accessed on 10 November 2021.

24. PTI, 'Jaishankar Defends NDA Government's Decision to Allow ISI Officials to Visit Pathankot Air Base in 2016', *The Economic Times*, 7 January 2020, https://bit.ly/3H7pGo2. Accessed on 10 November 2021.

25. DNA, 'Pak JIT Says Pathankot Attack Staged by India; No Evidence Attackers Entered from Pakistan: Report', *Daily News & Analysis*, 5 April 2016, https://bit.ly/3D4m042. Accessed on 10 November 2021.

26. IT, 'Pakistan's ISI Paid Kashmiri Separatists Rs 800 Crore to Fuel Unrest in Kashmir, Says Intelligence Bureau Report', *India Today*, 4 April 2017, https://bit.ly/30fOGZN. Accessed by 10 November 2021.

27. Nitin Gokhale, *Securing India the Modi Way: Balakot, Anti-Satellite Missile Test and More*, Bloomsbury, New Delhi, 2019, p. 113.

28. ET, 'PM Modi Warns Pakistan: Uri Attack Will Not be Forgotten', *The Economic Times*, 25 September 2016, https://bit.ly/3C1hFNR. Accessed on 9 February 2022.

29. Nitin Gokhale, *Securing India the Modi Way: Balakot, Anti-Satellite Missile Test and More*, Bloomsbury, New Delhi, 2019, pp. 114, 119, 120.

30. IANS, 'During Surgical Strikes, India Was Ready for Any Escalation from Pakistan', *Business Standard*, 28 September 2018, https://bit.ly/3wwSNfD. Accessed on 10 November 2021.

31. John Oneal, *Foreign Policy Making in Times of Crisis*, Ohio State University Press, Columbus, 1982, p. 4.

32. Rahul Kanwal, 'Inside Story of India's Daring Surgical Strikes Against Pakistan', *DailyO*, 7 October 2016, https://bit.ly/3KQD1Dm. Accessed on 24 January 2022.

33. Saikat Datta, 'Behind the Scenes: How India Went about Planning "Surgical Strikes" after the Uri Attack', *Scroll.in*, 29 September 2016, https://bit.ly/3F0ig45. Accessed on 10 November 2021.

34. Syed Sammer Abbas, 'Army Rubbishes Indian "Surgical Strikes" Claim as Two Pakistani Soldiers Killed at LoC', *Dawn*, 29 September 2016, https://bit.ly/3D4qRlM. Accessed on 10 November 2021.

35. Conversation with the author on 16 February 2021 in New Delhi.

36. DC, 'Surgical Strikes: Commandos Combed 250 km, 70-80 of Them Attacked Terror Launch Pads', *Deccan Chronicle*, 30 September 2016, https://bit.ly/3wxgXGO. Accessed on 10 November 2021.

37. Sujan Dutta, 'Indian Surgical Strikes on Terror Pads', *The Telegraph*, 30 September 2016, https://bit.ly/3qoLhCD. Accessed on 10 November 2021.

38. Vikram Sood, 'Talibanisation of Pakistan and the Growth of Jihadi Culture', in Satish Kumar, ed., *India's National Security: Annual Review 2009*, New Delhi, Routledge, 2010, p. 201.

39. Stanley Wolpert, *India*, University of California Press, Berkeley, 1991, p. 234.

40. Shyam Saran, *How India Sees the World: Kautilya to the 21ˢᵗ Century*, Juggernaut, New Delhi, 2017, pp. 98, 105.

41. Alex Stolar, 'To the Brink: Indian Decision-Making and the 2001–2002 Standoff', The Henry L. Stimson Center, February 2008, p. 26, https://bit.ly/3AFN1un. Accessed on 28 January 2022.

42. Daniel Markey, 'Shrewd Move: India's Surgical Strikes Delivered the Right Messages to Multiple Audiences at Once', *Scroll.in*, 2 October 2016, https://bit.ly/3kqvEH6. Accessed on 11 November 2021.

43. IANS, '3 Years Ago, I was Awake All Night: PM Modi on 2016 Surgical Strike', *The Tribune*, 29 September 2019, https://bit.ly/3F3Mh2Z. Accessed on 11 November 2021.

44. ANI, 'Come Back before Sunrise': What PM Modi Told Soldiers before Surgical Strikes', *Hindustan Times*, 1 January 2019, https://bit.ly/3wz5dUi. Accessed on 11 November 2021.

45. Bruce Stokes, 'India and Modi: The Honeymoon Continues', Pew Research Center, 19 September 2016, https://pewrsr.ch/3BbUX6L. Accessed on 8 February 2022.

46. PTI, 'Myanmar Operation: 70 Commandos Finish Task in 40 Minutes', *The Economic Times*, 10 June 2015, https://bit.ly/3qqpIBC. Accessed on 11 November 2021.

47. Ibid.

48. Sandeep Unnithan, 'The Indian Army's Surgical Strike Cannot Become a Template for All Cross-Border Operations', *India Today*, 11 June 2015, https://bit.ly/3s4fCFY. Accessed on 28 January 2022.

49. Amit Baruah, 'Hot Pursuit a Message to All, Says Govt', *The Hindu*, 11 June 2015, https://bit.ly/3n2y28u. Accessed on 11 November 2021.

50. PTI, 'Rajyavardhan Singh Rathore Lauds Army Operation in Myanmar, Says It Is Beginning', *The Economic Times*, 10 June 2015, https://bit.ly/3n3Qyxm. Accessed on 11 November 2021.

51. Harinder Baweja, 'Pak Isn't Myanmar, We Are a Nuclear Nation, Minister from Neighbouring Country Tells India', *Hindustan Times*, 11 June 2015, https://bit.ly/3CPxXtz. Accessed on 11 November 2021.

52. Harsh Pant, 'Introduction', in Harsh Pant, ed., *India's Evolving National Security Agenda: Modi and Beyond*, Konark, New Delhi, 2019, p. xiv.

53. NSC, 'Statement by NSC Spokesperson Ned Price on National Security Advisor Susan E. Rice's Call with National Security Advisor Ajit Doval of India', The White House, 28 September 2016, https://bit.ly/3D7d660. Accessed on 11 November 2021.

54. Saikat Datta, 'Behind the Scenes: How India Went about Planning "Surgical Strikes" after the Uri Attack', *Scroll.in*, 29 September 2016, https://bit.ly/3F0ig45. Accessed on 10 November 2021.

55. State, 'Daily Press Briefing', US Department of State, 29 September 2016, https://bit.ly/3ktJZTb. Accessed on 11 November 2021.

56. PTI, 'Surgical Strikes: India Briefs Envoys of 25 Countries Including the US, China, Russia, the UK and France', 29 September 2016, *The Indian Express*, https://bit.ly/3wCuM75. Accessed on 11 November 2021.

57. Vivek Chadha and Rumel Dahiya, 'Uri, Surgical Strikes and International Reactions', Manohar Parrikar Institute for Defence Studies and Analyses, 4 October 2016, https://bit.ly/3Fbv8EV. Accessed on 11 November 2021.

58. IANS, 'PM Modi's Call for Crackdown on Global Terrorism Finds Support at G20', *Business Standard*, 8 July 2017, https://bit.ly/3qt8bca. Accessed on 11 November 2021.

59. Indrani Bagchi, 'Pakistan Back on Terror Financing Watchlist as China Stays Silent', *The Times of India*, 24 February 2018, https://bit.ly/3D8BWCi. Accessed on 11 November 2021.

60. Rezaul H. Laskar, 'PM Modi Pulls out of Saarc Meet in Islamabad Citing Cross-Border Terror', *Hindustan Times*, 28 September 2016, https://bit.ly/3kpXbbw. Accessed on 11 November 2021.

61. Jayanth Jacob, 'Bangladesh, Afghanistan and Bhutan Follow India, Pull out of Saarc Summit', *Hindustan Times*, 28 September 2016, https://bit.ly/3ku2qXJ. Accessed on 11 November 2021.

62. IPRI, 'Regional Implications of Indian Hegemony in the SAARC', Islamabad Policy Research Institute, 20 March 2017, https://bit.ly/3G2ZM33. Accessed on 28 January 2022.

63. Arjen Boin, Paul 't Hart, Eric Stern and Bengt Sundelius, *The Politics of Crisis Management: Public Leadership Under Pressure*, Cambridge University Press, Cambridge, 2005, pp. 13, 70, 85.

64. India Today Web Desk, 'Surgical Strikes Happened in 2016. Our Politicians Still can't Stop Bickering about Them', *India Today*, 28 June 2018, https://bit.ly/3C72VNx. Accessed on 11 November 2021.

65. Lalit K. Jha and Yoshita Singh, 'Surgical Strikes Prove India Can Defend Itself: Modi', *Outlook*, 26 June 2017, https://bit.ly/3F7xdkW. Accessed on 11 November 2021.

66. Prabhash Dutta, 'Surgical Strike: What India Has Achieved in One Year by Crossing LoC into PoK', *India Today*, 28 September 2017, https://bit.ly/3F49KRD. Accessed on 11 November 2021.

67. Nitin Gokhale, *Securing India the Modi Way: Balakot, Anti-Satellite Missile Test and More*, Bloomsbury, New Delhi, 2019, p. 134.

68. Ali Ahmed, 'India's Strategic Shift from Restraint to Proactivism', *Economic & Political Weekly*, Vol. 51, No. 48, p. 10, https://bit.ly/3Aq7zXy. Accessed on 18 January 2022.

69. Vipin Narang, 'The Lines That Have Been Crossed', *The Hindu*, 4 October 2016, https://bit.ly/3HccQ81. Accessed on 11 November 2021.

70. Yudhijit Bhattacharjee, 'The Terrorist Who Got Away', *The New York Times Magazine*, 19 March 2020, https://nyti.ms/3F5lNhB. Accessed on 11 November 2021.

71. Rajat Pandit, 'Army Keeps Surgical Strike Option Open, While Also Honing Cold Start Strategy for Pakistan', *The Times of India*, 14 January 2017, https://bit.ly/3FaleDr. Accessed on 11 November 2021.

72. PTI, 'India Now Follows New Policy of Dealing With Terrorists: PM Modi', *The Economic Times*, 9 March 2019, https://bit.ly/3quo16e. Accessed on 11 November 2021.

73. C3S, 'Comparative Study of Sun Tzu and Kautilya on Military Affairs', Chennai Centre for China Studies, 25 May 2016, https://bit.ly/3qsP9m0. Accessed on 11 November 2021.

Chapter 2. Defiant in Doklam

1. Sun Tzu, *The Art of War*, Tuttle, Tokyo, 2008, p. 13.

2. Narendra Modi and Barack Obama, 'A Renewed US-India Partnership

for the 21st Century', *The Washington Post*, 30 September 2014, https://wapo.st/31Q5iaT. Accessed on 15 November 2021.

3. WH, 'US-India Joint Statement', The White House, 30 September 2014, https://bit.ly/30nEePu. Accessed on 15 November 2021.

4. WH, 'US-India Joint Strategic Vision for the Asia-Pacific and Indian Ocean Region', The White House, 25 January 2015, https://bit.ly/30hu1UR. Accessed on 15 November 2021.

5. WH, 'US-India Joint Statement', The White House, 27 September 2013, https://bit.ly/30jm6X8. Accessed on 15 November 2021.

6. Nitin Gokhale, *Securing India the Modi Way: Balakot, Anti-Satellite Missile Test and More*, Bloomsbury, New Delhi, 2019, p. 214.

7. Uday Mahurkar, 'What Modi Told Xi in Ahmedabad', *Rediff*, 7 July 2017, https://bit.ly/3Dt9BGY. Accessed on 15 November 2021.

8. IT, 'As Modi Raises Border Issue, Xi Agrees with a Chinese Yes', *India Today*, 18 September 2014, https://bit.ly/3DwyVfD. Accessed on 15 November 2021.

9. TNN, 'Chinese Incursion in Ladakh: A Little Toothache Can Paralyze Entire Body, Modi Tells Xi Jinping', *The Times of India*, 20 September 2014, https://bit.ly/3kzVPeg. Accessed on 15 November 2021.

10. MEA, 'Joint Statement between the Republic of India and the People's Republic of China on Building a Closer Developmental Partnership', Ministry of External Affairs, 19 September 2014, https://bit.ly/3FjEMFd. Accessed on 15 November 2021.

11. MOFA, 'In Joint Pursuit of a Dream of National Renewal', Ministry of Foreign Affairs, 19 September 2014, https://bit.ly/3DdaKm2. Accessed on 15 November 2021.

12. Dipanjan Chaudhury, 'China–Pakistan Economic Corridor is Illegal: India', *The Economic Times*, 6 February 2020, https://bit.ly/3qDRtHc. Accessed on 15 November 2021.

13. Tweet by Chinese Ministry of Foreign Affairs Spokesman Zhao Lijian, 21 December 2018, https://twitter.com/zlj517/status/1075826986776326144. Accessed on 15 November 2021

14. Maria Abi-Habib, 'China's "Belt and Road" Plan in Pakistan Takes a Military Turn', *The New York Times*, December 19 2018, https://nyti.ms/3cdOnkw. Accessed on 15 November 2021.

15. Arif Rafiq, 'The Pakistan Army's Belt and Road Putsch', *Foreign Policy*, 26 August 2020, https://bit.ly/3qDtacf. Accessed on 15 November 2021.

16. Manish Shukla, 'Just 90 Km Away from Indo-Pak Border, China Deploys Troops in Sindh', *Daily News & Analysis*, 21 March 2019, https://bit.ly/3FkIGxV. Accessed on 15 November 2021.

17. H.I. Sutton, 'China's New High-Security Compound in Pakistan May Indicate Naval Plans', *Forbes*, 2 June 2020, https://bit.ly/3ndwxVd. Accessed on 15 November 2021.

18. Ishaan Tharoor, 'What China's and Pakistan's Special Friendship Means', *The Washington Post*, 21 April 2015, https://wapo.st/3HnzDhl. Accessed on 15 November 2021.

19. Jamal Afridi and Jayshree Bajoria, 'China–Pakistan Relations', Council on Foreign Relations, 6 July 2010, https://on.cfr.org/31Sdsj2. Accessed on 15 November 2021.

20. Andrew Small, *The China–Pakistan Axis: Asia's New Geopolitics*, Hurst, London, 2015, p. 54.

21. PTI, 'Pak Bridgehead for China to Develop Ties with Muslim World', *Business Standard*, 15 January 2014, https://bit.ly/3kxrHjV. Accessed on 15 November 2021.

22. MEA, 'Speech by Foreign Secretary at Raisina Dialogue in New Delhi', Ministry of External Affairs, 2 March 2016, https://bit.ly/3nbQWKd. Accessed on 15 November 2021.

23. MEA, 'Inaugural Address by Prime Minister at Second Raisina Dialogue, New Delhi', Ministry of External Affairs, 17 January 2017, https://bit.ly/3HqJ3sG. Accessed on 15 November 2021.

24. Lin Minwang, 'Geopolitical Bias Hinders India in Benefiting from Belt & Road Initiative', *Global Times*, 29 March 2017, https://bit.ly/3r9EVqw. Accessed on 28 January 2022.

25. Raj Chengappa, 'NSG: The Great Wall of Xi', *India Today*, 30 June 2016, https://bit.ly/3ot5UuX. Accessed on 15 November 2021.

26. Cyril Almeida, 'Exclusive: Act Against Militants or Face International Isolation, Civilians Tell Military', *Dawn*, 6 October 2016, https://bit.ly/3Ci8jgS. Accessed on 15 November 2021.

27. Ayjaz Wani, 'China's Real Intentions Behind Its "Technical Hold" on

Masood Azhar', Observer Research Foundation, 21 February 2019, https://bit.ly/3FdD5cwm. Accessed on 15 November 2021.

28. Michael Kugelman, 'Masood Azhar Is China's Favorite Terrorist', *Foreign Policy*, 21 March 2019, https://bit.ly/3qLoMb0. Accessed on 15 November 2021.

29. CGTN, 'China Calls for Abandonment of Double Standards in Fight against Terrorism', China Global Television Network, 30 October 2020, https://bit.ly/3orvUa4. Accessed on 15 November 2021.

30. Yu Ning, 'Being a Pawn for US Containment Strategy a Trap for India', *Global Times*, 26 June 2017, https://bit.ly/35vMHTw. Accessed on 28 January 2022.

31. Thierry Mathou, 'Bhutan-China Relations: Towards a New Step in Himalayan Politics', in Karma Ura and Sonam Kinga, eds., *The Spider and the Piglet: Proceedings of the First Seminar on Bhutan Studies*, Centre for Bhutan Studies, Thimphu, 2004, pp. 390–391.

32. GS, 'Deng Xiaoping's "24-Character Strategy"', *Global Security*, https://bit.ly/3wL9F2m. Accessed on 15 November 2021.

33. Brahma Chellaney, 'China's Five-Finger Punch', *The Strategist*, 22 July 2020, https://bit.ly/3Hq1ZYg. Accessed on 15 November 2021.

34. Liu Xin, 'Pressure on Bhutan Reveals India's Hegemonism: Analysts', *Global Times*, 11 August 2017, https://bit.ly/3rVVcyE. Accessed on 28 January 2022.

35. Le Thi Hang Nga, Tran Xuan Hiep, Dang Thu Thuy and Ha Le Huyen, 'India–Bhutan Treaties of 1949 and 2007: A Retrospect', *India Quarterly*, Vol. 75, No. 4, 2019, p. 441, https://doi.org/10.1177/0974928419874547. Accessed 20 January 2022.

36. Claude Arpi, *Will Tibet Find Her Soul Again: India–Tibet Relations 1947–1962 Part 2*, Vij Books, New Delhi, 2018.

37. Shubhajit Roy, 'India, Bhutan to Work Closely on Security, National Interests', *The Indian Express*, 19 August 2019, https://bit.ly/3caUJ4a. Accessed on 15 November 2021.

38. P. Stobdan, 'India and Bhutan: The Strategic Imperative', Manohar Parrikar Institute of Defence Studies and Analyses, September 2014, p. 49, https://bit.ly/3CfiH91. Accessed on 15 November 2021.

39. Joel Wuthnow, Satu Limaye and Nilanthi Samaranayake, 'Doklam,

One Year Later: China's Long Game in the Himalayas,' *War on the Rocks*, 7 June 2018, https://bit.ly/3FiosF2. Accessed on 15 November 2021.

40. Ananth Krishnan, *India's China Challenge: A Journey through China's Rise and What It Means for India*, HarperCollins, New Delhi, 2020, p. 185.

41. Dipanjan Chaudury, 'Dokalam Standoff: No Easy Answers as China Quotes 1890, India 2012 Pact,' *The Economic Times*, 5 August 2017, https://bit.ly/3CiWRl9. Accessed on 15 November 2021.

42. Snehesh Philip, 'Operation Juniper—Inside Story of How Indian Army Pushed China Back from Doklam,' *ThePrint*, 17 October 2019, https://bit.ly/3Ch1cVV. Accessed on 15 November 2021.

43. Ibid.

44. MEA, 'Recent Developments in Doklam Area,' Ministry of External Affairs, 30 June 2017, https://bit.ly/3DlOrea. Accessed on 15 November 2021.

45. PTI, 'Chinese Army Conducts Live-Fire Drills in Tibet,' *The Economic Times*, 17 July 2017, https://bit.ly/3qLTW1Y. Accessed on 15 November 2021.

46. Ananth Krishnan, 'Now, China Moves Tonnes of Military Equipment to Tibet. Should India be Scared?,' *India Today*, 19 July 2017, https://bit.ly/3wQEItU. Accessed on 15 November 2021.

47. Jeff Smith, 'High Noon in the Himalayas: Behind the China–India Standoff at Doka La,' *War on the Rocks*, 13 July 2017, https://bit.ly/3DiMgb8. Accessed on 15 November 2021.

48. Sushant Singh, 'Doklam Faceoff: China Deployed More, Standoff Began Earlier,' *The Indian Express*, 25 September 2017, https://indianexpress.com/article/india/doklam-issue-india-china-deployed-more-standoff-began-earlier-4859674/. Accessed on 15 November 2021.

49. PTI, 'Back Off or China will Readjust Stance on Sikkim: Chinese Daily,' *The Economic Times*, 6 July 2017, https://bit.ly/3DdYmSO. Accessed on 15 November 2021.

50. PTI, 'No Dispute with Bhutan in Doklam: China,' *The Economic Times*, 5 July 2017, https://bit.ly/3cef7l0. Accessed on 15 November 2021.

51. Kiran Sharma, 'Detente in the Borderlands for India and China,' *Nikkei Asia*, 31 August 2017, https://s.nikkei.com/3wMCBHq. Accessed on 15 November 2021.

52. Ajit Kumar Dubey, 'Meet Prime Minister Modi's Key Men who Cracked Doklam for Him,' *India Today*, 30 August 2017, https://bit.ly/3wNCYRY. Accessed on 16 November 2021.

53. Iain Henry, 'What Allies Want: Reconsidering Loyalty, Reliability, and Alliance Interdependence,' *International Security*, Vol. 44, No. 4, 2020, p. 53, https://doi.org/10.1162/isec_a_00375. Accessed on 21 January 2022.

54. PTI, 'India is Nepal's "Elder Brother", Not "Big Brother": Sushma Swaraj,' *The Economic Times*, 22 February 2016, https://bit.ly/2YQ3my9. Accessed on 16 November 2021.

55. Indrani Bagchi, 'Doklam Standoff: China Playing Out Its "Three Warfares" Strategy against India,' *The Times of India*, 13 August 2017, https://bit.ly/2YOlV5G. Accessed on 16 November 2021.

56. Wang Qingyun, 'Indian Troops Must "Back Out" from Doklam, Foreign Minister Says,' *China Daily*, 25 July 2017, https://bit.ly/3nk9tnD. Accessed on 16 November 2021.

57. John Gong, 'Time for a Second Lesson for Forgetful India,' *Global Times*, 24 July 2017, https://bit.ly/3G2x96l. Accessed on 28 January 2022.

58. GT, 'Bhutan's Neutral Stance Embarrasses India,' *Global Times*, 11 August 2017, https://bit.ly/3rVZYft. Accessed on 28 January 2022.

59. PTI, 'Leave Sikkim Dokalam Area with Dignity or Be Kicked Out: Chinese Media,' *Business Standard*, 5 July 2017, https://bit.ly/3DgboPL. Accessed on 16 November 2021.

60. TH, 'Army Prepared for Two and a Half Front War: Gen Rawat,' *The Hindu*, 8 June 2017, https://bit.ly/3HspRL2. Accessed on 16 November 2021.

61. GT, 'Military Conflicts to Escalate if India Refuses to Withdraw Troops,' *Global Times*, 21 July 2017, https://bit.ly/3rXos8d. Accessed on 28 January 2022.

62. Prabhash K. Dutta, 'Chinese Media Thinks PLA can Annihilate Indian Army. Can They? A Fact Check,' *India Today*, 5 August 2017,

https://bit.ly/3oymlWL. Accessed on 16 November 2021.

63. GT, 'India Misjudges China's Hope for Peace', *Global Times*, 7 August 2017, https://bit.ly/343QN4s. Accessed on 28 January 2022.

64. GT, 'India will Suffer Worse Losses than 1962 if it incites Border Clash', *Global Times*, 4 July 2017, https://bit.ly/3Gds2A1. Accessed on 28 January 2022.

65. Simon Shen and Debashish Chowdhury, 'The Alien Next Door: Media Images in China and India', in Kanti Bajpai et al., eds., *Routledge Handbook of China–India Relations*, Routledge, Abingdon, 2020, p. 121.

66. EFSAS, 'The Doklam Standoff: A Template for Countering Chinese Belligerence and Expansionism', European Foundation for South Asian Studies, October 2018, p. 8, https://bit.ly/3FktP6x. Accessed on 16 November 2021.

67. FE, 'Independence Day 2017: Full Text of PM Narendra Modi's Speech from Red Fort', *The Financial Express*, 15 August 2017, https://bit.ly/3kIlHF8. Accessed on 16 November 2021.

68. Bijin Jose, 'Anti-China Protest: Gujarat Firm to Give Away "Made in India" Phones to its 400 Dealers', *India Today*, 19 July 2017, https://bit.ly/3DneyBc. Accessed on 16 November 2021.

69. Manjeet Negi, 'Inside Story of How India Achieved Breakthrough in Doklam Border Standoff with China', *India Today*, 28 August 2017, https://bit.ly/3Dkapy8. Accessed on 16 November 2021.

70. Nitin Gokhale, *Securing India the Modi Way: Balakot, Anti-Satellite Missile Test and More*, Bloomsbury, New Delhi, 2019, p. 199.

71. Shishir Gupta, 'The Doklam Stand-Off Was Resolved Because of Modi's Hamburg Initiative', *Hindustan Times*, 9 September 2017, https://bit.ly/3njeQDF. Accessed on 16 November 2021.

72. Frank O'Donnell, 'Stabilizing Sino-Indian Security Relations: Managing the Strategic Rivalry After Doklam', *Carnegie Endowment for International Peace*, 21 June 2018, https://bit.ly/327lVz9. Accessed on 16 November 2021.

73. Taylor Fravel, 'Stability in a Secondary Strategic Direction: China and the Border Dispute with India After 1962', in Kanti Bajpai et al., eds., *Routledge Handbook of China–India Relations*, Routledge,

Abingdon, 2020, p. 176.

74. ANI, 'No Talks until Indian Troops Withdraw from Doklam Border: China', *Daily News & Analysis*, 26 July 2017, https://bit.ly/3oxnyxv. Accessed on 16 November 2021.

75. John Ruggie, 'Multilateralism: The Anatomy of an Institution', *International Organization*, Vol. 46, No. 3, p. 571, https://doi.org/10.1017/S0020818300027831. Accessed 21 January 2022.

76. GT, 'Military Conflicts to Escalate if India Refuses to Withdraw Troops', *Global Times*, 21 July 2017, https://bit.ly/3rXos8d. Accessed on 28 January 2022.

77. Jayanth Jacob, 'Doklam Standoff: Japan Signals Support to India over Border Row with China', *Hindustan Times*, 18 August 2017, https://bit.ly/3Dl1HzH. Accessed on 16 November 2021.

78. Taylor Fravel, 'Why India Did Not "Win" the Standoff With China', *War on the Rocks*, 1 September 2017, https://bit.ly/3Dkq8gs. Accessed on 16 November 2021.

79. Cited in Yash Johri, 'Doklam Standoff: Why Did the Chinese Back Off? Did India Really "Win"?', *The Times of India*, 30 August 2017, https://bit.ly/327rfCD. Accessed on 16 November 2021.

80. Saibal Dasgupta, 'China Confirms Stoppage of Road-Work at Doklam, But Adds It Could Begin When Weather Permits', *The Times of India*, 28 August 2017, https://bit.ly/3kIRV2O. Accessed on 16 November 2021.

81. Sudha Ramachandran, 'Can Bhutan's New Government Avoid Doklam 2.0?', *The Diplomat*, 29 October 2018, https://bit.ly/3CiP5ru. Accessed on 16 November 2021.

82. Felix K. Chang, 'No Sanctuary: China's New Territorial Dispute with Bhutan', Foreign Policy Research Institute, 29 July 2020, https://bit.ly/3Fp03xz. Accessed on 16 November 2021.

83. Debashish Roy Chowdhury, 'China and India: Are War Clouds Gathering Over Doklam Again?', *South China Morning Post*, 27 January 2018, https://bit.ly/3nlJzjE. Accessed on 16 November 2021.

84. Keith Johnson, 'What Kind of Game is China Playing?', *The Wall Street Journal*, 11 June 2011, https://on.wsj.com/30tkR8m. Accessed on 16 November 2021.

85. Sumit Ganguly and Andrew Scobell, 'The Himalayan Impasse: Sino-Indian Rivalry in the Wake of Doklam', *The Washington Quarterly*, Vol. 41, No. 3, pp. 179, 187 https://doi.org/10.1080/016 3660X.2018.1519369. Accessed on 21 January 2022.

86. Lindsay Hughes, 'China, India and the Return to Doklam', Future Directions International, 31 January 2018, https://bit.ly/3Dotm2x. Accessed on 16 November 2021.

87. Manjeet Pardesi, 'India's Conventional Military Strategy', in Sumit Ganguly, Nicolas Blarel and Manjeet Pardesi, eds., *The Oxford Handbook of India's National Security*, Oxford University Press, New Delhi, 2018, pp. 114, 117.

88. ANI, 'Exercise Him Vijay Was Very Successful; Mountain Strike Corps Ready: Army Chief', *Asia News International*, 31 December 2019, https://bit.ly/3Ckz97W. Accessed on 16 November 2021.

89. Yogesh Joshi and Anit Mukherjee, 'Offensive Defense: India's Strategic Responses to the Rise of China', in Kanti Bajpai et al., eds., *Routledge Handbook of China–India Relations*, Routledge, Abingdon, 2020, p. 231.

90. Ananth Krishnan, 'Ahead of Ajit Doval's Visit, Chinese Editorial Calls Him "Main Schemer" Behind Doklam Standoff', *India Today*, 25 July 2017, https://bit.ly/3FjRFPU. Accessed on 16 November 2021.

91. Vijaita Singh, 'Ajit Doval: The Spy Who Came in From the Cold', *The Hindu*, 11 July 2020, https://bit.ly/3qHw8MT. Accessed on 16 November 2021.

92. Cited in Nitin Gokhale, *Securing India the Modi Way: Balakot, Anti-Satellite Missile Test and More*, Bloomsbury, New Delhi, 2019, p. 105.

93. FE, "Get Chinese Out of DHOKA-LAM": Rahul Gandhi Suggests Ideas for Modi's "Mann Ki Baat"', *The Financial Express*, 19 January 2018, https://bit.ly/3kCEiSH. Accessed on 16 November 2021.

94. TOI, 'Mega Times Group Poll: 71.9% of Indians Say They Will Vote for Narendra Modi as PM Again in 2019', *The Times of* India, May 26 2018, https://timesofindia.indiatimes.com/india/mega-times-group-poll-71-9-of-indians-say-they-will-vote-for-narendra-modi-as-pm-again-in-2019/articleshow/64324490.cms. Accessed on 16 November 2021.

95. Yun Sun, 'China's Strategic Assessment of India', *War on the Rocks*, 25 March 2020, https://bit.ly/3nidSrc. Accessed on 16 November 2021.

Chapter 3. Breaking Barriers in Balakot

1. Kaushik Roy, *Hinduism and the Ethics of Warfare in South Asia: From Antiquity to the Present*, Cambridge University Press, Cambridge, 2012, p. 142.
2. Raj Chengappa, 'Rules of the New Game: Can India Do Business with an Imran Khan-Led Pakistan?', *India Today*, 4 August 2018, https://bit.ly/3wU2Vzw. Accessed on 16 November 2021.
3. Cited in Ahmad Khalid, 'The Supreme Praetorian State of Pakistan', *Daily Times*, 28 June 2011, https://bit.ly/3cduEBH. Accessed on 16 November 2021.
4. Christine Fair, *Fighting to the End: The Pakistan Army's Way of War*, Oxford University Press, Oxford, 2014.
5. Adrija Roychowdhury, 'From Corruption Crusader to Taliban Khan, How Imran Khan Built Up His Political Innings', *The Indian Express*, 26 July 2018, https://bit.ly/3HqUDnv. Accessed on 16 November 2021.
6. IT, 'Imran Khan Wants Talks, Trade with India but Via Kashmir', *India Today*, 26 July 2018, https://bit.ly/3orovra. Accessed on 16 November 2021.
7. PTI, 'Afghans Have Broken "Shackles of Slavery": Pakistan PM Imran Khan', *The Hindu*, 16 August 2021, https://bit.ly/3ninzG1. Accessed on 16 November 2021.
8. DNA, 'Imran Khan's True Face Exposed, Pakistan Won't Mend Its Ways: New Delhi Takes Down Islamabad', *Daily News & Analysis*, 21 September 2018, https://bit.ly/3Dlq67X. Accessed on 16 November 2021.
9. MEA Affairs, 'Bilateral Brief: India–Pakistan Relations', Ministry of External Affairs, 7 February 2020, https://bit.ly/30Dx9L8. Accessed on 16 November 2021.
10. India Today Web Desk, 'Dear Modi Sahab: What Imran Khan Said in Letter to PM', *India Today*, 20 September 2018, https://bit.

ly/3wO5X8l. Accessed on 16 November 2021.

11. PTI, 'In a Letter to Imran, Modi Says India Looks for Meaningful Engagement with Pakistan' *The Hindu*, 20 August 2018, https://bit.ly/3qIpkOT. Accessed on 16 November 2021.

12. Maria Abi-Habib, 'Pakistan's Military Has Quietly Reached Out to India for Talks', *The New York Times*, 4 September 2018, https://nyti.ms/3kCaEx2. Accessed on 16 November 2021.

13. Jessica Stern, 'Pakistan's Jihad Culture', *Foreign Affairs*, Vol. 79, No. 6, November 2000, pp. 115–126 https://fam.ag/3qSGx84. Accessed on 18 January 2022.

14. Abhishek Bhalla, 'Pulwama Attack: Intel Warned of a Syria-Style Car Bomber, but No One Knew How to Stop Him', *India Today*, 14 February 2019, https://bit.ly/3oDPH5V. Accessed on 17 November 2021.

15. Sudhi Ranjan Sen and Mir Ehsan, 'Pulwama Recruiting Ground for LeT, JeM: Govt Report', *Hindustan Times*, 27 March 2019, https://bit.ly/3qJ3mvi. Accessed on 17 November 2021.

16. Kamaljit Sandhu, 'Long Convoy, Intel Failure: Multiple Lapses Led to Pulwama Terror Attack, Finds CRPF Inquiry', *India Today*, 4 September 2019, https://bit.ly/3CoSNzF. Accessed on 17 November 2021.

17. TH, 'Pulwama Terror Attack | NIA Arrests Man, Daughter', *The Hindu*, 3 March 2020, https://bit.ly/3KP7PUQ. Accessed on 28 January 2022.

18. Neeraj Chauhan, 'Pulwama Strike was Pushed Back a Week, JeM Man Tells NIA', *Hindustan Times*, 4 March 2020, https://bit.ly/3cgIC5P. Accessed on 17 November 2021.

19. Vijaita Singh, '2019 Pulwama Terror Attack Case: JeM Chief Masood Azhar among 19 in NIA Charge Sheet', *The Hindu*, 25 August 2020, https://bit.ly/3FkPP19. Accessed on 17 November 2021.

20. Hakeem Rashid, 'Jaish-e-Mohammed Claims Responsibility for Pulwama Attacks', *The Economic Times*, 15 February 2019, https://bit.ly/3o6FUGi. Accessed on 28 January 2022.

21. IE, 'Full Text: Pakistan PM Imran Khan Warns India of Retaliatory Action', *The Indian Express*, 19 February 2019, https://bit.ly/3cqpYIt.

Accessed on 17 November 2021.

22. ITV, 'Pulwama Attack: India Bids Farewell to CRPF Martyrs, Patriotic Slogans Reverberate as Scores Join in to Pay Tribute', India TV, 16 February 2019, https://bit.ly/3Hw48Ss. Accessed on 17 November 2021.

23. Arjen Boin, Paul 't Hart, Eric Stern and Bengt Sundelius, *The Politics of Crisis Management: Public Leadership Under Pressure*, Cambridge University Press, Cambridge, 2005, pp. 11, 38.

24. Scott Gates and Kaushik Roy, *Unconventional War in South Asia: Shadow Warriors and Counterinsurgency*, Routledge, Abingdon, 2016, p. 107.

25. J.P. Yadav and Piyush Srivastava, 'India's Blood Is Boiling, Says Modi', *The Telegraph*, 15 February 2019, https://bit.ly/3wThbby. Accessed on 17 November 2021.

26. Rezaul Laskar, 'Pakistan Slipped on Timelines to Curb Terror Financing: Global Watchdog FATF', *Hindustan Times*, 22 February 2019, https://bit.ly/3DnU9MA. Accessed on 17 November 2021.

27. PTI, 'We Support India's Right to Self-Defense: US to Ajit Doval on Pulwama Terror Attack', *India Today*, 16 February 2019, https://bit.ly/3oAapUy. Accessed on 17 November 2021.

28. PTI, 'Trump Says India Looking at Something 'Very Strong' After Pulwama Attack', *The Economic Times*, 23 February 2019, https://bit.ly/3FiHRFy. Accessed on 17 November 2021.

29. IE, 'Full Text: Pakistan PM Imran Khan Warns India of Retaliatory Action', *The Indian Express*, 19 February 2019, https://bit.ly/3cqpYIt. Accessed on 17 November 2021.

30. WB, 'Pakistan Seeks Urgent UN Intervention to De-Escalate Fresh Tensions with India', *Outlook*, 19 February 2018, https://bit.ly/3DqJlxd. Accessed on 17 November 2021.

31. Dipanjan Chaudhury, 'UN Security Council Condemns Pulwama Attacks despite Pakistan Efforts', *The Economic Times*, 21 February 2019, https://bit.ly/30uxVdH. Accessed on 17 November 2021.

32. Yu Jincui, 'Terrorist No. Could Be Better Addressed by India', *Global Times*, 17 February 2019, https://bit.ly/3wTx0z2. Accessed on 17 November 2021.

33. Nitin Gokhale, *Securing India the Modi Way: Balakot, Anti-Satellite Missile Test and More*, Bloomsbury, New Delhi, 2019, p. 30.

34. Amil Bhatnagar, 'Pakistan Expected Surgical Strikes, but We Took the Air Route: PM Modi', *The Indian Express*, 10 March 2019, https://bit.ly/3HtgnPE. Accessed on 17 November 2021.

35. Nitin Gokhale, *Securing India the Modi Way: Balakot, Anti-Satellite Missile Test and More*, Bloomsbury, New Delhi, 2019, p. 120.

36. Snehesh Philip, 'Why India Picked IAF over the Army and Navy to Hit Back at Pakistan', *ThePrint*, 27 February 2019, https://bit.ly/3oHGSbE. Accessed on 17 November 2021.

37. Rajdeep Sardesai, *2019: How Modi Won India*, HarperCollins, New Delhi, 2019, p. 191.

38. ANI, 'Inside Story: How Balakot Airstrike Became Operation "Bandar"', *The Economic Times*, 26 February 2020, https://bit.ly/3wXTPBB. Accessed on 17 November 2021.

39. Manu Pubby, 'After Pulwama Attack: Military Puts All Cards on the Table', *The Economic Times*, 16 February 2019, https://bit.ly/3kGbJ6T. Accessed on 17 November 2021.

40. TH, 'Balakot Air Strikes: When Key Naval Assets Were Put on Alert', *The Hindu*, 17 March 2019, https://bit.ly/3ouWE9m. Accessed on 17 November 2021.

41. Nitin Gokhale, *Securing India the Modi Way: Balakot, Anti-Satellite Missile Test and More*, Bloomsbury, New Delhi, 2019, p. 16.

42. Outlook Web Bureau, 'Full Statement by Foreign Secretary on India's Cross-LOC Air Strike', *Outlook*, 26 February 2019, https://bit.ly/3kK0Fpx. Accessed on 17 November 2021.

43. Conversation with the author on 3 March 2021 in New Delhi.

44. Reuters, 'PAF Chases Away Indian Jets after LoC Airspace Violation', *The Express Tribune*, 26 February 2019, https://bit.ly/3DrsXMH. Accessed on 17 November 2021.

45. IT, 'India Strikes Back: Pakistan Still in Denial Mode, Says Will Take International Media to Verify Claims', *India Today*, 26 February 2019, https://bit.ly/3FfwyhA. Accessed on 17 November 2021.

46. Web Desk, 'Pak Army Carried Away 35 Dead Bodies from Balakot after IAF Strike, Says Italian Journalist', *The Week*, 4 March 2019,

https://bit.ly/30uq3sB. Accessed on 17 November 2021.

47. IANS, 'Balakot Air Strike: Foreign Journalists, Diplomats Given Access to "Site"; Interactions Curtailed', *The New Indian Express*, 11 April 2019, https://bit.ly/3qLeCHq. Accessed on 17 November 2021.

48. Dhruva Jaishankar, 'Balakot Strike and Its Aftermath', *The Times of India*, 27 February 2019, https://bit.ly/3HqT2Ou. Accessed on 17 November 2021.

49. IT, 'Imran Khan to Chair Pakistan's Nuke Authority Meeting after Indian Air Force Bombs Jaish Camps in Balakot', *India Today*, 27 February 2019, https://bit.ly/3qI0wXl. Accessed on 17 November 2021.

50. Sameer Joshi, 'How Pakistan Planned to Hit India Back for Balakot—the Mission, the Fighters, the Tactics', *ThePrint*, 14 September 2019, https://bit.ly/3qMUpkG. Accessed on 17 November 2021.

51. Vishnu Som, '24 Pak Jets Tried To Cross Over, Intercepted by 8 Air Force Fighters', NDTV, 1 March 2019, https://bit.ly/3DgImij. Accessed on 17 November 2021.

52. IT, 'US Pulled up Pakistan for Misusing F-16s after Balakot: Report', *India Today*, 12 December 2019, https://bit.ly/3FmSvuZ. Accessed on 17 November 2021.

53. PTI, 'India Asks Pak to Immediately Return IAF Pilot, Ensure His Safety', *Business Standard*, 27 February 2019, https://bit.ly/3FmtfoP. Accessed on 17 November 2021.

54. PTI, 'Had Warned Pakistan of Consequences if Abhinandan Varthaman Not Returned: PM Modi', *The Economic Times*, 21 April 2019, https://bit.ly/30vmN08. Accessed on 17 November 2021.

55. Shishir Gupta, 'A Rare Phone Call, Secret Letter: How India Got Pak to Release IAF's Abhinandan', *Hindustan Times*, 27 February 2021, https://bit.ly/3kJcyMt. Accessed on 17 November 2021.

56. HT, 'Our Nuke Arsenal Is Not for Diwali: Modi at Rally', *Hindustan Times*, 22 April 2019, https://bit.ly/30xyUJn. Accessed on 17 November 2021.

57. ANI, '"COAS Bajwa's Legs Were Shaking": Pakistan MP Recalls Why IAF Pilot Abhinandan Varthaman Was Released', *Hindustan Times*, 29 October 2020, https://bit.ly/3qLWY6n. Accessed on 17 November 2021.

58. Sanjeev Miglani and Drazen Jorgic, 'India, Pakistan Threatened to Unleash Missiles at Each Other: Sources', *Reuters*, 27 March 2019, https://reut.rs/329QRyJ. Accessed on 17 November 2021.

59. Suhasini Haidar and Kallol Bhattacharjee, 'Abhinandan Varthaman Release: World Leaders Work Behind the Scenes to Avert India–Pakistan Conflict', *The Hindu*, 28 February 2019, https://bit.ly/3FmVbsx. Accessed on 17 November 2021.

60. PTI, 'IAF Pilot Abhinandan Varthaman's Return Our Diplomatic Victory: Amit Shah', NDTV, 1 March 2019, https://bit.ly/31ghgud. Accessed on 17 November 2021.

61. TNN, 'Rafale Jets Could Have Delivered Better Results: PM Modi', *The Times of India*, 3 March 2019, https://bit.ly/3Fpn1o9. Accessed on 17 November 2021.

62. IANS, 'In Show of Support for India, Pompeo Calls JeM Base Bombing "Counter-Terrorism actions"', *Business Standard*, 27 February 2019, https://bit.ly/3rLfiNr. Accessed on 9 February 2022.

63. IT, 'Nothing Justifies Terrorism: UN Chief Antonio Guterres's Message to Pakistan', *India Today*, 3 October 2018, https://bit.ly/3oDFZAx. Accessed on 17 November 2021.

64. Vasudha Venugopal, 'All India Radio Launches Website and App of Balochi Radio Service', *The Economic Times*, 17 September 2016, https://bit.ly/30CQEDM. Accessed on 17 November 2021.

65. Faisal Mahmud, 'Did the OIC's Dhaka Declaration Snub the Kashmir Problem?', *The Diplomat*, 11 May 2018, https://bit.ly/3CoKiVj. Accessed on 18 November 2021.

66. UNI, 'Chowkidar Giving Sleepless Nights to Cong, Terrorists: Modi', *United News of India*, 30 March 2019, https://bit.ly/3cp7qbO. Accessed on 18 November 2021.

67. PTI, 'PM Modi "Exploiting" Valour of Jawans, Says Rahul Gandhi', *The Economic Times*, 16 April 2019, https://bit.ly/3oF7iKX. Accessed on 18 November 2021.

68. Al Jazeera, 'Pakistan's Khan: India's BJP Conducted 2019 Air Raid to Win Polls', *Al Jazeera*, 18 January 2021, https://bit.ly/30xO5mb. Accessed on 18 November 2021.

69. Vinod Rajput, 'Pakistan Cried to World after Balakot Air Strike:

PM Modi', *Hindustan Times*, 9 March 2019, https://bit.ly/3HtB266. Accessed on 18 November 2021.

70. Arjun Subramaniam, *Full Spectrum: India's Wars, 1972–2020*, HarperCollins, New Delhi, 2020, p. 350.

71. Ipsita Chakravarty, 'In the BJP's 2019 Manifesto, Development Plays Second Fiddle to Politics of Fear', *Scroll.in*, 9 April 2019, https://bit.ly/3wVT7Vs. Accessed on 18 November 2021.

72. Ian Hall, 'India's 2019 General Election: National Security and the Rise of the Watchmen', *The Commonwealth Journal of International Affairs*, Vol. 108, No. 5, p. 515, https://doi.org/10.1080/00358533.2019.1658360. Accessed on 18 January 2022.

73. Harsh V. Pant, 'India's National Security Election: Why It's Advantage Modi', *The Diplomat*, 11 April 2019, https://bit.ly/3FquUJZ. Accessed on 18 November 2021.

74. Republic World, 'EAM S Jaishankar Speaks on "Bharat's Global Power Play" at Republic Summit with Arnab Goswami' [video], Republic TV, YouTube, 27 November 2019, https://bit.ly/3o79s6v. Accessed on 18 November 2021.

75. Alastair Smith, 'Diversionary Foreign Policy in Democratic Systems', *International Studies Quarterly*, Vol. 40, No. 1, 1996, pp. 133–134, https://doi.org/10.2307/2600934. Accessed on 18 January 2022.

76. ET Bureau, 'IAF Air Strike: Why "Non-Military Target" Wording?', *The Economic Times*, 27 February 2019, https://bit.ly/3noR2OS. Accessed on 18 November 2021.

77. B.S. Yediyurappa, 'Jawaharlal Nehru Was Adamant on Special Status for Jammu and Kashmir', *The Economic Times*, 25 September 2019, https://bit.ly/326xIxr. Accessed on 18 November 2021.

78. BBC, 'Musharraf Admits Kashmir Militants Trained in Pakistan', BBC News, 5 October 2010, https://bbc.in/3G8EOQn. Accessed on 28 January 2022.

79. TNIE, 'Retired Bureaucrats, Judges, Armed Force Officers Accuse Mufti, Farooq of Promoting Separatism', *The New Indian Express*, 5 November 2022, https://bit.ly/3rUJAMh. Accessed on 25 January 2022.

80. India Today Web Desk, '58% Back Modi Govt's Article 370 Move, 50%

Find J&K as UT Unconstitutional: MOTN', *India Today*, 23 January 2020, https://bit.ly/3nrmQm3. Accessed on 18 November 2021.

81. PTI, 'Pakistan Supported, Trained Terror Groups to Carry out Militancy in Kashmir: Pervez Musharraf', *The Economic Times*, 12 July 2018, https://bit.ly/3x4Kp7t. Accessed on 18 November 2021.

82. Elizabeth Roche, 'Pakistan Says Will Challenge Revoking of Article 370', *Mint*, 5 August 2019, https://bit.ly/3cqyeZ4. Accessed on 18 November 2021.

83. PTI, 'Imran Khan at UN General Assembly: India Must Lift "Inhuman Curfew"', *The Hindu*, 27 September 2019, https://bit.ly/3Cs0Bkc. Accessed on 18 November 2021.

84. Omer Farooq Khan, 'There Will Be More Pulwamas, Could Lead to War, Says Imran', *The Times of India*, 7 August 2019, https://bit.ly/3kNNjbU. Accessed on 18 November 2021.

85. 'Imran Khan: Time Right for Trump Mediation on Kashmir', *Gulf News*, 4 August 2019, https://bit.ly/3FqRwtR. Accessed on 18 November 2021.

86. Dipanjan Chaudhury, 'Donald Trump Repeats Kashmir Mediation Offer, India Says It's a Bilateral No.', *The Economic Times*, 23 January 2020, https://bit.ly/3HAYWwo. Accessed on 18 November 2021.

87. HT, '"PM Modi Really Feels He Has It under Control": Donald Trump on Kashmir', *Hindustan Times*, 22 June 2020, https://bit.ly/3oDCYR0. Accessed on 18 November 2021.

88. Arjun Subramaniam, 'IAF Operation Has Established Air Strikes as an Effective Tool of Deterrence in Sub-Conventional Warfare', *The Indian Express*, 27 February 2019, https://bit.ly/3kPXuwv. Accessed on 18 November 2021.

89. Special Correspondent, 'PM Urges Services to Abandon Legacy Systems, Practices', *The Hindu*, 6 March 2021, https://bit.ly/3oDB96y. Accessed on 18 November 2021.

Chapter 4. Turning the Tables in Ladakh

1. Carl von Clausewitz, *On War*, Princeton University Press, Princeton, 1976, p. 370.

2. PTI, 'Modi, Xi Stroll by Lake and Have a Boat Ride in Wuhan', *The Hindu*, 28 April 2018, https://bit.ly/3DsfGnm. Accessed on 18 November 2021.

3. Ananth Krishnan, 'With History in Sight and Lake-Side Walk on Itinerary, PM Modi Arrives in Wuhan', *India Today*, 26 April 2018, https://bit.ly/3qLi3On. Accessed on 18 November 2021.

4. PTI, 'How PM Modi and Xi Jinping's Informal Summit Could Improve India–China Ties', *Daily News & Analysis*, 22 April 2018, https://bit.ly/30xV3bb. Accessed on 18 November 2021.

5. Taylor Fravel, 'Stability in a Secondary Strategic Direction: China and the Border Dispute with India After 1962', in Kanti Bajpai et al., eds., *Routledge Handbook of China–India Relations*, Routledge, Abingdon, 2020, p. 174.

6. India Today Web Desk, 'Modi-Xi Jinping Bilateral Talks: India, China Reiterate Not to Let Differences Become Disputes', *India Today*, 5 September 2017, https://bit.ly/3kQrhVO. Accessed on 19 November 2021.

7. Pranab Dhal Samanta, 'One China? What About One India Policy: Sushma Swaraj to Wang Yi', *The Indian Express*, 12 June 2014, https://bit.ly/3HzLQQg. Accessed on 18 November 2021.

8. Jianwei Wang, 'Xi Jinping's "Major Country Diplomacy": A Paradigm Shift?', *Journal of Contemporary China*, Vol. 28, No. 115, 2019, p. 15–30 https://doi.org/10.1080/10670564.2018.1497907. Accessed on 19 January 2022.

9. PTI, 'Modi-Xi Summit in Wuhan Removed Several Misconceptions between India and China: Indian Envoy', *The Economic Times*, 16 November 2018, https://bit.ly/3nqfXRY. Accessed on 18 November 2021.

10. MEA, '2nd India–China Informal Summit', Ministry of External Affairs, 12 October 2019, https://bit.ly/32hqRl2. Accessed on 19 November 2021.

11. Pinak Chakravarty, 'Modi-Xi Mamallapuram Summit Not Purely Informal', *The New Indian Express*, 13 October 2019, https://bit.ly/3x0iAgu. Accessed on 19 November 2021.

12. Sachin Parashar, 'Ahead of Xi Jinping's Visit, China Ties Hit Bump:

Military Drill in NE', *The Times of India*, 5 October 2019, https://bit.ly/3qRcu0V. Accessed on 19 November 2021.

13. PTI, 'Article 370: China Says Opposed to Ladakh as Union Territory', *India Today*, 6 August 2019, https://bit.ly/324dxAf. Accessed on 19 November 2021.

14. Dipanjan Roy Chaudhury, 'Delhi's Indo-Pacific Strategy is Not Aimed at Containment of Any Power: Foreign Minister', *The Economic Times*, 29 August 2019, https://bit.ly/3coAbp4. Accessed on 19 November 2021.

15. Anirban Bhaumik, 'Modi Reminds Xi Accord to Respect Each Other's Concerns', *Deccan Herald*, 12 October 2019, https://bit.ly/3FvPN6I. Accessed on 19 November 2021.

16. Shaurya Karanbir Gurung, 'Number of Transgressions along India–China Border Have "Considerably" Reduced: Defence Ministry Report', *The Economic Times*, 18 July 2019, https://bit.ly/3Cth87v. Accessed on 19 November 2021.

17. Rajat Pandit, 'Post Wuhan, Guidance from Highest-Level Cut LAC Tiffs', *The Times of India*, 21 December 2019, https://bit.ly/3oCbuuW. Accessed on 19 November 2021.

18. Madan, Tanvi, *Fateful Triangle: How China Shaped U.S.-India Relations During the Cold War*, Brookings Institution Press, 2019.

19. WH, 'National Security Strategy of the United States of America', The White House, December 2017, p. 17, https://bit.ly/3FuftR1. Accessed on 19 November 2021.

20. Li Ruohan, 'Xi-Modi Meeting to Sustain Momentum of Improvement in Ties', *Global Times*, 23 April 2018, https://bit.ly/3IQ3Fuh. Accessed on 19 November 2021.

21. Mao Keji, 'Hints of Major Shift in Sino-Indian Relations', *Global Times*, 24 April 2018, https://bit.ly/3KMuOA5. Accessed on 28 January 2022.

22. Jim Gomez, 'Duterte: Philippines Can't Stop China Moves in Disputed Sea', *Yahoo News*, 19 March 2017, https://yhoo.it/3xa7tSs. Accessed on 19 November 2021.

23. Sreeram Chaulia, 'Coronavirus is China's Huge Political Failure', *The Asian Age*, 5 February 2020, https://bit.ly/3Gc4sUm. Accessed

on 25 January 2022.

24. Wenshan Jia, 'What Is an Alternative for a Dying US Democracy?', *Global Times*, 18 April 2020, https://bit.ly/3G9b0mA. Accessed on 19 November 2021.

25. Chloe Taylor, "Opportunity of the Century": How the Coronavirus Crisis Could Establish China as a Global Leader', *CNBC*, 31 March 2020, https://cnb.cx/3HDyDWH. Accessed on 19 November 2021.

26. Chris Buckley, '"The East Is Rising": Xi Maps out China's Post-Covid Ascent', *The New York Times*, 3 March 2021, https://nyti.ms/3x1NcOM. Accessed on 19 November 2021.

27. Kurt M. Campbell and Rush Doshi, 'The Coronavirus Could Reshape Global Order', *Foreign Affairs*, 18 March 2020, https://fam.ag/3FAMxXP. Accessed on 19 November 2021.

28. TE, 'Xi Jinping Wants China's Armed Forces to Be "World-Class" by 2050', *The Economist*, 27 June 2019, https://econ.st/3oOD34u. Accessed on 19 November 2021

29. Vijay Gokhale, 'President Xi's Long Game: World Is Dealing with a Leader Who Believes He Will Shape a Chinese Century', *The Indian Express*, 29 July 2020, https://bit.ly/30GuY9h. Accessed on 19 November 2021.

30. Chris Buckley, 'China's Combative Nationalists See a World Turning Their Way', *The New York Times*, 14 December 2020, https://nyti.ms/30J9Lfp. Accessed on 19 November 2021.

31. Liu Xuanzun and Guo Yuandan, 'Will US Aircraft Carrier Become Next Diamond Princess?', *Global Times*, 25 March, 2020, https://bit.ly/3o8Qv3p. Accessed on 25 January 2022.

32. Jay Pandya, 'China Stooge Calls US Backward and Barbaric; Predicts Its Decline on 244th Independence Day', Republic TV, 5 July 2020, https://bit.ly/3nvy1Kq. Accessed on 19 November 2021.

33. AFP, 'Why Beijing May Want to Keep Trump in the White House', *The Straits Times*, 20 October 2020, https://bit.ly/3qSpiDN. Accessed on 21 January 2022.

34. PTI, 'China Hikes Defence Budget to USD179 Billion, Nearly Three Times that of India', *The Economic Times*, 22 May 2020, https://bit.ly/34gUL9P. Accessed on January 25, 2022.

35. James Griffiths, 'Beijing May have Built Bases in the South China Sea, but that Doesn't Mean it Can Defend Them, Report Claims', CNN, 7 December 2020, https://cnn.it/34kHI7G. Accessed on 25 January 2022.

36. Geeta Mohan, 'China's Growing Territorial Aggression Amid Coronavirus Crisis', *India Today*, 26 June 2020, https://www.indiatoday.in/mail-today/story/china-growing-territorial-aggression-amid-covid-crisis-1692787-2020-06-26. Accessed on 25 January 2022.

37. Harsh V. Pant and Kartik Bommakanti, 'COVID19: The Chinese Military Is Busy Exploiting the Pandemic', Observer Research Foundation, 14 April 2020, https://bit.ly/3kT7rcK. Accessed on 19 November 2021.

38. Rahul Tripathi and Manu Pubby, 'COVID-19 Delayed Indian Exercise, Chinese Moved into Key Positions', *The Economic Times*, 3 June 2020, https://bit.ly/32gwSyp. Accessed on 19 November 2021.

39. Rahul Tripathi, 'Intel Alerted about PLA Movement in Ladakh in Feb-March', *The Economic Times*, 18 June 2020, https://bit.ly/3DwYblN. Accessed on 19 November 2021.

40. Mayank Singh, 'New Flashpoint? China Now Mobilising Troops in Depsang along LAC', *The New Indian Express*, 25 June 2020, https://bit.ly/3DtxoXs. Accessed on 19 November 2021.

41. Rajat Pandit, 'LAC Face-Off: Is Pangong Tso Just a Smokescreen and Depsang China's Main Target?', *The Times of India*, 18 September 2020, https://bit.ly/3qSf4Uk. Accessed on 19 November 2021.

42. Shaurya Gurung, 'In Making for Two Decades, DSDBO Road Now Upsets China', *The Economic Times*, 8 June 2020, https://bit.ly/2Z13lr5. Accessed on 19 November 2021.

43. Derek Grossman, 'Chinese Border Aggression against India Likely Unrelated to Pandemic', *The Diplomat*, 5 July 2020, https://bit.ly/32ltkep. Accessed on 19 November 2021.

44. Jason Scott and Iain Marlow, 'Chinese Official Pushes Conspiracy Theory US Spread Virus', *Bloomberg*, 13 March 2020, https://bloom.bg/30H9qty. Accessed on 19 November 2021.

45. Ananth Krishnan, 'Ladakh Standoff: After Talks Fail to Break

Impasse, China Blames India for Tensions', *The Hindu*, 13 October 2020, https://bit.ly/3FwpfSQ. Accessed on 19 November 2021.

46. Rezaul Laskar, 'Jaishankar Calls out China, Cites Its 5 Differing Explanations for Ladakh Violations', *Hindustan Times*, 9 December 2020, https://bit.ly/3qMGsDo. Accessed on 19 November 2021.

47. Hussain Haqqani, Aparna Pande and Satoru Nagao, 'China's Thrust into South Asia: Considerations for US Policy', in THI, 'A Global Survey of US-China Competition in the Coronavirus Era', The Hudson Institute, May 2020, pp. 16–17, https://bit.ly/30Hmy1m. Accessed on 19 January 2022.

48. Anurag Kotoky and N.C. Bipindra, 'After Decades of Neglect, India Builds Roads Along China Border', *The Economic Times*, 12 July 2018, https://bit.ly/33VUTvP. Accessed on 28 January 2022.

49. IANS, 'Chinese Daily Blames India for 1962 War', CNN News18, 13 December 2012, https://bit.ly/3r3ZfK6. Accessed on 25 January 2022.

50. Jonathan Ward, quoted in Ankit Panda, 'The Origins of Today's Sino-India Tensions', *The Diplomat*, 24 June 2020, https://bit.ly/3kTZrYH. Accessed on 22 November 2021.

51. PTI, 'China Makes Fresh Bid to Raise Kashmir Issue in UNSC', *The Economic Times*, 15 January 2020, https://bit.ly/3HFAuKp. Accessed on 22 November 2021.

52. Ananth Krishnan, 'Beijing Think-Tank Links Scrapping of Article 370 to LAC Tensions', *The Hindu*, 12 June 2020, https://bit.ly/3FB9HNt. Accessed on 22 November 2021.

53. Kelsang Dolma, 'Tibet Was China's First Laboratory of Repression', *Foreign Policy*, 31 August 2020, https://bit.ly/33SQaev. Accessed on 25 January 2022.

54. Suisheng Zhao, 'All Under a Chinese Heaven: China Uses an Idealised Version of Its Imperial Past to Promote a 19th Century Agenda', *The Times of India*, 13 July 2017, https://bit.ly/3r7TvPB. Accessed on 25 January 2022.

55. Prakash Katoch, 'China's Unabated Cartographic Aggression', *Indian Defence Review*, 6 July 2017, https://bit.ly/3L1sIwi. Accessed on 25 January 2022.

56. Taylor Fravel, 'China's Sovereignty Obsession', *Foreign Affairs*, 26 June 2020, https://fam.ag/3nADcsK. Accessed on 22 November 2021.

57. Jianwei Wang, 'Xi Jinping's "Major Country Diplomacy": A Paradigm Shift?', *Journal of Contemporary China*, Vol. 28, No. 115, pp. 25–26, https://doi.org/10.1080/10670564.2018.1497907. Accessed on 19 January 2022.

58. PTI, 'Chinese Soldiers in Large Numbers along LAC: Rajnath Singh', *India Today*, 3 June 2020, https://bit.ly/3kYkNEy. Accessed on 22 November 2021.

59. Dinakar Peri, 'Indian, Chinese Troops Face Off in Eastern Ladakh, Sikkim', *The Hindu*, 10 May 2020, https://bit.ly/3HIsE2B. Accessed on 22 November 2021.

60. MEA, 'India–China Meeting of Army Commanders on June 06, 2020', Ministry of External Affairs, 7 June 2020, https://bit.ly/3HFFwqr. Accessed on 22 November 2021.

61. PTI, 'China Suffered 35 Casualties during Galwan Clash: US Intelligence Reports', *The Times of India*, 17 June 2020, https://bit.ly/3HHSxjm. Accessed on 22 November 2021.

62. Express News Service, '45 Chinese Soldiers Killed in Galwan Valley Clash: Russian News Agency', *The New Indian Express*, 12 February 2021, https://bit.ly/3cyuO6T. Accessed on 22 November 2021.

63. TOI, 'Chinese Casualties in Galwan Clash Much Higher than Officially Acknowledged: Report', *The Times of India*, 3 February 2022, https://bit.ly/3gyT3nk. Accessed on 8 February 2022.

64. Hu Xijin, 'India Gained Only Casualties from Border Clash', *Global Times*, 24 June 2020, https://bit.ly/34hQ53O. Accessed on 22 November 2021

65. IT, 'China Very Sensitive about Galwan Casualties, Not to Release Numbers Unless President Xi Okays: Report', *India Today*, 18 June 2020, https://bit.ly/3HATjym. Accessed on 22 November 2021.

66. Liu Xin, Guoyuandan and Zhang Hui, 'China Unveils Details of 4 PLA Martyrs at Galwan Valley Border Clash for First Time, Reaffirming Responsibility Falls on India', *Global Times*, 19 February 2021, https://bit.ly/31d1Ozv. Accessed on 28 January 2022.

67. Geeta Mohan, 'China Planned Galwan Attack: EAM Jaishankar

Warns Chinese Counterpart of Serious Impact on Bilateral Ties', *India Today*, 17 June 2020, https://bit.ly/3cD715M. Accessed on 22 November 2021.

68. HT, 'Don't Underestimate Our Firm Will to Safeguard Territorial Sovereignty: China on Ladakh Face-Off', *Hindustan Times*, 18 June 2020, https://bit.ly/30Pbyz2. Accessed on 22 November 2021.

69. Mao Tse-Tung, *Selected Works of Mao-Tse-Tung, Volume II*, Pergamon Press, Oxford, 1975, p. 166.

70. XN, 'Full Text of President Xi's Speech at Opening of Belt and Road Forum', *Xinhua*, 14 May 2017, https://bit.ly/3Cz11FC. Accessed on 22 November 2021; Simone Van Nieuwenhuizen, 'China's "rule of law in international relations"', 1 August 2018, *The Interpreter*, https://bit.ly/3ltYYNd. Accessed on 22 November 2021; Astrid H.M. Nordin, 'Harmonious World: It Seems It Was Only a Dream', *International Studies Review*, Vol. 19, No. 2, June 2017, p. 328–329, https://doi.org/10.1093/isr/vix020. Accessed on 19 January 2022.

71. Gyan Varma and Anuja, 'India–China Face-Off: No Incursion, No Loss of Territory, Says PM Modi', *Mint*, 20 June 2020, https://bit.ly/3CGlSXJ. Accessed on 22 November 2021.

72. TNN, 'PMO Issues Clarification over Modi's Comments That No One Entered Indian Territory', *The Times of India*, 20 June 2020, https://bit.ly/3kWETyS. Accessed on 22 November 2021.

73. Kalyan Ray, 'Rajnath Singh Reviews Ladakh Situation; Commanders Given Freedom to Deal with Any Chinese Misadventure', *Deccan Herald*, 22 June 2020, https://bit.ly/3nEPtwr. Accessed on 22 November 2021.

74. BS Web Team, 'India Wants Peace, but Can Give Befitting Reply: PM Modi on Galwan Clash', *Business Standard*, 17 June 2020, https://bit.ly/3HIqtMF. Accessed on 22 November 2021.

75. L.N. Rangarajan, *Kautilya—The Arthashastra*, Penguin, New Delhi, 2000, p. 508.

76. Snehesh Philip, 'Stand-Off in Ladakh: Army Matching Wits with China, on Every Step', *ThePrint*, 23 May 2020, https://bit.ly/349LOiJ. Accessed on 25 January 2022.

77. Elizabeth Roche, 'We're Prepared to Hold Our Ground in Ladakh,

Says Army Chief', *Mint*, 12 January 2021, https://bit.ly/3FSE8PF. Accessed on 22 November 2021.

78. Manu Pubby, 'Defence Budget 2021: India Spent Rs 20,776 Crore on Emergency, Unbudgeted Defence Expenses Given China Challenge', *The Economic Times*, 2 February 2021, https://bit.ly/3nJ6yVQ. Accessed on 23 November 2021.

79. HT, 'Touch the Sky with Glory: PM Narendra Modi Welcomes Rafale Fighter Jets with a Sanskrit Tweet', *Hindustan Times*, 29 July 2020, https://bit.ly/3paW6WT. Accessed on 23 November 2021.

80. Rajat Pandit, 'IAF Watching Chinese Bases, Sure of Matching Air Power', *The Times of India*, 28 June 2020, https://bit.ly/3r0sPk0. Accessed on 23 November 2021.

81. PTI, 'AF's Strong Posturing during Ladakh Standoff Helped India Ward off Any Threat from China: Air Chief Bhadauria', *The Times of India*, 6 November 2020, https://bit.ly/3kXrart. Accessed on 23 November 2021.

82. Shishir Gupta, 'Gen Rawat Asks Tri-Services to Curb Peace-Time Activities in Deference to Deployed Troops in Ladakh', *Hindustan Times*, 26 October 2020, https://bit.ly/3l0B3Fc. Accessed on 23 November 2021.

83. Shishir Gupta, 'Navy's Forward Posture against PLA Aggression in Ladakh Muscles out Chinese Threat on High Seas', *Hindustan Times*, 20 July 2020, https://bit.ly/3r2jd8r. Accessed on 23 November 2021.

84. ET, 'Indian Navy's Marine Commandos or MARCOS Deployed in Eastern Ladakh to Deter China', *The Economic Times*, 16 December 2020, https://bit.ly/3FGt47S. Accessed on 23 November 2021.

85. Abhishek Bhalla, '"Secret Force" Comprising Tibetans Gets Award for Operation against China in Ladakh', *India Today*, 26 January 2021, https://bit.ly/32eIMZt. Accessed on 23 November 2021.

86. Krishn Kaushik, 'In Message to Beijing, Ram Madhav at Tibetan Unit Soldier Funeral', *The Indian Express*, 8 September 2020. https://bit.ly/3nKqXtP. Accessed on 23 November 2021.

87. Amrita Dutta, 'Army Plans to Keep 2 Strike Corps for Mountains Facing China amid Ladakh Crisis', *ThePrint*, 6 January 2021, https://bit.ly/3nDX8ed. Accessed on 23 November 2021.

88. Shishir Gupta, 'In India–China Border Disengagement Plan, Galwan Model Is the Template', *Hindustan Times*, 11 February 2021, https://bit.ly/3HVZehQ. Accessed on 23 November 2021.

89. Snehesh Philip, 'How Indian Army's Secrecy & Unorthodox Deployment Fooled the Chinese at Pangong Tso', *ThePrint*, 14 December 2020, https://bit.ly/3r2yQg0. Accessed on 23 November 2021.

90. Gaurav Sawant, 'Op Snow Leopard: Inside Story of How Army Reclaimed Heights in Eastern Ladakh', *India Today*, 16 September 2020, https://bit.ly/3CGR3lp. Accessed on 23 November 2021.

91. DNA, 'Here's How the Indian Army Forced China to Retreat in Eastern Ladakh', *Daily News & Analysis*, 18 February 2021, https://bit.ly/3xim7a7. Accessed on 23 November 2021.

92. Pradip R. Sagar, 'Ladakh: China Opening New Fronts by Occupying Lesser Guarded Heights along LAC', *The Week*, 1 September 2020, https://bit.ly/3nK6GEK. Accessed on 23 November 2021.

93. Gordon G. Chang, 'The Chinese Army Flops in India. What Will Xi Do Next?', *Newsweek*, 11 September 2020, https://bit.ly/32qMsaN. Accessed on 23 November 2021.

94. Online conversation with the author on 14 October 2020.

95. PTI, 'TikTok Anticipates a Loss of over $6 Billion from India's Ban: Report', *Business Standard*, 3 July 2020, https://bit.ly/3d4Sxvn. Accessed on 29 November 2021.

96. Sutirtho Patranobis, 'India's Imports from China Dropped 13%, Exports Went up by 16% in 2020: State Media', *Hindustan Times*, https://bit.ly/3nJpK5Q. Accessed on 23 November 2021.

97. Neha Alawadhi and Subhayan Chakraborty, 'India Blocks Automatic FDI Route for Neighbours to Curb Hostile Takeovers', *Business Standard*, 19 April 2020, https://bit.ly/32snAzt. Accessed on 23 November 2021.

98. Celia Chen, 'India to Slowly Phase out Huawei and Other Chinese Vendors from Its Telecoms Network, FT Reports', *South China Morning Post*, 25 August 2020, https://bit.ly/3r33LZx. Accessed on 23 November 2021.

99. Ananth Krishnan, 'India, China Foreign Ministers to Establish

Hotline', *The Hindu*, 26 February 2021, https://bit.ly/3nGQxzG. Accessed on 23 November 2021.

100. PTI, 'India–China Relations Going Through a 'Very Difficult Phase': Jaishankar', *Business Standard*, 5 May 2021, https://bit.ly/30SwhCo. Accessed on 23 November 2021.

101. Express News Network, 'Trade Associations Announce Boycott of 3,000 Chinese Products', *The Indian Express*, 11 June 2020, https://bit.ly/3DJJQTf. Accessed on 23 November 2021.

102. Sachin Dave, 'We Will Boycott All Chinese Products Say 87% of Indians: LocalCircles Survey', *The Economic Times*, 19 June 2020, https://bit.ly/3nEhDHH. Accessed on 23 November 2021.

103. MOFA, 'Wang Yi Speaks on the Phone and Reaches Positive Agreement on Easing Border Situation with Indian National Security Adviser Ajit Doval', Ministry of Foreign Affairs, 6 July 2020, https://bit.ly/3HKp0W4. Accessed on 23 November 2021.

104. Times Now Digital, 'After 20 Soldiers Martyred in Ladakh, Anti-China Protests Erupt Across India; "Boycott China" Calls Grow', Times Now, 17 June 2020, https://bit.ly/313I2pz. Accessed on 29 November 2021.

105. ED, 'Full Text: PM Modi's Address to Indian Armed Forces in Leh', *The Indian Express*, 5 July 2020, https://bit.ly/3xiqaU6. Accessed on 23 November 2021.

106. IT, 'Dr S. Jaishankar Speaks on India's External Management at India Today Conclave South' [video], *India Today*, YouTube, 13 March 2021, https://www.youtube.com/watch?v=uvPLrys1NoY. Accessed on 23 November 2021.

107. Jay Pandya, '"If Someone Provokes Us, We Won't Spare Them": Rajnath Singh Warns China on Expansionism', Republic TV, 30 December 2020, https://bit.ly/3DNIab6. Accessed on 23 November 2021.

108. HT, 'PM Modi Questions Previous Regimes Over Ladakh's Daulat Beg Oldi, Says They Compromised on Security', *Hindustan Times*, 3 October 2020, https://bit.ly/3nHJnuY. Accessed on 23 November 2021.

109. Sutirtho Patranobis, '"China–US Relations Facing Most Serious

Challenge": Minister Wang Yi', *Hindustan Times*, 9 July 2020, https://bit.ly/3cHODIK. Accessed on 23 November 2021.

110. Subrahmanyam Jaishankar, *The India Way: Strategies for an Uncertain World*, HarperCollins, New Delhi, 2020, p. 11.

111. Liu Zongyi, 'US, India to Remain Strange Bedfellows Regardless of Any Military Pact', *Global Times*, 10 October 2020, https://bit.ly/3IHYOuX. Accessed on 23 November 2021.

112. Shubhajit Roy, 'US Signs Key Defence Agreement with India, Mike Pompeo Says China "No Friend To Democracy"', *The Financial Express*, 28 October 2020, https://bit.ly/3FCHx4T. Accessed on 23 November 2021.

113. Christopher Woody, 'The US is Helping India Keep an Eye on China's Military, Top US Commanders Say', *Business Insider*, 23 December 2020, https://bit.ly/2ZdIRLR. Accessed on 23 November 2021.

114. Reuters, 'Quad Nations Meeting to Announce Financing to Boost India Vaccine Output: Report', *The Indian Express*, 10 March 2021, https://bit.ly/3o2qt2k. Accessed on 29 November 2021.

115. Global Times, 'India Seeking Courtship with Quad a Negative Asset of BRICS, SCO', *Global Times*, 12 March 2021, https://bit.ly/3CGolBf. Accessed on 23 November 2021.

116. John Oneal, *Foreign Policy Making in Times of Crisis*, Ohio State University Press, Columbus, 1982, p. 314.

117. Elizabeth Roche, 'Rajnath Gets Russia Assurance of Speedy Completion of Defence Deals', *Mint*, 24 June 2020, https://bit.ly/3xmhgor. Accessed on 23 November 2021.

118. Rezaul H. Laskar and Sutirtho Patranobis, '"Implement Agreed Actions": India Reminds China on Disengagement at LAC', *Hindustan Times*, 27 August 2020, https://bit.ly/3nHyHMZ. Accessed on 24 November 2021.

119. PD, 'China Must Resolutely Counterattack India's Opportunist Move', *People's Daily*, 1 September 2020, https://bit.ly/3CNgt0P. Accessed on 24 November 2021.

120. Yang Sheng, 'Biden "Smoother" to Deal With', *Global Times*, 19 August 2020, https://bit.ly/3r6Z94e. Accessed on 24 November 2021.

121. AP, 'Biden: China Should Expect "Extreme Competition" from US', *The Associated Press*, 7 February 2021, https://bit.ly/3DNcAKT. Accessed on 24 November 2021.

122. Indrani Bagchi, 'How India Changed Playbook and Took China by Surprise', *The Times of India*, 12 February 2021, https://bit.ly/3xvRnCV. Accessed on 24 November 2021.

123. TW, 'Indian Army Releases Footage of Pullback by China at Pangong Tso', *The Week*, 16 February 2021, https://bit.ly/3xhIDju. Accessed on 24 November 2021.

124. Snehesh Philip, 'Why LAC Could End up Like LoC with More Indian Army Deployments After China Tensions Ease', *ThePrint*, 14 September 2020, https://bit.ly/3H8iPKP. Accessed on 28 January 2022.

125. Deeptiman Tiwary, 'We Have Strategies for Depsang… Trust Deficit Exists: Army Chief', *The Indian Express*, 25 February 2021, https://bit.ly/3r5Wb0y. Accessed on 24 November 2021.

126. Snehesh Alex Philip, 'Indian Army Has New Strategies for Pakistan, China: Punitive Deterrence, Credible Deterrence', *ThePrint*, 24 May 2021, https://bit.ly/30Uh2sM. Accessed on 24 November 2021.

127. Jonathan M. Roberts, *Decision-Making during International Crises*, Macmillan, London, 1988, p. 98.

128. Deepanjan Roy Chaudhury, 'India, China May Slip into Conflict that Neither Wants: US Report', *The Economic Times*, 10 April 2021, https://bit.ly/3FJI1Gg. Accessed on 24 November 2021.

Epilogue: Operation Nation

1.   Vibha Sharma, 'India Will Fight and Win as One: Modi', *The Tribune*, 28 February 2019, https://bit.ly/311dhSm. Accessed on 24 November 2021.

2.   Conversation with the author on 10 March 2021 in New Delhi.

3.   Michael Mandelbaum, *The Fate of Nations: The Search for National Security in the Nineteenth and Twentieth Centuries*, Cambridge University Press, Cambridge, 1988, pp. 132, 202, 260.

4.   Conversation with the author on 11 March 2021 in New Delhi.

5. Brahma Chellaney, 'The Non-Violence Myth: India's Founding Story Bestows Upon it a Quixotic National Philosophy and Enduring Costs', *The Times of India*, 3 February 2019, https://bit.ly/3KO0g0F. Accessed on 28 January 2022.

6. A.K. Singh and Narender Kumar, *Battle Ready for the 21st Century*, Centre for Land Warfare Studies, New Delhi, 2021, p. 28.

7. 'My Diwali Is Not Complete Without Being with the Soldiers: PM at Longewala', Narendra Modi, 14 November 2020, https://bit.ly/3FFqQFZ. Accessed on 24 November 2021.

8. Subrahmanyam Jaishankar, *The India Way: Strategies for an Uncertain World*, HarperCollins, New Delhi, 2020, p. 65.

Index

25